The Quality of Mercy

The Quality of Mercy

A Revolutionary Lady's Tale

BY

WILLIAM CIBBARELLI, PH.D.

XULON ELITE

Xulon Press Elite
2301 Lucien Way #415
Maitland, FL 32751
407.339.4217
www.xulonpress.com

© 2022 by William Cibbarelli, Ph.D.

All rights reserved solely by the author. The author guarantees all contents are original and do not infringe upon the legal rights of any other person or work. No part of this book may be reproduced in any form without the permission of the author.

Due to the changing nature of the Internet, if there are any web addresses, links, or URLs included in this manuscript, these may have been altered and may no longer be accessible. The views and opinions shared in this book belong solely to the author and do not necessarily reflect those of the publisher. The publisher therefore disclaims responsibility for the views or opinions expressed within the work.

Paperback ISBN-13: 978-1-6628-5183-4
Hard Cover ISBN-13: 978-1-6628-5184-1
Ebook ISBN-13: 978-1-6628-5185-8

DEDICATED TO

D.F.P.

W.C.D.

C.C.K.

Mercy Otis Warren by John Singleton Copley (1763)
Museum of Fine Arts, Boston, MA

CONTENTS

Introduction xi
Chapter 1. The Beginning 1
Chapter 2. Life's Lessons Learned Early 5
Chapter 3. Reader Today, Leader Tomorrow 13
Chapter 4. The Conspiracy 33
Chapter 5. Love is Blind 45
Chapter 6. Family is Everything 57
Chapter 7. Catalyst for Change 71
Chapter 8. Silence is the Virtue of Fools 75
Chapter 9. The Die is Cast 87
Chapter 10. The Pen is the Tongue of the Mind 101
Chapter 11. Freedom is Won, Never Given 113
Chapter 12. The Propagandist 123
Chapter 13. The Columbian Patriot 133
Chapter 14. The History 151
Chapter 15. The Saucy Lady 159
Chapter 16. The Celebrated Lady 185
Chapter 17. Lady Constantia 209
Chapter 18. A Life Worth Living 239
APPENDIX
Mercy Warren's Reading List 255

BIBLIOGRAPHY 281

INTRODUCTION

This revolutionary tale has Mercy Otis Warren, a self-educated eighteenth-century woman, dramatist, poet, pamphleteer, historian, propagandist, and consummate letter-writer, preparing a fictional journal during the last year of her life. The novel is a blending of fact, fiction, and speculation built around the life of this unique lady; recognized by the Founding Fathers as an expert in constitutional and English Common Law, as well as a major participant in and contributor to the debates prior to and during the Revolution and constitutional debates. She authored the pamphlet, *Observations on the New Constitution,* which offered eighteen amendments to the proposed Constitution, and was the first woman to write a history of the American Revolution. Although known to American historians, I believe Mercy Warren's contributions to the founding of America are worthy of being known by all Americans. Her story is a tale of individual courage and determination in confronting and overcoming outdated social conventions regarding women's intellectual capabilities and political status, from which contemporary readers can learn and benefit.

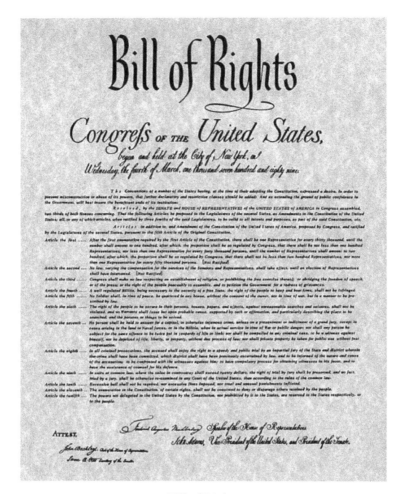

Bill of Rights

Her friends and correspondents included Abigail Adams, Catharine Sawbridge Macaulay, Judith Sargent Murray, Hannah Winthrop, John and Samuel Adams, Patrick Henry, John Hancock, Thomas Jefferson, Alexander Hamilton, Eldridge Gerry, and George Washington, to cite the most notable. Her contributions to the founding of America earned her the appellations as the "Conscience of the American Revolution" and "Mother of the Bill of Rights," the latter coming a century later when a descendant, Charles Warren, discovered her authorship of the

Observation while emptying her Plymouth home attic. He found an old chest with her personal correspondence and drafts of her plays, poems, history, and the aforementioned pamphlet.

The author's fictitious journal of Mercy Otis Warren's life grew from his doctoral dissertation, *Libraries of the Mind: A Study of the Reading Histories of Mercy Warren, Abigail Adams, and Judith Sargent Murray (1728-1820)*, which explored the intellectual development of these three women by creating their reading dossiers and studying, through their personal correspondence and public writings, how what they read shaped their thinking on the issues confronting late eighteenth-century America. Mercy Warren's life and works have been studied by historians which, like the author's dissertation, were based on written evidence in her personal correspondence and published works. This method of investigation mitigates any speculation beyond the known facts shaping her life, unless the preponderance of documentation allows an educated opinion or, more appropriately, guess.

In the case of Mercy Warren, however, there were large gaps in her life where there was no factual documentation, such as early childhood, education, courtship, and marriage, to cite a few. Having studied her intellectual persona from a purely academic perspective, I asked myself, "Could I fill in these gaps using my knowledge of eighteenth-century social and cultural traditions, and political events gathered during my dissertation research that shaped her life for which I, and a curious reader, might want to know more, even if only speculative?"

An example of this construct was her involvement as a permanent member of the Committee of Correspondence in 1773 with Samuel Adams (leader of the Sons of Liberty) and Dr. Joseph Warren (no relation), who planned the Boston Tea Party. The raid was not a spur-of-the-moment event. There were approximately 115 raiders boarding three East India Company vessels and dumping the colonists' much-loved beverage into the Boston Harbor, which lit the fuse in the powder keg of revolution. The raid required detailed planning, timing, security, and a dispersal plan to protect the raiders from British capture and reprisals. Mercy's involvement in this Committee of Correspondence, of which I was unaware during my dissertation research, sparked my interest and I asked myself, "What was Mercy Warren's involvement in the planning? Why was she named to the permanent committee?" I knew from previous research that neither Samuel Adams nor Dr. Warren were lawyers. I also knew from my previous dissertation study that Mercy was a recognized expert in English statutory and Common Law by colonial leaders searching for a response to the British government reaction to the *Gaspée Affair of 1772* and subsequent passage of the *Tea Act of 1773*. Like this and other episodes in the novel, the author takes liberties with what is known by creating a speculative or, more appropriately, fictitious account of Mercy's involvement.

I thought the best vehicle for presenting the narrative was to construct a fictional journal written by Mercy Warren during the last year of her life for future generations of the Warren family. From my study of this unique woman, I knew she avoided self-promotion or self-glorification and would have not written an autobiography applauding her achievements. With all her actual accomplishments, she did not need to seek fame because male and female contemporaries recognized her intellectual prowess. She was an enthusiastic supporter and believer in the democratic vision of the American republican experiment. It takes little conjecture to realize she was fastidious, saving letters, published works, and personal items that eventually found a home with the Massachusetts Historical Society and other American museums.

Mercy Warren grew to adulthood in a society shaped by religious values and centuries-old traditions defining gender roles. But there were ordinary questions rarely addressed by scholars when studying the broader issues that confronted American society. Mercy Warren's life and experiences would have differed little from other young girls growing up in eighteenth-century colonial America. For example, did Mercy play games as a young girl and what were the games common in eighteenth-century Colonial America? How did she deal with the births and deaths of brothers and sisters? How detailed was her pre-university tutorial education, and how was it conducted? Exactly how did she meet her husband, with whom she fell deeply in love? What were the common menu foods in the Bay Colony?

I address these and other questions by describing the socio-cultural environment in which she lived. One example of contextual construct was understanding Mercy Warren's non-traditional learning, which needed exploration of the eighteenth-century education system beyond the first homeschooling under her mother's supervision.

From the earliest founding of the colonies, and regardless of class, the Protestant immigrants emphasized women learning to read because they were their child's first teacher, with the primary book of learning being the Bible. Conversely, writing was considered a predominantly male skill, linked to occupation and class. Lawyers, clerks, scholars, physicians, clergy, and businessmen needed to be able to write. Most women, along with farmers, artisans, non-whites, and the lower classes, did not need to know how to write. These groups only needed to make their "mark" on official documents. Mercy Warren would have been no exception to these social norms, except for her stubborn personality.

There were three levels of formal schooling for young boys: the Latin School, also known as the grammar or English school, the pre-university tutorial for entry into a college, and college itself. To put this in perspective, the Latin School is comparable to our present-day grammar and high school. The pre-university tutorial is equivalent to our contemporary undergraduate baccalaureate programs, and the last to the current graduate level master's degree. The student had to complete each level to advance to the next. This education system was only open to young boys and men from socially prominent or financially prosperous families, like the Warrens. To put it bluntly, the Latin School and institutions of higher learning were closed to females. These were male-only bastions and no exceptions were tolerated. Therefore, Mercy's participation in the Latin School reading curriculum and her brother's pre-university tutorial proved a major societal milestone in a time when this opportunity was non-existent for young girls and women.

To participate in the pre-university tutorial, Mercy would have had to study the Latin School curriculum, which included the translations of Cato, Cicero, Corderius, Aesop, Erasmus, Ovid, Justinus, Homer, and Virgil. Many of these authors appeared in the dual Latin-to-English or Greek-to-English translations available by the eighteenth century, while other subjects in the program emphasized grammar, proper diction, elements of rhetoric, logic, moral and natural philosophy, geography, ethics, and writing in prose and verse. She would have also read the histories of Greece, Rome, and England, *The Adventures of Telemachus, Spectator, Guardian*, and English authors John Milton, John Locke, Joseph Addison, Alexander Pope, Jonathan Swift, and William Shakespeare, among others. This was not an easy task even by modern grammar and high school standards, and Mercy was about thirteen years of age when she undertook the challenge of reading these writings.

Mercy Warren's uncle, Reverend Jonathan Russell, a certified tutor for Harvard College, concentrated the pre-university reading in classical and humanist authors, theology, divinity, Latin, Greek, and French while revisiting the Latin School curriculum. The tutorial expanded her reading into Ancient, Medieval, Renaissance, Reformation, and Enlightenment authors covering history, poetry, drama, political theory, law, and philosophy. As the reading list at the end of the novel illustrates, this was a challenging reading program that typically lasted one year, two at the most. Once the tutor certified the student, he entered college to study a chosen profession in law, science, medicine, business, or the ministry. Of course, eighteenth-century society denied Mercy Warren and other young girls access to Latin School and Harvard College, as these were male bastions. She and other females were also deprived of the ability to practice in the professions. Simply put, the public world of the professional was a male-only club.

Lastly, the novel blends the known facts of Mercy Warren's life with the author's speculation to fill in the gaps in her life and is organized from Mercy's earliest recollections as a young girl to the present-day preparation of the fictional journal. The dates at the end of each chapter are my fictional invention for how Mercy Warren kept track of the journal's progress. There were practical reasons for this timeline. She was eighty-five when she undertook the fictitious journal and, for years, suffered from severe attacks of migraine headaches, failing eyesight, temporary bouts of blindness, and arthritis. These ailments, along with her normal correspondence with family and friends, household and estate management duties, and regular weekend visits by her son's family and grandchildren, would have limited her writing time.

In the novel, conversations on specific topics and issues in Mercy's life are paraphrased versions found in her letters and those of her correspondents. Personal quotes were also useful in adding more depth to the conversations between her friends, family members, the Founding Fathers, and other political power brokers and prominent Americans. I then sprinkled eighteenth-century vocabulary, terminology, and phrases throughout the novel, such as Chief Magistrate to describe what we call today the President of the United States.

The reader will find no in-text citations or footnotes in the narrative to impede their reading. If a reader wishes to further explore a topic, an author, individual, or event, the bibliographical sources at the end of the novel provide ample information for more in-depth research. Finally, I have also included an appendix, an updated version of Mercy Warren's reading history, so the reader can experience what this unique woman studied. This list also offers the reader the opportunity to explore those authors who influenced her intellectual development and political thinking. The author hopes readers will embrace the narrative as a blending of fact, speculation, and fiction, enjoying the journey of this very accomplished woman to whom America owes a great deal of thanks.

Chapter 1

THE BEGINNING

It was a pleasantly warm Monday morning in May 1813 while sitting in the library of my Plymouth home, relishing the soft ocean breeze filling the air with its salty aroma, mixing with a sweet pine and floral scent, that I came to my epiphany. I looked through the sculpted panes, feeling the warm light dancing across the unlit silver candlesticks in their crimped saucer bases, a birthday gift from James: the love of my life, my partner, and my confidant in all things. Staring out the window, I mused how my life had become too predictable. Here I was sitting, day after day, at a weathered pine desk, finishing letters to family and friends, doing a little gardening, strolling the estate, watching the grandchildren on weekends, and helping with the cooking, cleaning, and reading.

I might be eighty-five, but there must be something to do to relieve this feeling of boredom and uselessness. I wished for those halcyon days when revolution was in the air and I was an active participant, contributing my mind and pen to the cause. Those times were exhilarating, empowering, and threatening. I was alive then and, with James at my side, there was no obstacle I could not overcome. I needed to think about something new, something to excite my mind, and it certainly was not writing another letter inquiring about people's health, what was new in their lives, the births of distant relatives, the all-too-frequent death notices, and other tidbits of innocuous gossip.

Worse still, in the last few years, I only read and wrote during the day because the flickering candlelight aggravated my failing vision, even with my spectacles, and then came the incessant headaches and episodes of temporary blindness. The doctor kept recommending remedies like strong coffee, tea, or stroking my forehead with nutmeg and vinegar to ease the headaches. Shaking my head, *Nutmeg and vinegar, he could not be serious! I sometimes wondered if the man studied with a witch doctor. Next, he will want to apply leeches and bleed me.* Here I was complaining, another sign of old age. I know my doctor was trying his best, and that worried me. I decided to take a walk to clear my mind.

I felt another of those endless headaches coming on, so I best get moving before the pain crippled me or caused one of those bouts of temporary blindness that sometimes attended them. Leaving the library, I strolled into the kitchen where the cook was preparing a light breakfast of poached eggs, fried ham, hot brown bread, and coffee. I could hear my son Henry's children stirring, and I knew it best to get going; otherwise, they would consume the morning. Rushing through the meal and putting on my shawl, I was interrupted by Henry, who peering into the kitchen told me he was going into town for supplies and was there anything I needed.

I told him to buy more ink, paper, and a fine-tipped stylus or two, and reminded him to tend to the icehouse and bring in more wood for the fireplaces and bathing rooms. As he closed the door, I realized how grateful I was that he and his wife, Mary, and the children visited on the weekends from their farm in Eel River, less than three miles distance from my home. Their proximity made me feel better, knowing in the event of an emergency, he and Mary were a short carriage ride away. Mother once told me a benefit of marriage were the children and grandchildren who could care for me in my old age. I had not given it much credence at the time, but now I appreciated this piece of adult wisdom shared with a young girl who was wrapped up in reading more

The Beginning

than worrying about who she might marry. Reminiscing, another sign of aging; I needed to shake this darn mood.

Standing on the porch, I stopped for a moment and realized this had been my home for sixty years. I remember questioning James when he bought it, not believing we needed so much living space. I could not have been more wrong. We came to need the five bedrooms (each lit and warmed by a fireplace), three bathing chambers, kitchen, parlor, library, and spacious porch overlooking a large estate, with a well-tended garden, stable, barn, and icehouse. Without Henry and the family, I would only have the cook, housekeeper, and estate workers for company. Oversized though the house was, it was home. Yes, James had been right.

My musings were interrupted when I realized there were letters owed to my friends, Abigail and Judith, but I would do that after my stroll. As I left the porch, feeling the sun's rays warming my face, the germ of an idea began swirling in my head. *Why not write a self-reflective journal describing my life through specific moments in time? I could recapture those bygone, exhilarating days when revolution was in the air for future generations of the family, describing our contributions to the founding of our great country. What a great idea.* As I strolled, the outline formed in my mind. I would look back from childhood to now. Smiling, I remembered my dear tutor, Uncle Jonathan, telling me that before I put pen to paper, I needed to create an outline. That way I would avoid the marginal notations, which had furrowed his brow so many decades ago.

A journal would be perfect, bonding the past to the present. I could describe the influential people, friends, and events that had shaped my life. In this way, future generations of my family would know of their ancestors' contribution to the founding of America. On the selfish side, revisiting my history would allow me to get over this boredom by doing something new and challenging. I can write a little each day, using the simple outline I made, beginning with my experiences as a young girl, advancing though the various stages of my life to the present day. I will track each chapter's progress by inserting a completion date at the end. In this way, I would not forget details of the events and people, about which I was writing, because there was great deal of information to recall and set to paper.

I also needed to review each narrative to insure I was not forgetting a topic, event, or personage while paraphrasing important conversations, as remembering them word for word would be impossible. In this regard, I needed to review my correspondence, and those of my correspondents, that might stimulate my memory of an event or conversation. At least, readers would get the gist of the conversations from what I share. The journal will not be published and known only to, and read by, our immediate family.

Returning to the house after a shorter walk than planned, I went into the library to check that there was enough paper and ink to begin. I was glad that Henry would be buying more writing materials and supplies today. In the meantime, I sat and began writing the letters owed to my dear friends, Abigail and Judith. After that, I would start the journal.

Plymouth, Monday, 10 May 1813

Chapter 2

LIFE'S LESSONS LEARNED EARLY

Awakening at five am the next morning, I was excited to begin writing. I poured myself a cup of coffee, entered the library, and opened the window to let in the cool sea breeze. The weather was milder than normal for Plymouth on this May day, but not unusual when the wind blew out of the northeast. After taking a sip of coffee, I donned my calf skin writing gloves, which were a gift from Henry when he had noticed my old pair was threadbare with thick, ink-stained fingertips. He had recommended cutting off the tips of my right-hand glove to minimize the ink staining them, saying they would last longer. *Clever idea*, I thought, but kept the old pair as a standby. I did, however, cut off the fingertips. Taking a couple sips of coffee, I took pen in hand but before beginning leaned back in my chair and let my mind wander back to those innocent, early days of my youth.

My earliest recollections from childhood became lasting lessons learned, which I carried throughout my life. I was born into the prominent Otis family on 14 September 1728 in Barnstable, Massachusetts. Every day, I helped Mother (Mary) with the cooking, cleaning, gardening, and practicing my reading and writing. I played different games like horseshoes, Sackstraws, kite flying, jump rope, and London Bridge, where two players held hands and made an arch with their arms while others passed through in single file. The arch is then lowered at the song's end to catch a player. We also played hopscotch, marbles, Blind Man's Bluff, and Spinning Tops with my brothers and sisters. My favorite was Huzzlecaps, where you captured other players' pennies by tossing your pennies to land on top.

Another favorite was Jackstraws, where we dropped thirty-one wheat straws and picked up one at a time without moving any other, with the winner having the most sticks at game's end. But my sisters and I also enjoyed jump rope, Blind Man's Bluff, hopscotch, and hide-and-seek. I sometimes played hoop racing with my brothers and, a few times, Rounders, featuring a wooden bat, a leather-covered ball, and four sacks of straw in a diamond formation, with the scoring based on touching each straw sack. Later, these were the same games my sons played. My daily concentration as a young girl, however, was on domestic chores and learning to read and write. Of all these chores, it was the gift of reading that stimulated my curiosity and opened the world of imagination to me.

I learned my letters using a simple, single-page hornbook, with a handle hanging by a cord of my dresses girdle. I recall Mother constantly declaring, "Mercy, dear girl, remember, recitation and memorization, recitation and memorization; practice makes perfect." The hornbook became a constant companion. At every chance between chores, and before and after playing games, I would pick up the paddle and recite the alphabet, vowels and consonants, and the Lord's Prayer, concluding with the Roman numerals. I must have been about three or four years old when I could recite everything on the paddle from memory without referring to the chunk wood banging against my leg when I walked or ran.

As time progressed, Mother introduced me to the more challenging *New England Primer,* which repeated the alphabet, vowels, and consonants, adding words from two to six syllables, religious maxims, illustrations, alphabet assistants, contractions, catechism answers, and moral lessons. Challenging though the Primer was, I was happy to be relieved of the cumbersome hornbook. Mother also gave me John White's *The*

Countryman's Conductor in Reading and Writing True English, a speller which offered more words and reading drills based on previously learned and new vocabulary. I also began reading the *King James Bible*, but it was learning my hand that proved the most demanding.

The task of learning penmanship was shared by my mother, father, and older brothers, Joseph and James. I practiced the basic English Round copperplate, the cursive Gothic minuscule, and the elegant Italian *cancellaresca* hand, the latter becoming my preferred script. My reason for the choice was simple: the script was pretty and elegant, and still is. Although I cannot recall its name or author, I spent hours copying script from the phrases and words into a copybook. The biggest test of my dexterity, patience, and concentration, however, was learning how to hold a quill, trimming the tip with a small knife, and preparing the black ink by mixing a teaspoon of copperas, tannic acid, a pinch of gum Arabic, and a pint of water. This was something I did until my husband gifted me with an Italian gilt-bronzed and silver scrollwork inkstand with two inkwells, into which I dipped a metal-tipped wood stylus pen. *What a luxury,* I thought at the time. No more struggling with trimming quill tips and preparing ink.

I can only smile now thinking about those early attempts at writing, finding more ink on my fingers than in the mixing plate. Practicing penmanship was as laborious as my learning the essentials of domesticity, child-rearing, domestic medicine, and household management under Mother's tutelage. My father and brother James reminded me that an excellent hand said as much about an individual's intelligence as the books they read, for without a legible, graceful script, one could not express their ideas with clarity. For me, writing was exhilarating and liberating because I could express my opinions and exercise my creative spirit at the same time. At the time, however, I did not realize all this education was designed to reinforce my role as a future wife, mother, and household manager.

Mother was born in 1702 into the prominent Allyne family whose proud lineage, like that of my family, dated back to the early establishment of the Plymouth Colony in the 1620s and 1630s. She and Father married in 1720 when both were eighteen years of age. Mother was a traditional woman who schooled my sisters and me in the domestic skills necessary to becoming dutiful wives and mothers. This also meant preparing us for marriage to the right man who came from a socially and financially prominent family, who would enhance our family's position in Massachusetts Bay society. Of course, as a child, the idea of marriage, children, and social position were alien to me. But I was wedded to family and social traditions, and the image of the Otis family was everything. However, our family's prominence could not avoid tragedies, which seemed to come in a deluge.

Between 1730 and 1739, Mother was continually pregnant and although my household responsibilities increased, I was always excited about welcoming new brothers or sisters into the family. My sister Mary was born in 1730 and Hannah arrived in 1732. Although I became more involved in household chores during Mother's later pregnancies, my responsibilities included tutoring my younger sisters, Mary and Hannah, in their reading, a role for which I barely felt qualified. I was thankful Father and my brothers, James and Joseph, helped when they could, finding myself spending more time helping Mother with the chores and gardening as each pregnancy progressed. When time allowed, I continued my studies albeit without the aid of Mother who, by day's end, was exhausted. However, I learned during these nine years how to manage my time and deal with the tragedies of life.

In 1736, my sister Martha was born but died within six weeks, from what the doctor guessed was an unknown respiratory ailment. We lost my sister Abigail in 1738 after four weeks. Once again, the doctor could only guess at the cause. In 1739, my sister Elizabeth, the first so named, passed away after her first birthday in 1740. In her case, the doctor identified the cause as the grippe because she had a high fever, cough, chills, sore throat, and runny nose. When Mother became pregnant again in 1739, we were a family wearied by death. So, when Samuel was born in 1740, we held our collective breaths for the first year, after which we all felt relieved.

In 1746, Mother was forty-four when she became pregnant again. Even at eighteen, I knew this was dangerous, forty-five being an advanced age for child-birthing. We had suffered so many losses during the 1730s, we were fearful for Mother's health, no less for the child she was carrying. Stillbirths and mothers dying from a variety of known and unknown ailments during childbirth were common enough in younger women, but at forty-five, it was a far more serious matter entirely. I only learned later that Mother had given birth to two stillborn children earlier in her marriage before my brothers, Joseph and James, were born. Over her life, Mother gave birth to fifteen children, of which only seven survived to reach adulthood. But childbirth was not the only reason all ages of men and women died.

This was a time in our colony's history when diseases like typhoid, the bloody flux (dysentery), grippe (influenza), the dreaded black pox (smallpox), and putrid fever (typhus) flourished with devastating results, and a child's sniffle, sneeze, or fever would send parents into a panic. I knew later as a mother feeling the same anxiety when one of my boys caught a fever or coughed. Then, there was the consumption disease, which afflicted and took the lives of many colonists. From personal experience, I came to know this disease for which there was no cure. I recall Mother telling me that the first order of business for her and other newlyweds was to buy a book on domestic medicine, which offered homemade remedies, and finding a local midwife or doctor, the latter being rare. What I did know was these diseases struck with no distinction to class or station in life; rich and poor alike suffered and died equally.

So, with all this in mind, I remember, as if it were yesterday, in 1747, when Mother called to Father to have the doctor come quickly. She knew it was her time. To my surprise, when the doctor arrived, he asked me to help in the delivery. I did not recall Father ever attending Mother's childbirth events, although I never came to know why. The doctor's orders were explicit. I was to hold Mother's hand and wipe her forehead with a wet towel to keep her calm. Although I had experienced the births and deaths of newborns, I was scared being in the room while Mother cried out in pain. Every time she let out a yell and squeezed, my hand and fingers went numb. It may have hurt me but nowhere near what Mother was experiencing.

I did not dare look down at the doctor's struggling hands. He was in a wild sweat, and I remember, above Mother's cries of pain, the doctor exhorting her to "Push, push, breath, push, breath, push. Do not despair; we are almost there." Then, suddenly, I heard a wail and looking down, I saw Elizabeth in the doctor's bloody hands. Mother had decided when she first became pregnant that if she gave birth to a girl, she wanted her named Elizabeth to honor her recently deceased namesake. I thought it was a miracle that Mother and Elizabeth survived; an amazing, if not a scary, experience and one I would remember when my time came.

I recalled Mother at once releasing her grip and looking up to me, saying, "Mercy, what are you doing here, child?" I responded in a soft voice, "The doctor needed my help. How are you, Mama?" She smiled, "I am fine now, child." Before I could respond, the doctor, who had gently cleaned the infant and swathed little Elizabeth in a soft coverlet, said, "Mercy, say hello to your little sister and please place her in the crib." I looked at the little bundle in my arms, kissed her forehead, welcomed her into the family, and softly murmured, "I am your older sister, Mercy," before doing as I was told.

Everyone was ecstatic, especially Father, who feared for the loss of his beloved wife and partner. Now we held our collective breaths, hoping Elizabeth would survive her first year. The doctor was surprised that mother and Elizabeth had survived, considering Mother's age and the difficulty of the birth. As I look back through the sometimes-clouded vision of my life, I realized that in my youth, I bore witness to the strength and fragility of life; lessons learned I took with me later into life when lying in my own birthing bed. At that time, I thought this was the one time men were not the stronger sex, which was why husbands did not attend childbirths.

After Elizabeth's birth, I noticed everyone looked at me differently. I was no longer their little girl; I had become a young woman. Although my daily schedule had become busier, ranging from rising at five in the morning until ten in the evening, I did not let it interrupt my studies with Uncle Jonathan. Just as important in my life, the events and ordeals of those years made me more self-confident, self-aware, and self-disciplined. This was exemplified by my non-traditional education and reading curriculum, but more about this episode of my life in the next chapter.

Plymouth, Friday, 21 May 1813

CHAPTER 3

READER TODAY, LEADER TOMORROW

I was always curious about the books in the family library, so exploring this private space accessible only to my father and brothers became an obsession. Even Mother only entered this private domain when invited, or to dust and clean. I recall walking past the library, peering through the crack in the door, looking at the shelves of books, and listening to my father and brothers recite phrases in some alien language. I asked myself, *What was this foreign tongue and what was in those books?* My curiosity only increased my desire to sneak more than a peek and get into Father's guarded domain. I wanted to read the books, but this was Father's inner sanctum and one entered by invitation only, which did not include my sisters and me. Of course, I was admittedly a stubborn child who only abided rules with which I agreed and ignored those with which I did not. The forbidden library was one such rule I did not tolerate.

My first test of Father's rule and patience came during a game of hide-and-seek. In my haste to best my brother James, I opened and closed the door to the library quietly, believing it would be the last place he would look. There I stood, giggling and hiding, behind the door when I heard footsteps approach. Thinking it was James, I ran to Father's desk and hid underneath it. Unknown to me, it was not James but Father who entered. He closed the door and sat in his chair. I curled into a ball and squirreled away into the furthest recess of the desk, hoping his foot would not discover my hiding place. Then I heard the door open and James inquiring if he had seen me. Father retorted, "Why should she be in here? She knows entry into this room is forbidden. Now go away and find your sister. I am busy. Stop interrupting me."

My feeling of relief lasted only for a moment as I saw Father's right foot shuffle forward touching my leg and looking up, saw him peering down at me with a cocked head and saying, "Mercy, you know better. Now come out of there." I stood up and fixed my dress, replying to Father that I was sorry but thought James would not look for me in the library. I thought it was a great idea and told him so. Smiling, Father said I was only half right, because he had found me. He then told me, "His little scamp" as he often called me, to run along and I might find a better hiding place in the bathing room tub next to his and Mother's bedroom. James would never think of looking for me there. I clearly recall, as if it were yesterday, him saying, "Run along now and don't tell anyone you were in here. You might need a good hiding place in the future." I smiled, nodded, and ran off like the wind. Looking back now, I realized Father was not angry with me.

There was something about the special bond between Father and daughters. In my experience, I have seen how fathers dote on their daughters. I think this bond has to do with fathers believing their little girls need protection from the vagaries and dangers of life. This notion was certainly an extension of the age-old idea that men generally viewed women as the weaker sex who needed their guidance and protection. Father always seemed to forgive my obstinate and challenging behavior, often telling me I was his little imp whom he loved very much, even though I drove him to distraction. He was certainly not that understanding or forgiving when it came to my brothers, Joseph or James. But that was not the end of my quest. I had survived entering Father's inner sanctum, but now I thought, *How do I get at those books?* My older brother Joseph was off to Harvard, so I had to rely on James.

My scheme was simple. I would have James become a party to my plot. This was not the last time I roped poor James into one of my schemes.

I convinced him when he could, and without Father knowing, to sneak books he thought proper for me from Father's library. I would read them and have him return them to the shelf, believing Father would be none the wiser. I read Joseph Addison's and John Dryden's poetry, Shakespeare's plays, *Aesop's Fables*, *Pilgrim's Progress*, *Robinson Crusoe*, and *Gulliver's Travels*. I was mesmerized by Defoe's and Swift's adventure novels, the beauty of Addison's and Dryden's verses, moral and often humorous lessons in *Aesop's Fables*, and Bunyan's allegorical description of his journey from a devastated city to the city of God. One of my favorite authors, though, was Shakespeare. His comedies and tragedies were entertaining; his histories offered a window into the intrigues of the English royal houses, and his sonnets were beautifully crafted. I would reproduce their lines in my penmanship copybook so I could remember them. Even then, I was still hearing Mother's voice, "Recitation and memorization, Mercy. Memorization and recitation."

But I was greedy and wanted more of this knowledge, resolving to get it by the direct approach of asking Father, or through chicanery. I discarded the direct approach, believing it was too risky. If Father said no, then my hopes would be dashed. So, deception it became. Once again, my poor and lovable brother James became my co-conspirator. I wanted to take part in his scheduled university tutorial with our uncle, Reverend Jonathan Russell. I was thirteen and knew James, who was sixteen, had completed Latin School, would need to complete his tutorial for acceptance into Harvard College. James told me our uncle would tutor him for about a year. This concerned me because if he went off to Harvard before I could take part in the tutorial, the chances of me enhancing my education would be difficult, if not impossible.

James thought me crazy, or in the colloquialism of the day, I was as as mad as a hatter. A young girl studying the classics, history, political theory, and philosophy? He said it was absurd, believing it an impossible dream. But, nonetheless, he said he would help, if for no other reason than to see how Father, Mother, and Uncle Jonathan would react to my ludicrous request.

James told me the university tutorial would reinforce the Latin School curriculum in grammar, spelling, reading, penmanship, speech, composition, and rhetoric, also adding ethics, history, geography, logic, political theory, law, and moral and natural philosophy. He would read the best English authors (Milton, Locke, Addison, Pope, Swift, Addison and Steele), and translations of Ancient Greek and Roman writers. I knew my grammar, spelling, reading, penmanship, speech, and composition were as good as his, but I could not say the same about the other authors, books, subjects, and foreign languages. I would be asking our uncle to let me take part in the tutorial, even though I had not attended Latin School. Also, as a female, the tutorial was certainly not the normal training regimen for a young lady in the 1740s, or even today for that matter.

I knew Uncle Jonathan well. He had presided over each baptism and funeral, and often came to our Sunday suppers with his lovely wife, and my namesake, Mercy Otis Russell. Although Aunt Mercy had given birth to six children, none had survived. The causes for their deaths were unknown because Aunt Mercy and Uncle Jonathan never spoke of them. I can only assume they were victims of the numerous diseases and childhood ailments common in the colonies at the time. Uncle Jonathan was well-educated and open-minded with an extensive library, a graduate of Harvard College, and a certified tutor for that institution. The challenge was convincing Father and Mother to let me study with James while they intervened on my behalf with Uncle. I knew this would not be an easy task. Having already roped James into the plan, I asked him to convince Father of my request while I took on the difficult mission of convincing Mother.

My duties at home had become less onerous because Hannah and Mary were taking on more responsibilities. With the exception of teaching Samuel his reading and writing lessons, I had more leisure time, so my attendance at the tutorial would not be a burden on the family, or so I innocently rationalized. I was placing my hopes on my brother's shoulders, but I knew him well. He would fight for me, being a very convincing advocate who took winning personally and hated losing at anything.

James approached Father, who was not surprised by the unusual request. He knew me too well, but a young lady wanting to study the classics, law, philosophy, and history? "To what end?" Father told James. "She cannot pursue a public career. Young ladies are taught reading, writing, arithmetic, child-rearing, household management, French, dancing, and music. But that is all. This is what potential suitors from prominent families expect from future wives and mothers. No man would court, no less marry, a young lady who was as well-read or more so than himself." But James was more persistent, pointing to my curiosity and passion for books, and my natural intelligence. He admitted to sneaking me books from the library and how I consumed them quickly and always demanded more. Before he could continue, Father told him he had known he had been sneaking books from the library for his precocious, little scamp. James was surprised that Father had said nothing, asking him why he had not. Father told him, "It was fun having you and Mercy think you were pulling the wool over my eyes." James then noted how I had matured as a young woman, and to put a damper on this opportunity to improve my intellect would be morally wrong.

James told him I would speak with Mother and, if she approved, would he and Mother intercede with Uncle Jonathan on my behalf? He nodded and said, "Let us see what Mother thinks and then I will speak with Mercy before approaching Uncle Jonathan." When James informed me of Father's decision, I was ecstatic, adding that he had always known about our little plot about the library books. I could only smile at this revelation, knowing Father would deny me few requests because of his special bond with me and my sisters. But now came the difficult task of convincing Mother, which would not be easy.

When I mentioned my request to her, she did not seem surprised, which made me think she might have already spoken with Father. She obviously had not, as her next statement proved it. She wondered aloud, quite disparagingly, how it would appear to a prospective beau that I had a professional's education. She pointed out men only cared about how, "You might enhance his family's social and financial prominence, give him children, teach them their letters, and keep a household." They did not need or want a highly educated woman. It was a threat to them and then, pausing for a moment, she mused that at times, this might be a good thing and chuckled. Her last comment caught me off guard. I had always thought of Mother as a traditional, practical woman who cared little for higher education.

She may have appeared traditional, but I suspected deep down she would have liked to achieve more in her life. She said if our uncle agreed to tutor me and believed he would, because he had a high opinion of me, the study would be very intense and challenging. Another surprise. I hardly thought he noticed me, but Mother pointed out we children were not always privy to adult conversations. "You will, of course, need to speak with Father but, if he agrees, you have my blessing," she told me. I was overjoyed and at once ran off to ask Father.

Excited, I dashed into the library without knocking and saw Father and James sitting side by side, reviewing a lengthy document. I knew our oldest brother, Joseph, had gone through the same process and been tutored by Uncle Jonathan, but he was finishing his legal studies at Harvard College so I had no point of reference as to what the tutorial was all about. Without excusing myself, I blurted out that Mother had approved my studying with James. Looking up, he smiled, saying he knew she would, but our uncle was quite another matter. Stunned, I simply asked, "Then you agree?" Frowning at me, he said, "Did you really think I would say no?" I also recall him saying, "Mercy, you are sometimes a recalcitrant child, my little scamp, but you have a special gift, and I do not want to see it wasted." He then beckoned me to sit down next to him and James to see the document they were reviewing. It was the reading curriculum for the tutorial. He looked and told me I would be taking on a difficult undertaking. As I scanned the paper, I was excited and stunned at the same time, thinking to myself, *How am I to read authors in Latin, Greek, or French?* I knew nothing of these foreign tongues.

James must have sensed my anxiety, for he touched my hand and told me books on the list had been translated into English and others were in dual translations. So, I could read the English text while learning the important phrases of the other language. Relieved, I then asked Father if he thought Uncle would agree. I remembered James saying count on it, but Father simply frowned and said nothing. In my mind, I was cautiously celebrating victory. I had connived my parents, with the help of my brother, to convince them in giving me the opportunity of expanding my education. Now, all that remained was convincing our uncle, and Sunday supper would be the event to persuade. And in this case, Mother would become my heroine.

On Sunday, Mother left nothing to chance, making every effort to impress, so-to-speak. I had never seen her concentrate so much, preparing a sumptuous meal with vegetable soup, roast turkey, cranberry sauce, sausages, vegetables, corn bread, pudding, coffee, and tea. Dessert included dough encrusted Blueberry Duffs, breaded spiced Apple Betties (my favorite), with both coated in powdered sugar, and a peach brandy cordial. Hannah and Mary oversaw the preparation of the desserts while I helped Mother with the other courses. At one point, Mother turned to Hannah and Mary, chiding them about eating the Duffs and telling them, as she always did, they would spoil their appetites. She pointed out that Duffs and Betties were the favorites of Uncle Jonathan and Aunt Mercy. Hannah asked Mother why she was preparing so much food while she and Mary stole another Apple Betty from the tray. Mother replied it was an especially important day for me but to remember the rule that a man with a full stomach was easily manipulated and controlled, and she planned to get to Uncle Jonathan through his belly. "By the by, I expect all of you to be on your best behavior at the table," she said.

As the meal progressed, the look on Uncle Jonathan's face was priceless. He was in epicurean heaven, smiling with each bite and complimenting Mother for as fine a meal as he had ever eaten. This drew a scowl from Aunt Mercy, whose smile suggested, *See what you get for your next supper*. I recalled grinning at this experience. Poor Uncle Jonathan who, noticing Aunt Mercy's scowling look, became tongue-tied as he tried to first explain himself to his frowning wife and finally apologized to her in defeat. But when Mary and Hannah served the desserts, Uncle's pained look turned euphoric. He sipped his tea, had one of each cake, and when Father brought out the peach brandy, he was hooked. While Mother, Father, Uncle Jonathan, Aunt Mercy, and James retired to the parlor, we girls cleared the table and began washing and drying dishes, glasses, and cutlery. As I scrubbed and dried, my thoughts were in the parlor, wondering how my parents were arguing my case to Uncle. Although I was as nervous as our cat waiting for the field mouse to stir, I had to keep a calm demeanor, for I would know soon enough.

Then a serious-looking James peeked into the kitchen and told me my presence was requested. I dropped my cloth, shed my apron, brushed my dress, fixed my hair, and followed James into the parlor. My heart was pounding so hard I thought it would burst from my breast. I walked into the parlor to four dour-looking faces staring at me. I thought, *This did not look promising* and fully expected unwelcome news. Father asked me to sit down, saying they had been talking about my request. He would let Uncle Jonathan have the floor. I could not help but feel downtrodden, expecting the worse. Mother, on the other hand, had the look of self-satisfaction but for what reason I could not fathom.

Looking at me seriously, Uncle Jonathan told me, after considering my parents' and Jameses arguments, he had decided to take me on, with my brother, as a student for the university tutorial. I was elated but before I could thank him, he continued by telling me that I had not had the benefit of a Latin School training, so he would need to alter my curriculum without hindering Jameses studies because studying the university curriculum was meaningless without a point of reference. Selected parts of the Latin School curriculum would supply the necessary foundation. I would also take part in Jameses university training program at the same time. He said this would be challenging because I would also be reading the tutorial authors. In other words, I would be doing twice the amount of reading, but his goal was to have me as well-educated as any college candidate or graduate.

He asked if I understood, to which I nodded, thanking him and my parents for the opportunity and promising to not let anyone down. Smiling, Uncle Jonathan said I might not thank him after seeing the reading schedule. Aunt Mercy rose and gave me a kiss on the cheek, saying how happy she was for me, and she knew I would do well. Then, getting in another sly comment about Uncle Jonathan's meal blunder, added to not let Jonathan bully me. Musing, I told myself she was still annoyed over the meal comment and poor Uncle Jonathan would never live it down. I nodded and thanked her for the support and slowly left them to their brandy and conversation. I skipped and hopped down the hallway, smiling widely at my good fortune. I had done it. Over the years, I have pondered why Uncle Jonathan agreed to tutor me. But Mother had once told me that since Uncle Jonathan and Aunt Mercy were childless, having buried six children at young ages, she believed they saw me as the daughter they never had, further noting two of the children lost had been my namesakes. Mother may have been correct in this assessment. She was rarely wrong when it came to reading people's motives.

The next day, Monday, James, and I drove the family carriage to Uncle Jonathan's home in West Barnstable, five miles from our farm in Barnstable. I could not hold my excitement, chattering the entire trip, going on and on about the subjects and authors I would be reading. To his credit, James let me babble on without comment, suspecting he was less enthusiastic and more apprehensive about the challenging curriculum he was undertaking. When we arrived at Uncle's, I started to spring from the carriage before it stopped, and poor James had to pull back abruptly on the reins to force a short stop. Uncle's stable boy came out and took control of the horse and carriage. James asked him to walk the horse, wipe him down, and give him feed and water. The young man nodded while I pulled at Jameses sleeve, my enthusiasm overwhelming me. I wanted to start. James shook his head and turned toward the front door. Before he could knock, Aunt Mercy opened the door, gave me a hug, kissed me on the cheek and beckoned us to follow her to the library.

Stepping inside, I stood in the doorway, dumbfounded. I never imagined so many books in one place. The library simply dwarfed our family's collection. I strode over to the shelves and scanned, tier upon tier, of books in English, Latin, Greek, French, German, Spanish, and Italian, some in dual translations covering every subject one could imagine. I could not believe my good fortune, wondering how anyone could digest all the knowledge in these books. For me, it was a dream come true and I could not wait to start. Uncle Jonathan strolled in and, looking at me, simply said, "Impressive, yes?" Tongue-tied, all I could do was nod. Without any further conversation, we got to work. He told us Aunt Mercy would prepare a light dinner at midday so we could keep up our strength. Uncle noted casually that mental exertion is sometimes as tiring as playing games or physical labor. At the time, I thought this an exaggeration but, as time progressed, I came to realize he was correct.

He sat at his desk, offering us chairs in front of him, and went ahead to explain his approach to the tutorial. Upon our arrival, we would be given a reading assignment in the morning to complete by the dinner hour. After dinner, we would discuss the book, focusing on the author: where he was from, when he was writing, the book's subject matter, why he was writing, and the audience he hoped to reach. We would also take texts home and prepare essays, which we would discuss at the next session. Some books could not leave the library because they were rare and expensive, so we would read them in the library or, in my case, the parlor.

Uncle did not intend to lecture or teach. His method was to listen to our explanations of the readings and, in our discussions, dissect the author's arguments. Turning to me, he told me based on the schedule he had worked out, I would take more books home, read them, and prepare essays covering the who, when, what, why, book themes, and author's audience. Most of these books would be from the Latin School curriculum readings that James had already completed. He then went ahead to lay out our schedule.

For the first month, my schedule would be Mondays, Wednesdays, and Fridays, while James attended five days a week. After the first month, Uncle would adjust my schedule accordingly, but he expected to see me at least twice a week to discuss my readings and essays. By agreement with my mother, he noted my readings should not interfere with my household responsibilities. Considering this warning, he would send me home with enough reading material to accommodate the schedule so if unforeseen events surfaced, I would not fall behind. I nodded my understanding. Interestingly enough, Mother's last pregnancy was one such unforeseen circumstance.

Having completed his recitation, he wasted no time and, turning to James, handed him a copy of Matthew Bacon's *A New Abridgement of the Law*, telling him to begin reading the first two chapters. They would discuss Bacon after dinner. I later came to appreciate Bacon's work when I began studying English Common Law. His three volumes, an accumulation of the dissertations and treatises of Sir Jeffrey Gilbert, Lord Chief Baron of the Exchequer, was the standard encyclopedia of the Common Law in eighteenth-century America. But I digress; I need to stay on topic or will drift into unnecessary narratives.

Turning to me, he outlined my reading program. The plan was simple and comprehensive. I would do my reading in the parlor in the mornings. We would review and discuss the readings in the parlor, while James did his reading in the library. His rationale was that these were Latin School authors, so there was no need to waste Jameses time. We would follow the same routine in the parlor for my essays, reviews, and discussions in the mornings. After dinner, I could take part in the review and discussions of Jameses subjects or continue my reading in the parlor. In this way, I would continue my Latin School curriculum readings while gaining a familiarity with Jameses college-level subjects. He hoped this schedule would bring me up to Jameses reading level before he left for Harvard. Uncle smiled and said I would be doing a great deal of reading and writing, noting that the latter would have the added advantage of improving my hand.

Uncle then turned to a table behind him and placed three books in front of me, saying that I could start by reading Arthur Golding's translation, *The Commentaries of Caesar*. I would take it home and prepare an essay on the *Commentaries* for our next session on Wednesday. After completing the *Commentaries*, I would begin reading John Dryden's translation of *Lives of Illustrious Greeks and Romans* by Plutarch and Philemom Holland's, *History of the Twelve Caesars* by Suetonius.

Ahering to our schedule, and while James did his morning reading assignment in the library, Uncle Jonathan and I would retire to the parlor to review and discuss the *Commentaries*. The essays on the translations of Plutarch and Suetonius would follow the same pattern, which became the standard practice; that is, reading, writing, reviewing, and discussing. I nodded and thought to myself, *What have I gotten myself into?*

After dinner, I joined Uncle Jonathan and James in their discussion of Bacon's compilation of English Common Law. Although I could have continued my reading in the parlor, I knew the *Commentaries* could wait until I got home and prepared my essay for Wednesday's session. But I was curious about Jameses college-level reading, which, in this case, had to do with the evolution of the English legal system. This decision became an important moment in my intellectual development because the subject of the constitutional and English Common Law so intrigued me that it became less of a subject to study and more a passion, an avocation.

From what I overheard, the English system was based on the principle that rulings made by the King's courts were the common custom of the realm versus decisions made in local and manorial courts, driven by provincial laws and customs. English Common Law owed its creation to the legal reforms of King Henry II and evolved through succeeding monarchs, based on the precedents of the Court of the King's Bench, Exchequer, and Court of Common Pleas. I discovered common law was different from the statutory laws, enacted by parliamentary legislation because it was based on legal precedent.

I was intrigued by what constituted a legal precedent and asked Uncle Jonathan to explain the concept. Without comment, he turned to James and asked him to explain it to me. James told me precedent was a principle or rule set by an earlier legal case that was binding on other later tribunals, when deciding cases with similar issues. The English legal system, he explained, placed great importance on deciding cases according to consistent rules so that similar facts yielded similar and predictable results. I nodded my understanding and decided to return to my reading which, I might add, was remarkably interesting and informative about one of the most well-known celebrities in history, with whom I was only familiar from Shakespeare's drama, *The Tragedy of Julius Caesar*. I could ask James for more information on the English legal system on our ride home, but I did not want to intrude on his schedule. He was being groomed for college while I was being groomed for who knew what.

Uncle Jonathan was correct; even with a light dinner, I was mentally drained by the end of the day. I could not wait to get home, finish the *Commentaries*, and begin preparing my essay, after which I would plunge into Dryden's and Holland's translations. On our ride home, I commented that the discussion of English Common Law was fascinating, and I would definitely like to explore more of the subject. However, I knew Uncle would want me to be better prepared with other readings. James simply commented that Uncle Jonathan was giving me the Latin School reading to prepare me for the more complicated subjects in history, philosophy, political theory, constitutional and English Common law, and in the languages of Latin, Greek, and French. He chuckled, saying that at least he would not be subjecting me to science, mathematics, and geography. However, I had not thought about foreign languages but held my tongue, knowing full well their study would be very demanding.

When we arrived home, my parents asked how the first day went. I regaled them with the reading assignments and what I had learned about the English legal system. They could see we were tired, so Mother took us into the kitchen for a light supper, telling me to go to bed afterwards. When I asked about my chores, she simply said my education was more important than household duties, and Hannah and Mary knew I would be tired so they did them. As I went to my room, I stopped in to thank them for helping Mother. They just smiled and told me to get to bed.

Rising early the next day, I helped Mother prepare breakfast and then retired to my room to finish the *Commentaries* and begin drafting my essay. In my haste to complete the essay, I began scribbling rapidly, forgetting the rule that a legible, well-crafted hand was important for understanding what I wrote about. So, I quelled my enthusiasm and slowed down. I really wanted to make a good first impression on Uncle Jonathan, who had broken with the social tradition about a young girl's education.

On Wednesday, we traveled to Uncle's home. I was excited, looking forward to impressing him with the first essay. When we entered the library, Uncle Jonathan gave James copies of the Henry II's *Assizes of Clarendon; Magna Carta Libertatum*; legal opinions of Sir Edward Coke, Chief Justice of the Court of Common Pleas; John Selden's *History of Tithes*, and the last two volumes of Bacon's *Abridgement*, telling him to begin reading the *Assizes* and *Magna Carta,* which they would discuss after dinner. The Coke, Selden, and the remaining parts of Bacon's work James would take hone. The authors would be discussed at the next session. This process offered me the opportunity to sneak-a-peek and review the subject matter with my brother, thereby advancing my reading while not intruding on Jameses schedule. Retiring to the parlor, he turned to me with a slight smile and asked to see what I had written about Caesar. The decisive moment had arrived, and my nervousness showed.

He read the two-page essay, then began turning the essay clockwise and counterclockwise, reading my marginal notes. With a chagrined look, he asked, "Why all the marginalia?" I explained that after reading the completed text, I noted overlooked facts, so I went back to those paragraphs and made notes in the margins. He was neither impressed nor pleased with my reasoning, telling me before putting pen to paper, I should create an outline of what I wanted to say. He repeated his first day's lesson: "Ask yourself who was the author, where was he from, when was he writing, what was the book about, why was he writing, and who was the intended audience? Then, and only then, could you offer an opinion on the author and work in an organized, coherent manner. Doing this would end the need for marginalia."

He even extended this notion to personal correspondence and professional publications. I nodded, now feeling annoyed with myself. He did add that I had a beautiful hand, the Italian script being a very elegant, educated style. Though I did not feel very complimented, I had learned a valuable lesson. Before putting pen to page, I need to create an outline. In this way, I would eliminate the margin notations. Unfortunately for my correspondents, I continue using marginalia in personal letters. There are some habits impossible to break.

He then asked what I thought of the *Commentaries* and its author. I launched into my description of the book and the man. When done, Uncle Jonathan noted that I had done an excellent job of describing the what, where, how, and, to a limited degree, the who, but I did not answer the why. Answering the why would allow me to know more about the man and the motivation for penning the work. He did not expect me to know this at present, which is why he gave me Plutarch's, *Lives of Illustrious Greeks and Romans* and Suetonius, *History of the*

Twelve Caesars. Their observations would supply more context about Julius Caesar, bearing in mind as a reader or writer, I must always think in terms of context and motivation. Another important lesson learned.

While at dinner, I told James about the idea of capturing an author's context and motivation for authoring the book. After we returned to the library, James asked Uncle Jonathan what he meant by motivation and context. Uncle told us contexts were the circumstances surrounding a person or event, while motivation was what drove the author to undertake the work. Using the *Commentaries* as an illustration, he explained Caesar came from a socially and politically prominent family. He was a highly effective orator, lawyer, general, and politician. The *Commentaries* were not only the story of his conquest of Gaul. The Gallic War was his context, but his motivation was to realize political power, wealth, and social prominence, which would increase with his journal, describing how he conquered Gaul and expanded the Republic. After reading of his triumphs over Pompey, and consolidation of power with victories in Spain, Greece, Asia Minor, Egypt, and North Africa, one got a fuller understanding of Caesar's motivation. The *Commentaries* describing his conquest of Gaul was the context which motivated his goal, the rule of an empire.

He continued by noting no author wrote without a reason; there was always a context and a motivation. Historians, philosophers, political theorists, and jurists, even poets, novelists, and dramatists, published in the context of their times, motivated by their ideologies, opinions, or desires for personal gain or power. In the end, all authors looked to impress an individual or group. The Roman historian Suetonius looked to impress the emperor Trajan, while Machiavelli wanted the favor of the Borgia Pope and Medici bankers. Conversely, Thomas Becket and Thomas More were motivated by religious principles in the context of unchecked royal power. They did not impress, and Henry II and Henry VIII executed both. He emphasized that we must never forget that the study of an author, individual, or idea was always about context and motivation. I came to realize how important motive and context would be in my future works, and I must always create an outline before taking my quill in hand.

After the first month, the schedule changed. Uncle Jonathan supplied books either at Sunday supper, or Wednesdays and Fridays when I attended in person. Jameses schedule did not change, as Uncle wanted him certified for Harvard College within six months. Knowing James was proficient in Latin, Greek, French, mathematics, astronomy, composition, philosophy, theology, and natural philosophy, he concentrated on law, Jameses chosen vocation. After James left for Harvard, and except for other students, I had Uncle's library to myself, with an open invitation to come and go at will.

My schedule did not change. Every Wednesday and Friday, I would discuss assigned readings and my essays. Knowing Uncle's schedule with other students, I found myself visiting the library on Saturdays, spending the entire day reading books not required by Uncle's program. I especially explored books on the law. The law became a passion for me because it offered a window into the evolution of great societies and cultures. When I explored the histories of ancient and modern civilizations, the common thread to their greatness was their legal system. Without law, society would devolve into chaos leading to the rule of the mob and ultimately the rise of the tyrant.

The months stretched into years, and I found myself visiting the library, his tutoring schedule allowing, three, four, and sometimes five days a week to continue my reading there in political theory, philosophy, law, history, drama, novels, and poetry. When reading Latin or French texts, I selected the dual Latin-English and French-English translations to enhance my skill in reading these languages while using the English portion to delve into the authors' ideas. Many times, during these exploratory visits, Uncle Jonathan would ask me to sit and discuss my readings, which were not assigned or for which I was preparing essays. We still adhered to our Wednesday and Friday tutoring schedule, but I did notice a change in our sessions, becoming more an exchange of opinions about authors and subjects.

Once Uncle realized my interest in law, he showered me with the books James had read during the tutorial. I also asked Father to buy books for our library, especially works on the English statutory and Common Law, a passion born from understanding that the law blended history, philosophy, and political theory. When I read the historians studying the Roman Empire or English monarchy, renowned ancient and modern philosophers, and political theorists, their texts always included the legal principles upon which their societies were founded. Simply stated, the law had its own history, philosophical foundation, and political reality reflective of the society in which it functioned.

Although Uncle Jonathan knew of my preoccupation with the study of law, he was intransigent about the reading of other authors and subjects. He taught me that philosophy, political theory, and history, especially the latter, were equally, if not more important. In his judgment, these subjects intersected and had to be viewed through the broader perspective of history. Law, like political theory and philosophy, evolved over time, and the study of their history was the only way to understand the development of social and cultural traditions. He believed there was a direct connection between authors like Aristotle to Machiavelli, Locke and others, in the same way there was a historical connection between Rome's *Twelve Tables*, the *Assizes of Clarendon* and *Magna Carta*, and English Common Law. There was no subject studied without knowing its history. This axiom even applied to poetry, drama, and novels. Besides his continual focus on context and motivation, the historical theme was a frequent element in our discussions of authors.

My visits to Uncle Jonathan had another less intellectual benefit. I was becoming an accomplished equestrian and carriage driver. On Sundays, after Father and Mother relented, I would take the reins of the carriage and drive to church. At other times, I would simply take one of the horses and ride down to the shore, book in hand, to read and enjoy the cooling salt air breeze. I thought my life was perfect, but life has a way of changing quickly. Before I move on to other matters, I must first describe a poignant tragedy in my life.

In May of 1750, Aunt Mercy, Uncle Jonathan's charming wife, passed away suddenly, leaving Uncle alone. She was fifty years old and over the years, Uncle had buried six children, so Aunt Mercy was all he had left. Father was deeply affected by the loss of his sister, his only remaining sibling with whom he had been very close. Father had previously lost his sister Mary in 1732, age forty-seven, and brothers Nathaniel in 1739, age forty-nine, and Solomon at childbirth in 1696. Aunt Mercy and Uncle Jonathan always managed to visit on a Sunday to dine with the family. She was the favorite of the whole family and her death affected all of us, especially me because I remembered how supportive she had been when I was requesting to study with Uncle Jonathan. Although I cannot prove it, I believe she spoke up for me when my parents, Uncle Jonathan, and James were debating my request.

Although Uncle continued to tutor me, I could see the pain in his eyes and feel his melancholy. At times during our discussions, his mind would wander momentarily, lost in memory of his beloved wife and life partner. I realized he was lonely, so I began spending more time with him, traveling to his home five times a week. Mary and Hannah often came along to bring a little joy into his life. They were more than happy to attend, for they too were saddened by Aunt Mercy's death and Uncle's loneliness. We never forgot to bring along a good supply of freshly made Duffs and Betties, his favorites. Even Samuel and Father came with me when their schedules allowed to spend time with him.

We wanted him to know he was very much a part of our family and loved by us. No matter the time we spent together, I could see there was an empty space in his life and heart. I came to appreciate the depth of his loss and feelings of loneliness when in 1808 my beloved husband, James, died. And even with children and grandchildren to fill the void in my heart, I remained heartbroken. Losing a life partner with whom you shared love was something you never get over.

Sad though he was, Uncle continued to guide my reading and education with the same enthusiasm he had showed prior to his loss. But I knew Uncle Jonathan felt as if he had no one, and as much as we tried to make him know he was family, part of his being was somewhere else. From the moment he lost Aunt Mercy, his life became a matter of waiting patiently until he could join her. Even after my marriage and move to Plymouth, I still made it a point of having James drive our carriage to his home on Saturdays to spend the day. Uncle Jonathan and James got along very well, and James made it a priority to have him spend weekends with us in Plymouth, regardless of the season or the weather. As I told James, "I cannot tell you how much this man has meant to my life. He was not just a teacher and tutor, but a collaborator, confidant, and dear friend." When he passed in 1759, I believe his wish had come true. He would now be with his Mercy. Every time I read a book, I think of this wonderful man who opened a world of knowledge to me.

Plymouth, Thursday, 24 June 1813

Chapter 4

THE CONSPIRACY

Although I helped Mother and my sisters with the household and farm chores, my schedule and studies of the great authors with Uncle Jonathan consumed my life. I thought my life was perfect, but Mother and Father took a different view. I was twenty-five, unmarried, and had no prospective beau on the horizon. The subtle hints started with Father noting to what end I was gaining all my knowledge. He pointed out I could not practice law, hold public office, or even publish because female writers were frowned upon in our religiously centered colony. Our society, he noted sarcastically, was not ready for a Justice Mercy Otis. I might be smarter than most men, but men did not want a wife who was more intelligent.

Mother was less subtle, telling me that if I persisted in pursuing an education, I would be known by the dreaded title, the Spinster of Barnstable. She then mentioned, not too diplomatically, the negative influence I was having on Hannah and Mary who, even though younger, seemed more interested in reading and learning unnecessary subjects than finding husbands. She did not want to be known as the mother of three spinsters, with little chance of loving on grandchildren or having family to care for her in old age. Mother then sadly noted Uncle Jonathan's lonely life. I could not argue her last point, but then I knew Uncle had us to look after him. Nonetheless, Mother and Father persisted with their concern for my marital status.

Courtship and marriage were part of our inherited European and English tradition. Men like my brothers Joseph, James, and Samuel were expected to marry and if they chose not to, they could lead productive and successful lives without social criticism. This was not so with women. We were expected to marry into prominent families who would enhance the family social and financial status in society. We were being groomed to breed civic minded children who strengthened the social order. The spinster, therefore, became a social outcast who diminished a family's prominence in society because people would ask what a family had done wrong to have a spinster or spinsters living at home. So, I could understand mother and father's concerns for their unwed daughters. I was twenty-five, Mary was twenty-three, and Hannah was twenty-one at a time when young girls married between the ages of sixteen and twenty. Even Elizabeth, my youngest sister, who was sixteen, was approaching the marrying age.

When I spoke with Hannah and Mary about Mother's protestations, they were hearing the same story and, like me, they had no prospects on the horizon. We attended Sunday church services and events, social gatherings, occasional parties, and the weddings of friends, but I for one was disinterested in seeking a mate. However, I knew we would continue hearing Mother's line, "Do you want to spend your life as a spinster: alone, unloved, with no children to look after you in old age, with only books to cuddle up with at night?" As I recall, paraphrasing her comments, Mary noted that Mother came from a different tradition, an older generation, and did we need men to make us happy? She thought not. Hannah was equally outspoken, proclaiming she would not marry a man simply because it was the only way she could be fulfilled. She then added with the siblings we had buried and diseases like Black pox, typhoid, grippe, Bloody flux, and putrid fever that ravaged our communities, why would any woman want to marry? She agreed with Mary and would choose whom she married, and it would not be an arranged marriage as was customary among the prominent families in the colony.

I reminded them Mother and Father might appear broad-minded, but we came from a prominent family dating back to the first settlers of this colony. Our education's goal was to attract the right husband, a man who supported us financially while enhancing our family's social and political status in society. When it came to traditional values like marriage, I told them Mother and Father were not open-minded. Their comments suggested we had too much education, which was not good for finding a mate. We might agree to avoid arranged marriages or chose to marry when we wanted, but as we were soon to discover, their fixation on this subject had taken on a life of its own. And little did I know there was a conspiracy afoot to nullify my part of the agreement led by my parents to make me the target of their "marry-off Mercy" game.

Unknown to me, they had enlisted my brother James to play the role of matchmaker. Had I known this at the time, it would not have been just ludicrous but downright hilarious. James was the least romantic person I knew, and to this day, I try to imagine my dear brother, bow and arrow in hand, pretending to be Cupid with little flapping wings and pointing his arrow at some unlucky man or me. The image was ridiculous, but I soon learned his aim would be perfect.

There are dates one never forgets, and Saturday, 15 December 1753, was one such example. Returning home after visiting with Uncle Jonathan, who was ill, I noticed a stranger sitting with my brother and father in the parlor. They rose and James introduced Mr. James Warren, a college friend who was passing through on his way to Plymouth. Holding out his hand, James slightly bowed, expressing his pleasure at making my acquaintance. As we shook hands, my brother James turned to him, asking if he would join us for supper. After some forceful back and forth between him, my brother, and my father, he accepted. Father rose and told me to inform Mother we would have a guest for supper. I turned and retreated to the kitchen to tell Mother. As I think of it now, at the time, I was more interested in reading John Starkey's translation,

The Works of the Famous Nicolas Machiavel: The History of Florence, The Prince, The Discourses, The Art of War that Uncle Jonathan had given me rather than attend a supper with someone I did not know. I wish my dear husband, James, was still with me. He would understand and have a good laugh.

In any case, I informed Mother to add another setting for Jameses guest, Mr. Warren. Carrying out her part of the charade perfectly, she looked over her shoulder and murmured, "Who is this Mr. Warren?" I told her he was a friend and classmate of James from Plymouth. She shook her head, annoyed at being inconvenienced, and told me to set a place for him next to James and Father. I finished the setting and, after excusing myself, retired to my room to freshen up. I closed the bedroom door quietly and gazing around appreciated that this was my special place, my inner sanctum. My quills, sheafs of paper, and books were arranged below the window facing the beautiful landscape. Taking off my walking dress and standing in my camisole, I filled the washstand with water, adding a little scented rose water, and dabbed at my face, hands, arms, and legs. Putting on a blue walking dress, I collected the crocheted shawl Mother had fashioned for me, draped it over my shoulders, and made my way to the dining room.

Everyone was seated and as I entered, Mr. Warren stood and bowed slightly. James offered the seat next to him, which put me directly across from Mr. Warren. Father bowed his head and repeated the oft-heard John Wesley prayer, "Be present at our table, Lord. Be here and everywhere adored. These creatures bless and grant that we may feast in paradise with thee. Amen." We all repeated amen, and Mother began serving the food. Mother had prepared turnip soup, roast mutton and currant jelly, carrots, potatoes, brown bread, stewed fruit, coffee, tea, and, for dessert, breaded spiced Apple Betties coated with powdered sugar and a tray with glasses for the peach brandy cordial. Mary, Hannah, and I thought Mother had made every effort to impress. Of course, I never realized she was applying her age-old axiom that had worked on Uncle Jonathan: the way to a man's heart was through his stomach. In this case, the stomach was Mr. Warren's, and the heart was mine. Even the seating had been pre-arranged so I would be facing Mr. Warren.

During dinner, Father, James, and Mr. Warren talked politics and legal matters. From an early age, I was aware of the political nature of our family. At this time, Father was a successful lawyer, Colonel in the Massachusetts militia, and Attorney General of Massachusetts. Later, he became a judge in the Massachusetts Bay General Court and, later, a highly respected member of the Council of Massachusetts. When chosen for the latter post, he had expected an appointment as Chief Justice of the Massachusetts Supreme Judicial Court, but the position went to Thomas Hutchinson, which created an enmity between our family, or should I say between my brother and the Hutchinsons. This would lead to tragic events in the future, but more about this matter later. So, Father's opinions on subjects, such as British rule and colonial representation in Parliament, were no surprise to me. He was one of those early patriots who were rare at the time in the colonies.

My brother James was no less outspoken on these issues of British and colonial governance and parliamentary representation, adding that the colonial governments needed to address other issues like slavery and a woman's right to a better education. Once again, this was part of the set-up with which I was unaware. When arguing the women's issues with Father, he continually held me out as an example of an educated young lady: the kind of woman who could vote, pursue a profession, and hold public office. But Father, liberal though he thought he was, strongly disagreed with James on this issue. This came as no surprise because their relationship had always been contentious, but even the disagreement between Father and James was part of the charade. They wanted to engage me in the conversation so I could impress Mr. Warren, who spoke little but when he did was thoughtful and laconic in his responses.

As chance would have it, he raised Father's eyebrows by agreeing with James on the loathsome treatment of women, which he compared to indentured servitude, if not a form of slavery, both institutions which he adamantly abhorred. Mother, who had moved to my side after supper, softly elbowed my side and smiled. I thought she enjoyed James and Mr. Warren getting his goat, but this too was part of the farce. She was pleased that poor Mr. Warren had not only taken the bait but did so by opening the discussion that she knew would include me.

To my surprise, Father turned the tables on everyone and asked, considering I was more educated than most men, what did I think about their opinions on women's education, voting, or holding public office. I noted Mother stiffening and scowling at Father, seeming to say without speaking, *What in the Lord's name are you doing?* Being totally in the dark as to what the family was up to, I thought Mother was frowning because she was worried Father's comment would undo her carefully contrived sumptuous meal, filled-stomach, capture-the-man's-heart strategy. Again, all this posturing was part of the deception.

Taking a deep breath, I said my sex was no less capable than men when it came to learning and intelligence. If women had the responsibility as their children's first teachers, should they not also learn subjects other than religion? I offered the opinion that a well-educated, intelligent young lady was an asset to a future husband, and not property bartered in a marriage lottery. To prove my point, I asked them to consider the celebrated women of history.

I expounded on the rights and status of Roman women who, in the late Republican and Imperial periods, could own property and land, write contracts and wills, inherit goods, work outside the home, appear in court, and run their own businesses. They may not have been able to vote or hold office, but they played public roles in the sphere of religion as vestals. For Roman women, divorce was legal and codified in the *Twelve Tables*. A wife simply had to leave her husband's house and take back her dowry. This was far more advanced than our current legal status and political condition, no less the social traditions hampering our educational opportunities and intellectual development.

Taking a sip of brandy, I continued that there were other examples of medieval and modern European women who were very celebrated by their peers. Sir Thomas More's daughter, Margaret Roper, was considered the most learned women of sixteenth-century England. She published a Latin-English translation of Erasmus, *A Devout Treatise upon the Paternoster*. Although I had not read Isotta Nogarella's works, Uncle Jonathan informed me she was an Italian author and intellectual of great note, being the first major female humanist. And there was the French classicist Anne Dacier, who translated the works of Horace, and *The Iliad* and *Odyssey*.

Lady Mary Wortley Montagu challenged contemporary English social attitudes toward women and their intellectual and social growth. Her *Turkish Embassy Letters* were the first secular work by a woman describing the Muslim east, and she was credited with introducing and advocating for smallpox inoculation in Britain upon returning from Istanbul. In the colonies today, women's role in society was governed by outdated traditions, offering us none of these opportunities because of religious beliefs.

We were subjected to the Puritan view of women's role in society. Their dogma perpetuated the idea that women were farmhands tending vegetable gardens, whose responsibilities as wives focused on caring for husbands, household management, and producing and guiding future generations of Puritan children. In contrast, Quaker women had more power in their denomination, and they strongly encouraged women to get an education. They allowed women to hold leadership positions in their churches and could travel to practice the ministry. We lived in a province where theological despotism has created a social structure where young girls and women were no more than servants, and I did not believe the Lord intended this to be the case.

I clearly remember at this point Father shook his head, saying that he should not have asked, and Mother retorted, "Then why did you? You know our Mercy is very outspoken." James chimed in, saying he could see Uncle Jonathan's tutoring had not gone to waste, stating that I had moved from simply reading texts to developing opinions about what I read. Mr. Warren noted he thought I had hit the mark and wanted to know more about my views on how to improve women's education and the institution of slavery. I remembered replying he should call me Mercy. But I could not see Mother grinning, never realizing she was thinking to herself, *I got him, and soon I will get her.* I was a pawn being moved around on the marital chessboard by a master of the game: my mother, the queen.

Continuing my recitation, I told them each town or borough should set up a girls' academy similar to the Latin School, with a curriculum emphasizing the classics, history, philosophy, political theory, French and Latin, arithmetic, drama, poetry, novels, and penmanship. The young ladies attending the school would also study the celebrated women of history to improve their self-confidence. These academies would be open to all, not just the rich or socially prominent. The affluent would pay for their daughters to attend while those without the means would attend for free, their tuition paid based on a tax levied on each household by the city, town, or borough. I also hoped in the future that young women, when male minds were more predisposed, could attend college and enter professions like medicine, law, politics, and ministry. This was my dream, but being a realist, I knew this would require a major change in male attitudes toward women's role in our society.

I then turned my attention to the abhorrent institution of slavery, noting I would emancipate all slaves in our colony, if any still were enslaved, as well as those in bondage in other colonies. Unfortunately, I did not believe this would happen in our southern colonies where agricultural production relied on the cheap labor of the enslaved. I would also reform the laws of indentured servitude, which I personally found repugnant and demeaning to the individual who was not paid for their work, could be physically abused, and had no access to apprenticeships.

Finally, on a separate issue, I would lobby for a change in the outmoded laws of coverture. Being lawyers, they knew that when a woman marries, her legal rights and obligations were subsumed to those of her husband, creating a single legal entity. The woman had no rights, and should her husband die or end up in debtor's prison, she became responsible for paying his financial liabilities. This often had the effect of forcing the wife and family into poverty. I asked, "If you were a woman, would you want to marry knowing you could end up in poverty versus remaining unmarried, wherein you can own property and make contracts in your own name?" I ended my recitation, looking around at faces frozen in disbelief. I thought, *Had I been too candid?* Interestingly enough, it was worth noting that after our marriage, James made provision that I be considered a separate entity after his death, thereby protecting me from this outdated law.

After digesting what I said, Mr. Warren, who asked me to call him James, said that my opinions were based in sound thinking, telling me I would make a dynamic and effective advocate in court and, he for one, would not want to be the opposing lawyer. My brother nodded in agreement, telling the table that he would not want to challenge me on any subject. "She had always been the smarter one with a special gift for learning," he added. Looking toward James, my brother noted that Uncle Jonathan, whom he knew, had often said Mercy was his best student. I was surprised by this piece of gossip, as I had not known my uncle's opinion of my intellectual capability.

Noting the time, James said he had to be on his way before it became too dark. He had a long ride to Plymouth and needed to be in Boston the next afternoon. He turned to Father and Mother, thanking them for their hospitality and wonderful feast. Mother then did something unusual, unheard of actually. She told him it was too late in the day to travel and offered to have him stay the night, and that it would be no inconvenience. Father agreed, adding it was a chilly night and he would feel terrible if he fell ill. My brother agreed. Then, for an inexplicable reason, I found myself agreeing with all of them, wondering to myself why I had done so. But I said to myself, *This man is intriguing.* He was not patronizing and seemed genuinely interested in what I had to say. He realized there was no winning the argument and accepted the invitation.

Later in the evening, while soaking in the bathtub, I asked myself why this man fascinated me. As I sprinkled lavender scent into the bath, I kept wondering why. The water was warm, comforting on this chilly night, and reaching for the soap plate, I realized my experiences with men were limited to my father, brothers, and Uncle Jonathan. Those experiences were not exactly the romantic encounters of Richardson's *Pamela*, Shakespeare's *Romeo and Juliet*, *Much Ado About Nothing*, or his superbly composed sonnets. No, my experience with men was not just limited; it was non-existent. Yet, this man moved my heart and I wanted to know more about him. Toweling off, I mused, *Let me see what happens tomorrow.*

That night, I tossed and turned in bed, my mind cluttered with images of James Warren. In the morning, I made certain to look my best. Entering the dining room, I purposely sat across from him, wanting to see his countenance and try to discover the reason for my infatuation. As we dined on poached eggs, hot brown bread, fried ham, and coffee, I quickly glanced at him while he, Father, and James spoke about colonial governance matters, which might have normally interested me but not this morning. James was an attractive man with a round face, sharp nose, rosy cheeks with penetrating brown eyes and hair, and a soft-speaking voice. He was a fine figure of a man with a regal bearing, and his demeanor spoke of self-confidence but not arrogance. Overall, I thought he was handsome and charming. As my mind dwelled on him, I did not hear Father calling my name.

He tapped my arm, asking me where my mind was, and that James had asked me a question. While apologizing, I offered the excuse for my mental dalliance by simply saying I had not slept well. Mother asked if I were feeling ill. No, I replied simply, saying I just could not get comfortable last night. I then asked James to repeat his question. He wanted to know my opinion on the representation of each colony in the Parliament. Thinking for a moment, I offered the thought that the rights of the individual and good governance should be the primary goal of government. If we stay colonies, we will be treated as foreigners, not citizens or equals, used for the benefit of the Crown and Parliament with no voting rights. I agreed with John Locke , the renowned philosopher and political theorist, that if a government claimed the power to levy and collect taxes on its people, they needed their consent, or it was a breach of the fundamental law of property and subverted the authority of the government, inevitably leading to tyranny. Mr. Warren seemed surprised for a moment, then, with a serious look, said that he could not have said it better.

My brother, scanning the group, said that we should send me to the royal court and Parliament to argue our claim. He thought they would be awed by my arguments and seriously consider changing their policy. Mr. Warren agreed, further noting that I would be a worthy representative and advocate for our cause. I told him thank you for his kind words but noted that a well-read, intelligent woman would be a distraction, as they were unaccustomed to strong-willed women. I then offered that the renowned Machiavelli had noted that feminine wiles had no place in politics, and that they were the most charitable and troublesome of creatures, but the man who shunned them passed up the troubles and the benefits. I then noted, "As the saying goes, there is no honey without bees." Everyone laughed, Father noting my special gift for language. This was when I noticed Mr. Warren staring at me, and it did not make me feel uncomfortable. As I smiled back, I felt a shared awareness in our glances, a sense of mutual understanding beyond the spoken word.

Mr. Warren said he would like to stay longer but he had to be on his way. Turning to Father and Mother, while glancing at me, he asked permission to visit me again. I felt my heart pounding, hoping Mother and Father would approve. Father looked to Mother, and they nodded their approval. And then, turning to me, he asked that if I agreed, what day would be most convenient. Finding myself momentarily tongue-tied, I blurted out he could visit any Saturday or Sunday. Then not realizing what I was saying, I added, "With Father and Mother's permission, you might stay the weekend." *Had I said all of this? Not just one day, a weekend.* I felt myself blushing like a young girl complimented by her first beau, and here I was twenty-five years old. *What must he think?* He simply smiled, which calmed my nerves. As Father led him to the door, I noticed Mother with a broad smile, and later, I learned, it was a smile of the victorious. The chicanery of my brother and parents had worked to perfection.

Plymouth, Friday, 16 July 1813

Chapter 5

LOVE IS BLIND

On Monday, I visited Uncle Jonathan to return Pufendorf's *Introduction to the History of the Principal Kingdoms and States of Europe*, Raynal's *History of the Two Indies*, and Filmer's *Patriarcha or the Natural Power of Kings*. I wanted to discuss Filmer because his defense of the divine right of kings had prompted Locke to publish *Two Treatises of Government*. As we began to discuss Filmer, I found myself unable to concentrate; all I could think about was James Warren.

I suddenly heard Uncle Jonathan's voice telling me that I seemed preoccupied. "Is everything all right at home? Are you ailing?" Shaking my head, I said, "I was having trouble gathering my thoughts." With a concerned look, he pressed that it was not like me to lose my focus, asking me to tell him what was troubling me. After what he had done for me, I felt obligated to tell him about my feelings for James Warren. But I had to be circumspect, not wanting him to think I was acting like a girl influenced by a romantic Richardson novel or Aphra Behn's, *Love-Letters Between a Nobleman and His Sister* or *Poems upon Several Occasions*.

I then related the events of the weekend when a friend of my brother's, James Warren of Plymouth, stopped by to visit with him. Uncle Jonathan interrupted saying that he knew the family but was only slightly acquainted with their son James. If memory served, his father was a distinguished and prominent citizen of our colony and Justice of the Peace. He noted the Warrens, like our family, were among the original settlers of the colony. Apologizing for running on, he asked me to continue.

I explained my parents invited him to supper. He asked my opinion on various topics, and I found myself becoming intrigued by him. He was intelligent, articulate, and soft-spoken, and genuinely interested in what I had to say. By the time we finished eating, it was late, and my parents recommended he stay the night. He agreed and when I retired for the evening, I found myself thinking about him to the point I could not sleep. Uncle Jonathan looked at me and said it sounded to him that I had become smitten with Mr. Warren. I resumed at morning breakfast with our conversations, which focused on the subject of parliamentary authority to levy taxes. I recommended a commission be sent to the mother country to argue the case that we were citizens of the country deserving of representation and not foreign colonists to be treated like castaways. Uncle Jonathan's brows furrowed and eyes narrowed and with a curious look inquired, "Well, how were your comments received?"

Replying, I thought I had committed a social error in speaking of matters not associated with a woman's role, but to my amazement he was complimentary, even suggesting I argue our case to Parliament, believing I would be a most effective advocate. Then we kept stealing glances across the table for the rest of the meal. Thinking to myself, this was a man I wanted to get to know better, then came the unexpected. He asked, with the proper permissions, to visit with me again. Looking at Uncle Jonathan, he was smiling broadly.

While continuing to grin, he offered, "Dearest Mercy, unless I am too old to appreciate youthful exuberance anymore, I believe you have been struck by Cupid's arrow. It sounds like you are falling in love with James Warren." Surprised by his frankness, I blurted how could he say that. I hardly knew the man. Uncle countered that it appeared to him that I knew Mr. Warren well enough, noting the ways of love have always been a mystery to men and women. "When I was a young man, and even today, prominent families like ours arranged marriages in the hope the two people would, over time, grow to love each other. Personally, I did not subscribe to this way of thinking. Love should come as a surprise, an inexplicable burst of emotions and passion defying explanation in words, whether romantic prose or poetry. You have found the man with whom you can share a life." As I looked at him, the serious furrowed brow was replaced by those bright sparkling eyes and the broad grin I had come to appreciate.

He continued, "You know, your Aunt Mercy, God rest her soul, and I met very casually and fell in love without either of us knowing it at first. It was a wonderous discovery." He seemed melancholy for a moment and, pointing to the Filmer tome, he looked at me and said, "I can see how you would have impressed Mr. Warren. You are a special person with a special ability. Cherish the gift, share it with others. Do not hide it inside." He then reached and opened the drawer of his desk and took out a small pamphlet. Pushing the small folio to me, I remember clearly what Uncle Jonathan said: "This is a gift for you. I have wanted to give it to you for some time, and this is the right time." Looking at the title page, I was surprised. It read *Dante Alighieri, La Vita Nuova, translated by Reverend Jonathan Russell, 26 December 1716.*

I said to Uncle, "I know this work by the great Italian author but have not read it because my Italian is poor, and it had not to my knowledge been translated. I did not know you had done so." Uncle Jonathan then related the story of the translation. When he and Aunt Mercy married the day after Christmas in 1715, she was twenty-two and he twenty-five. They were very much in love, and Uncle decided he wanted to give her a special gift for their first anniversary, so he decided to translate Dante's *La Vita Nuova* into English and every anniversary thereafter, he would read it to her. Becoming melancholy for a moment, he said, in an unbelievably soft voice, the poem became especially important after the recurring deaths of his children. To break what were obviously sad memories, I asked him how he had chosen the author and this poem over so many others.

He considered *La Vita Nuova*, a combination of prose and verse, the finest poem expressing medieval courtly love ever written in any language. The poem focused on Beatrice who, for Dante, was the embodiment of the absolute, all-embracing love, blending the desire aroused by beauty with the longing of the soul for divine magnificence. "Even my English translation captured the beautifully crafted and flowing lyrical cadence of the Italian language," he said, stating he read this poem to Aunt Mercy every year since their first anniversary, the last time the day before she passed. I could see his eyes well up, but stifling tears, he simply said he wanted me to have it as a gift from him and your namesake, Aunt Mercy.

Holding back my tears, I gently slid the folio back, telling him I could not accept such a personal, emotional gift. Putting his hand over mine, he stopped me and said it was his way of keeping the memory of his beloved wife alive, saying he had neither children nor heirs who would guard it. He knew I would cherish it. He then asked if I knew how my parents had come by my name, to which I replied, "I assumed after Aunt Mercy." He said that was partially true, "But you need to know early in our marriage, we lost two daughters within six months of their birth whom we had named Mercy. Your mother and father chose to name you Mercy out of respect for your aunt and our losses. So, you see, Mercy, you are more bonded to my family than you realize. Every time your aunt and I saw you, we saw our daughters."

He then said, "You know how I go on about context and motivation." I was confused for a moment, but he then said, "Open the book to the first short stanza and read the English translation for me." Doing as instructed, I read, "In that part of the book of my memory before which little can be read, there is a heading, which says: *Incipit vita nova*: Here begins the new life." Uncle looked at me and said this line was the most succinct statement of an author's context and motivation he had ever read. I rose from the chair and went around to Uncle, kissing him on the forehead and thanking him for his trust in me. I told him I would protect this folio and his and Aunt Mercy's memory unto death. He simply smiled that smile I had come to know so well when we discussed authors.

Departing, I felt ingratiated that this man who, being so much a part of my education and intellectual development, trusted me enough with this singularly personal keepsake. But I was also incredibly sad and took my time riding back home. My mind was racing with more questions about my feelings for Mr. Warren, for which I had few answers, and wanting to read *La Vita Nuova*. Arriving home, I showed Father and Mother the folio. They both sighed, sniffled, and wiped a tear from their eyes. They knew how special this little folio meant to Uncle and, as Mother pointed out, his gift was like someone giving a part of their heart and soul to someone else. At all times, I have kept this very personal memento near me and when my mind wanders to my late James, I open it, read it, and know he is in Dante's paradise, patiently awaiting my arrival.

Back to the main situation of this journal entry, I still needed to address the questions about my feelings for James Warren. The most prevalent thought was how to proceed without appearing too aggressive. I decided to speak to Mother; she would know what to do. I found her in the garden and, sitting next to her on the bench overlooking the front yard, I related my feelings to her. Thinking for a moment, she told me I should not be too bold, reminding me a young lady must be reserved and let the man express his feelings first. Having offered this piece of advice, she simply asked if I was in love with him or thought so. More importantly, she added, "Do you see yourself living a life together and having children with him?" Based on my feelings, I told Mother of my uncertainty, my feelings being confused. She noted that was why we had courtship; getting to know the man to make sure of your feelings.

Sitting back, she noted being in love was not enough. She knew he could support me financially and his family reputation in the colony was well-known, but would he support my educational and intellectual goals? I thought he would and said so. She said, "Learn as much as you can during the courtship because in the end, this will be your choice. Of course, if he were a serious suitor who wanted your hand, he would need to speak with Father." As far as she was concerned, I had her support regardless of my decision. I rose and thanked her, and then we hugged. She played her part in the scheme so well it would be fool's errand to play a game of Whist with her. Mr. Hoyle would be proud. She had given me much to think about, but before doing so, I wanted to read *La Vita Nuova*. Uncle believed the poem was relevant to my situation, so I wanted to discover why.

Sitting in my room by candlelight, I opened Uncle's translation, which included the original Italian, a language with which I was barely familiar. But the poem would provide opportunity to gain more experience with this beautiful language. The lengthy poem was a peculiar blending of prose and verse as Uncle had described. But when reading the first lines, I understood Uncle's attraction to the work. Reading them again with no distractions, my mind captured the depth of Dante's love. "In that part of the book of my memory before which little can be read, there is a heading, which says: *Incipit vita nova*: Here begins the new life." Even in English, those lines and the rest of the work had a beautiful, lyrical, and measured rhythm that drew me into the story. I could understand why Uncle had translated the poem and agreed with his assessment that this work was the best love poem ever penned.

But I asked myself, *How did the poem relate to my situation?* Dante related his sporadic meetings with Beatrice, starting when she was ten years old and he nine until her death. When he saw her much later in the company of two older women, attired in a brilliant white outfit, he was terrified as to what might be her reaction at seeing him again. He became intoxicated when she greeted him with the greatest virtue and grace. Throughout the poem, he praised her beauty and goodness, recounting his intense reactions to her kindness and telling of the events in both their lives, which explained the nature of his feelings for her. When Dante learned of her death, he vowed to write nothing more about her, distraught beyond his or anyone's understanding. What Uncle wanted was for me to be Beatrice to Jameses Dante, a man totally dedicated to me and our love. Much later in life, I read it in the original Italian and discovered it was even more beautiful than the translation. But I have digressed enough from the family's chicanery surrounding my courtship and marriage to James.

It was only after our marriage that my brother informed me of the conspiracy, promising that James knew nothing of the scheme. When I informed Mother and Father that I knew what they had done, they first blamed each other and, at one point, said they may have created the plan, but James supplied the man. At this point, my brother's quizzical look said it all; each was blaming the other to avoid embarrassment. Sitting there, my James looked as perplexed but, in the end, we had a good laugh, with me noting I had gotten the best of them because I had landed the perfect partner.

It was not long after our marriage in November 1754 that Hannah began courting Nathaniel Bird, whom she wed in 1756. They moved to Rhode Island and had two daughters, Deborah and Susan. Hannah, Deborah, and occasionally Susan, continue to correspond with me. My youngest sister Elizabeth, who I had first held in my arms when she was born, chose to pursue her own path to happiness. She met and was courted by a dashing, young British officer, and knowing Father would never consent to their marriage, eloped with him in the early 1760s. Surprisingly, she had clandestine support in her endeavor from our mother who told me later that she would never let radical political views get in the way of any of her daughters' happiness. Mother never ceased to amaze me. Elizabeth moved to England with her husband. We correspond regularly and she continues to be happy and very much in love. Mary married last. She was thirty-one when she married John Gray in 1761. I knew Mother felt relieved, believing Mary would be a spinster. She lived a quiet and happy life, and we both sat for our John Singleton Copley portraits in 1763. Unfortunately, Mary passed away suddenly in 1763 after losing her son, John, six days after his birth.

Although we never discovered the cause of death, I have always believed it had to do with losing little John. She was so excited when she became pregnant, telling me how much she wanted a child to love on and care for. His loss devastated her, and she simply gave up living. This may not sound logical, but it was what I believe. I still wear the mourning ring her husband made for the family as a necklace, my fingers being too swollen at times to get it on or off. As I lift it and look at the gold with black enamel, center amethyst, and two cut crystals, I can still read the inscription *M: GRAY OB:5 NOV 1763 Æ 33*. Even now, I can still see her beautiful smile, bright eyes, and playful demeanor; more memories stored in the recesses of my mind.

Mary Otis Gray mourning ring (1763) gold, enamel, amethyst, and crystal commissioned by John Gray on the death of Mary Otis Gray for Mercy Otis Warren with inscription, M: GRAY OB:5 NOV 1763 Æ 33. Collection of the Massachusetts Historical Society

But I must return to describing my courtship. Needless to say, Jameses next weekend visit led to weekly excursions in his carriage. We drove to Plymouth and the ocean, or just spent afternoons sitting in the garden speaking about any topic that spurred our interest. With each visit and conversation, I found myself falling deeper in love with him. His visits then became more frequent, sometimes twice or three times a week. We could not get enough of each other's company. Then one day in June, after driving to the shore, he turned to me and asked if I would consent to becoming his wife. Without hesitation, I said yes to his proposal and assured him Father and Mother would approve. However, he said the proprieties must be followed; a young man must always ask a father for his daughter's hand, which I was definitely not going to argue. Then I thought of the special bond between father and daughter, which might explain the tradition of asking a father for his daughter's hand in marriage. On our carriage ride back to Plymouth, I thought to myself, *I could not believe my good fortune. I had not been looking for a husband and by sheer coincidence, I had met the perfect man.*

On 14 November 1754, with a smiling Uncle Jonathan officiating, Hannah, Mary, and Elizabeth acting as my ladies in waiting, and my brother standing with Mr. Warren and his father in attendance, we were married at the Barnstable estate. Oh, how I remember the day. My dress was a blue wool gown. Mother, Hannah, Mary, and Elizabeth had decorated the wedding table with white paper chains and two white cakes: one for the groom, the other for the bride. Tradition held that the guests ate the groom's cake, leaving the bride's untouched to save in a tin of alcohol for their first wedding anniversary. We dispensed with tradition and both cakes disappeared, with Uncle Jonathan enjoying them the most. It was one of those rare moments when Uncle Jonathan seemed genuinely happy, as if he were giving away his own daughter and, in a way, he was. He had been my tutor, my intellectual alter ego, and, to a degree, confessor to whom I could divulge my deepest secrets.

Mother and my sisters outdid themselves in preparing the wedding feast. There was clam chowder, poached oysters, roasted pig, duck, potatoes, baked rye bread, and pumpkin casserole with trays of Apple Betties and Blueberry Duffs, coffee, and tankards of spiced hard cider, combined with sugar, lemons, and limes. We even had Sack-posset, compliments of my brother: a rich, thick concoction of boiled ale, eggs, and spices dating back to Shakespeare's time. Reminiscing now, the day was the best in my life, a life which all too quickly became frenetic and complicated. Although we did not know it at the time, we had gotten married at the start of the French and Indian War between England and France. But this event I will leave to a later chapter because of its importance to our country's founding. Needless to say, even had we known, we would not let a foreign war ruin our wedding day.

As we were leaving, Hannah, Mary, and Elizabeth hugged me and said they would miss me and promised to visit. Mother, with tears in her eyes, kissed me on both cheeks and simply said, "I love you." Father, his eyes welling up, kissed my cheek, hugged me, and said how he was proud of me. At the doorway, Uncle Jonathan was waiting with a large package, which he thrust into Jameses arms, hugged me, and exclaimed he was going to miss his best student. I told him he would not be rid of me that easy, as I would be visiting to continue my studies. Thanking him for his gift, we turned, got into his carriage, and set off for our new life in Plymouth.

The night was windy and chilly as James steered the carriage along the dark road. I found myself cuddling up to him and resting my head on his shoulder to keep warm. Turning and kissing my forehead, he told me how happy he felt, and that he was the luckiest man in the world. As he spoke, I realized the cold had become less troublesome, but he insisted on covering my head with a scarf. He turned and asked what I thought Uncle Jonathan had given me. It was heavy, so he assumed books. I muttered he was probably correct. The ride of thirty miles along the bumpy post road kept us alert. This was no time to throw a wheel, so the trip took longer than normal. But, after a couple of hours, we reached our new home.

Our home was a small, single-story affair with two bedrooms, bathing chamber, kitchen, parlor, and small anteroom we used as our library. The phrase "our library" fostered memories of growing up and passing Father's library, which was his personal domain. Even when I was in Uncle Jonathan's library, as comfortable as he made me feel, I still felt like an intruder, a thief stealing books from someone else's home. At that time, tradition held men owned libraries and women did not, or rarely did. To enter a man's library was like invading a foreign land, but here I was in my own library, an equally shared space with my husband. The idea made me feel empowered and special.

Speaking of Uncle, I would be remiss in not mentioning his wedding gift. The two neatly wrapped packages included Anne Bradstreet's *The Tenth Muse Lately Sprung Up in America*, *Don Quixote*, *Canterbury Tales*, *The Works of William Congreve*, and Aristotle's *A Treatise on Government*. In his own quiet way, he too was recognizing my intellectual equality. Back to my musing about my first day, or should I say first night of marriage.

Looking back through my life's journey, I thought my first night with James was glorious. I never thought of myself a passionate person but that first night taught me better. Then again, it proved to be one of so many I cannot count. The passion in me reflected the love we shared, and neither he nor I ever took the love, the passion, or our mutual respect for granted. We did everything together, and I came to know being in love took work, for to ignore the slightest part, like tending a garden, would kill it. But I am straying into my secret world, and that is for me to know and no one else.

Needless to say, and regardless of the war ravaging the colonies, our first two years were about building the foundation of our lives. James was not just considerate but enthusiastically supported my intellectual goals and development. Whenever he travelled to Boston on business, he always managed to return with a book he knew would interest me. Whenever travelling peddlers trundled by to sell their wares, he would go out to inspect the products (kitchen utensils, pots, pans, dishes, and the like), but he always searched and bought books, pamphlets, or broadsides I might find interesting or useful in my studies.

In late 1756, our lives changed when I became pregnant, and James began looking for a larger home. In 1757, just before the birth of our son, James bought the Winslow estate, a beautiful two-story house with a pitched gabled roof, wainscot wood paneling and multiple bedrooms, bathing chambers, a large kitchen, parlor, and library. I thought our new home too much, but he insisted I deserved no less. Unconsciously, I followed in Mother's footsteps, giving birth to James in 1757, Winslow in 1759, Charles in 1762, Henry in 1764, and George in 1766. Unlike the experiences of my youth, each of the boys were strong and healthy. With each pregnancy, I hoped for a little girl, thinking I could school her as I had been, but this was not to be. Looking back, James had been correct in buying a large home for our growing brood. Our joy was tempered by the loss of Jameses father, who passed away quietly after a short illness just after we moved into the new home. He was a wonderful man who always made me feel loved, sometimes telling me I reminded him of his beloved wife, Penelope, who had passed away years before in 1737.

Plymouth, Friday, 30 July 1813

Chapter 6

FAMILY IS EVERYTHING

It is difficult to reduce a family history to a few pages when I could pen a lengthy narrative on everyone. Mothers remember everything about their spouses and children. They remember the first wail at birth to every little scratch, illness, unrestrained laughter, tears, real and imagined fears, sleepless nights, and successes and failures. Memories are etched into my consciousness, recalled during quiet moments in old age as I question if James and I were good parents. Did we succeed in offering greater opportunities to our children than we experienced? My feeble attempt to highlight the individual child or selected parts of their lives is an injustice to their memories. It is also an injustice to my partner, the man who shared the responsibilities of parenting.

I did not raise my children alone. Without the support of my beloved James, I could not have achieved the successes resulting from my parenting or dealt with the tribulations attendant to raising children, especially sons. James often reminded me we can only guide, offer advice, and supply the means for our children to succeed. In the end, however, each of them had to make their own decisions and chart their courses in life. He was always by my side, telling me not to blame myself for their failures, often chiding me that seeking perfection was a fool's errand, for we are all imperfect creatures. He once joked even our Lord must have been imperfect because He had created imperfect creatures, saying he believed it was a purposeful mistake, designed in God's infinite wisdom, to challenge us each day to live as perfect of a life as possible.

Having five precocious boys challenged my educational experience, intellectual skills, and patience as a mother and first teacher. One thing was certain: my involvement was direct, demanding, and comprehensive. I began using the same recitation and memorization method taught and tolerated in my youth. Growing up has a way of changing long-standing opinions, and it was no different with me. I often heard my mother, father, or Uncle Jonathan's voices telling me, "Wait, you will come to know." Besides reading, writing, arithmetic, and religious principles, I looked to instill in them the same passion for books and knowledge I had come to love. I avoided too much concentration on religious texts.

In my childhood, religious reading was an everyday activity. This was especially true for young girls who when they married were expected to be their children's first teacher. Religion informed our daily lives and was thought to be the foundation of a civil society. At an early age, we memorized the *Lord's Prayer* and read sermons, psalms, *Book of Common Prayer*, and works by famous religious authors. Although I adhered to this tradition, I had my boys studying geography, history, political theory, and philosophy at a very early age. I believed then, and still do today, that a civil society demands well-educated citizens who are guided by, but not slaves to, religious principles.

Being my boys' first teacher was important to me, as serious as anything I did later in life in support of my beloved America. Each of them needed to understand the qualities necessary to become successful individuals and responsible adults. I may not have been able to achieve perfection, but I was sure going to try and get as near as humanly possible. This brought me back to my first meeting with James.

I recalled saying at the supper table that the importance of a mother's role in children's education demanded improvements in a young girl's education. It was not enough for a future mother to teach reading by parroting Bible phrases and sermons. A mother also needed to learn how to write and the basics of arithmetic, going as far as to recommend girls receive formal schooling similar to the Latin School. I was convinced then, and still believe today, that mothers are more than household domestics; they are the foundation of a civil society. I know of an all-girls private school, opened by a dear friend, Judith Sargent Murray, which has achieved a modicum of success, but I will speak of this later in the journal.

The schooling of my children proved arduous, but it did not interrupt my personal reading and intellectual growth. Of course, without the help of James, I could not have accomplished my goal. He was there every day, reinforcing my teaching method and warning the children that success demanded a well-informed, well-educated, and well-read individual. He often told them our family name and prominence were no guarantee of success. Each of them would be judged based on their character, personal behavior, education, and intellect.

Early in their education, I reinforced the principles needed to become successful adults by creating a teaching tool, *This Alphabet*, which combined learning their letters with moral principles or character traits, such as the letter "T" standing for truth, the strong garb of dignity and virtue, or "W" for wisdom, the necessary aid to serve decisions, which were two examples of this exercise.

There were other homespun homilies, as my sons called them, like, "He who lies down with the dogs rises with fleas," or "Be civil to all, sociable to many, familiar with few, friend to one, and enemy to none." I also found the moral lessons in Samuel Coxall's book, *The Fables of Aesop*, useful, like "Fine clothes may disguise, but silly words will disclose a fool," or "The smaller the mind, the greater the conceit." Each of these and other quotes from this well-known ancient storyteller and moralist became points of emphasis in my teaching method.

Parents expect each child to have a different personality, and my boys were no different. James, my oldest, had a disciplined, self-confidant, dependable, and thoughtful demeanor. He was the quickest to learn his letters and penmanship, and devoured books in the same way I did. He later attended Latin School and Harvard College. In fact, all my boys attended Latin School and each, except one, attended their father's and brothers' alma mater. James helped with the reading and penmanship lessons of his younger brothers, Charles, Henry, and George. He could have moved to Boston or elsewhere to practice law and avoid the Revolutionary War, but he chose to serve in our infant navy. However, he sustained a wound requiring the amputation of a leg, which limited his mobility but not his desire to be successful. He still visits me occasionally, but his disability and his estate responsibilities make it difficult. Yet, he manages to write me letters on a regular basis.

My second son, Winslow, was another matter entirely. He was clever, stubborn, intelligent, but undisciplined, with an independent streak that became a challenge to James and me. He gave me the greatest grief and although he was intelligent and personable, he showed a fondness for the hedonistic lifestyle, which I attributed to youthful defiance of authority. In this case, his rebelliousness tested my patience, not to mention Jameses. But when he showed a fondness for Philip Stanhope, the Earl of Chesterfield, and his treatment of women in his *Letters Written to His Son*, I had James buy a copy of this work. After reading it, I was appalled and could not believe a son of mine would consider this individual an exemplar of gentlemanly behavior toward women.

With the wisdom born of being a mother who understands her child, especially a mother who had the experience of cajoling her parents, I recognized my son's penchant for stubbornness demanded a more tactful approach. Writing Winslow, who was residing in Boston, I noted Lord Chesterfield had many saving qualities when it came to his opinions on politeness and social graces, but his recommendations about the treatment of women were abhorrent and immoral. It certainly was not the behavior of a gentleman, especially one raised by this mother.

When my friend, Abigail Adams, read the letter, she sent it without consulting me to the *Independent Chronicle*, who published it. In the end, Winslow listened to his mother's counsel, but when he refused to attend Harvard College, his decision proved a great disappointment to us. Instead, he leapt from job to job, career to career, seeking satisfaction and success but achieving neither. Finally, in 1790, we were proud when he was commissioned as a Captain in the United States Army and posted to Fort Recovery, Ohio. He served in the command of General Arthur St. Clair and died at the Battle of the Wabash, fighting an Indian Federation. We were both crushed and, to this day, I miss his wayward personality.

It may seem illogical to say, coming from a disciplined individual such as myself, but he was my favorite. I did not show him any more attention than my other sons, but somehow, I was closer to him in spirit. He was the black sheep of our family. Looking back, I saw in him a reflection of myself: the young girl, the rebel; demanding more education, challenging existing social conventions, and risking personal safety during the Revolution War and thereafter. Obstinate though he was, he was still my darling. Only Winslow, with directness and honesty, could have challenged me to write my last two plays with new themes other than the American Revolution and Thomas Hutchinson.

My third son, Charles, was like his brother James, a disciplined student who excelled in school. He took to reading the classics, enjoyed Shakespeare and Pope, and, later, my satirical plays and poetry written during the Revolution. He thought my article on Lord Chesterfield a wonderful defense of propriety and morality. Grinning, he once told me his adventurous spirit, something he had in common with Winslow, came from me, and how could it not when I took so many personal risks with the British army, navy, and loyalists surrounding us during the Revolution. But this happy, intelligent, and carefree boy was a sickly child with chronic breathing problems. His health aside, upon graduating from Harvard College, he planned to pursue a legal career, but the coughing and fevers were becoming more severe, which our family doctor finally diagnosed as the consumption disease.

So, in 1782 and 1783, we sent Charles to Spain on the advice of the doctor, who thought the climate might improve his health and cure the disease. After each journey, his breathing seemed to improve but not enough to cure the consumption. On his third trip and after being ill for months, he passed away in Saint Lucar, Spain in early 1785. I blame the evil of tobacco, which he began smoking at an early age. Our young men believe it stylish to sniff or smoke the foul-smelling, horrible weed in pipes. I just wish Charles could have been convinced of tobacco's danger but, as James said, he probably would have looked at me, and said, "Mother, you are being too serious over nothing. There are more important things in the world to worry about." I do not believe he realized that he, like my other sons, was the most important person in my life. But it matters not, I still mourn his loss to this day.

My fourth child, Henry, born in 1764, was like James and Charles, very disciplined and well-educated. He devoured my lessons, graduated from Latin School and Harvard College with high marks. He had a good mercantile education with a general knowledge of science. In 1788, he served as Aide-de-Camp to Major General Benjamin Lincoln, who was in command of the Massachusetts forces during Shays' Rebellion. He later served for a year as clerk to General Lincoln, who was the collector of the customs for Boston. Having resigned this position due to ill health, he was later appointed collector of customs for Plymouth by President Thomas Jefferson in 1803. He continues to farm in Eel River, Plymouth.

Of all my sons, Henry was the only one to marry and give me the grandchildren I so dearly treasure. As noted earlier, he chose after Father's death to begin visiting every weekend with the family to look after me. As memory would have it, Mother warned that spinsters could not look forward to children or grandchildren taking care of her in old age. Every day that I see Henry, Mary, and the children, her words come to mind. Strange of late, I have been finding myself increasingly recalling Mother's maxims and advice.

My last child, George, was born in 1766. He too was a good student and, after graduating Harvard College, moved to Maine to pursue a farming and a mercantile career. From his letters, we knew he was happy with his career choice and position in society, but he died a bachelor in February 1800 at age thirty-four. We never discovered the cause of his death, but I suspected consumption again. He was another one of my children who used tobacco on a regular basis.

As an aside, after Charles's death, I recalled reading the pamphlet penned by King James I of England in 1604 titled, *A Counterblast to Tobacco,* in which he described smoking, "As a custom loathsome to the eye, hateful to the nose, harmful to the brain, dangerous to the lungs, and the black stinking fume thereof, nearest resembling the horrible Stygian smoke of the pit that is bottomless." I only wished I had read this pamphlet earlier to Charles and George; it might have saved their lives, or at least warned them of the risks of tobacco. But as my James correctly pointed out, we can educate, mentor, and guide but in the end, they chose their lives' direction, right or wrong though their choices might be. This evil habit is as dangerous and deadly as alcohol, but no one seems to listen, especially to overprotective mothers and grandmothers.

The Warren and Otis clans were a large, extended family with uncles, aunts, and a host of nephews, nieces, and cousins. My brother James married Ruth Cunningham, a lady of good breeding, well-read and well-educated. She passed away in 1789, six years after my brother's death from an unknown cause, although I suspected consumption. They had three children: Mary Otis Lincoln, James Otis III, and Elizabeth Otis Brown. James III passed away in 1775, while Mary married Benjamin Lincoln's son, Benjamin Lincoln III, and had two boys: Benjamin Otis Lincoln and James Otis Lincoln. By the by, this Benjamin Lincoln was the same man for whom my son Henry worked. My second niece, Elizabeth, married Captain Leonard Brown, a British army officer, and left the country with him during the war. Except for a brief trip to Massachusetts in 1792, when she visited me, she never returned to America. We occasionally exchange correspondence, and it is gratifying to know she still remembers me as her celebrated aunt. I did recall her marriage and alliance with the British so deeply offended her father, my brother, he only left her five shillings in his will.

I do need to speak about my mercurial brother, James, with whom I had a close relationship. As mentioned earlier, James had a combative relationship with Father because of Jameses volatile temper and argumentative personality. He could lose his temper in an instant and then, just as quickly, become calm and composed. I knew Father was beside himself when Harvard banished James for some infraction of their rules to Watertown, a rural community about seven miles from the main campus in Cambridge. After this exile, I remembered Father sending a letter expressing his disappointment with Jameses behavior and encouraging him to seek God's righteousness to better himself. I never learned the transgression, as neither Father, Mother, nor James spoke of it, but it must have been serious to call for an exile from Harvard, a college well-known for its raucous students' lifestyle.

What I thought was merely an independent streak may have been an early sign of a mental decline, which worsened as he became older, especially after his pummeling at the hands of Governor Hutchinson's supporters. From what I heard, or so the story went, he and company of friends were in local Boston public house loudly criticizing the colonial administration and Governor Thomas Hutchinson in particular. Upon taking leave of his associates, he was set upon by the Governor's supporters who beat him senseless. It was after this event that I began noticing his mental lapses and extreme changes in behavior even before the one leading to his resignation as the Advocate General of the Admiralty Court, an event of which I will speak about in a future chapter. But as unpredictable as his personality could be with others, he was always thoughtful, calm, and attentive to me, which brings me to an unusual event that marked a turning point in my life.

One day in early May, two weeks after the Lexington and Concord skirmishes on 19 April 1775, James and his wife Ruth showed up unannounced at our door. This was peculiar because my sister-in-law was what we called a "High Tory," believing our cause was morally wrong. I knew this had been a long running cause of disagreement in their marriage, dating back to Jameses first attacks on the British colonial administration and Parliament's taxation policies. Yet, James told me she was a loving, caring wife and mother. The surprise visit came about because he was concerned that the impact of recent events would adversely affect our family. I told my brother and husband that I would join them after making Ruth comfortable. She seemed tired and needed some time to relax after their carriage trip.

While my brother and James went into the library to discuss the matters at hand, Ruth and I sat in the kitchen sipping coffee. Then, to my astonishment, the usually guarded Ruth unburdened herself. She told me since Lexington and Concord, James had become more irrational with wild mood swings and verbal outbursts, first condemning the British and then denouncing the rebels; it was like living with two men. She was clearly distraught and scared. I asked if she and the children felt threatened. "Not in the least," she replied. She was more concerned he might hurt himself and although they might disagree politically, she loved him dearly and was very worried for his mental state.

This is when I realized Ruth was more bonded to James than previously believed, knowing from experience political differences could easily destroy personal relationships, even marriages and families. She asked if we could find a reason for James to stay with us for a while, reasoning that my close bond with him might help in recapturing his mental clarity. Ruth was clearly troubled and had convinced James to visit us on the specious excuse that the changing situation in the colony might affect our families negatively. She admitted she was grasping at straws, but she was trying anything in her power to find a way to improve his mental health. I told Ruth we would find a reason for James to visit before they left. She thanked me, and I could see her eyes tear up.

When they were leaving, I asked my brother to come back for a visit. To my surprise, my brother said he had already been asked to visit again to discuss family and business matters in light of what was going on. James agreed to return at the end of May or early June. Ruth and I exchanged glances, seeing we did not need to invent an excuse. After they left, I told my husband James about my conversation with Ruth, and asked why he invited him back. James said he noticed how my brother seemed confused at times during their conversation. He was terribly upset about the recent events and troubled all our negotiations had come to naught. Knowing there were no ongoing negotiations, and Lexington and Concord had certainly negated any future dialogue with Britain, he realized James was more than confused.

James then decided to invite my brother back under the pretext that current events made it necessary to discuss how to protect the family from whatever happened in the future. I then told him about Ruth's concern about his wild mood swings and mental health. She had convinced him to visit us on the pretense of discussing the impact of recent events on the family to get our opinion.

As I dwell on it now, I had not really known Ruth, except as a Tory sympathizer, but there was in her voice a genuine distress and tears in her eyes. This was not the Ruth I had come to know. She was always a quiet lady, laconic in conversation, and reticent about speaking of political matters. I had first met Ruth in 1754 when I began courting James. She and my brother had been courting for a year or so before I met my James. She came from a prominent and wealthy Boston merchant family and, as the only child, was heiress to a large fortune worth £10,000. She and James had married in 1755 and although their politics differed, they were very attached to each other. As I look back, I realize she had a hard life. She survived my brother with whom she was very much in love, and her son's death while in British captivity in 1777 aboard a prison ship in Boston Harbor. One daughter married a British officer and moved to England, while the other daughter married the son of Continental Army General Benjamin Lincoln. Unfortunately, Ruth died alone in 1789 with the family split. I may have disagreed with Ruth politically, but respected that she never wavered in her loyalties, affirming her preference for the British government to the very end.

Then an even stranger event than the unannounced visit soon occurred. In early June 1775, James arrived at the estate as promised, and the change in his demeanor proved heartwarming. He recaptured his clarity of thought and was not melancholy or confused. Then one morning, James asked where my brother had gone. He was last seen riding toward Boston and asked if he had informed me he would be traveling. I answered no, wondering what my brother was doing or where he was going. As it turned out, the fool had commandeered a musket, and joined the siege of Boston by our militiamen and taken part in the battle of Bunker Hill. We only heard of his foray when a dispatch rider bellowed the news of our victory and that Dr. Joseph Warren, a dear friend of whom I will speak of later, had been killed, and the renowned James Otis had been one of the defenders of Boston and the colony.

To say the least, when James returned unhurt, I was beside myself with anger born of fear for his safety. It was the only time I lost my temper with anyone in the family. Reproaching him, he apologized, saying he felt the need to do more than simply sit by and watch while others fought and died for our country. I stormed off and told my estate workers and groom that he was never to have a horse unless approved by me. Even though his mind was clear as to why he decided to take part in the battle, this episode only served to prove his mental condition was deteriorating more rapidly than I had thought.

In the end, James died on 23 May 1783, the result of a lightning strike while staying at an old friend's home in Andover, where he had gone to recover his mental clarity. Odder still was his premonition concerning death. In his last letter to me, he said he hoped to die by direct lightning strike. Truly a strange omen and to this day, I cannot fathom how he knew. I told James, it was as if he called upon the Lord to end his life in a fashion reflecting the unpredictable nature of his personality. His death crushed us all, especially when we discovered, unknown even to his friend, that he had burned most of his personal papers without explanation. I remember President Adams saying of my brother, "The

American Revolution did not start in Philadelphia, or at Lexington and Concord. Instead, it was born February 24, 1761, when in the Boston's Massachusetts Town House, he rose to defend American liberty."

My oldest brother, Joseph, who passed in 1810 at eighty-five, served proudly, like my husband, during the Revolutionary War. He was a Colonel, commanding the First Barnstable County Regiment of Militia in August 1775. In 1776, he was promoted to Brigadier General of militia and reinforced the Continental Army, commanded by General Washington. He had first married Rebecca Sturgis in 1753, who passed away in 1761 at age thirty-one. She gave birth to Rebecca Otis Williams, James Otis, Elizabeth Otis Osgood, a second Elizabeth Otis, Joseph Otis, and two children who were stillborn. .

In 1770, Joseph, who was forty-five, remarried the twenty-seven-year-old Maria Walter, who gave birth to Dorothy Otis Smith, Joseph Otis, Nathaniel Walter Otis, John Otis, Thomas Otis, Charles Otis, Mary Allyne Otis Gay, William Otis, Arthur Otis, Maria Otis Colby, and one stillborn child. She was a remarkably busy lady birthing so many children, but she still occasionally corresponds with me. Rebecca was the most productive of the Otis clan, and with five boys of my own, I could not imagine the chaos and confusion in that household. However, she always seemed content with her life. I occasionally hear from the children of his two marriages, but Joseph wrote me frequently before his death.

As I mentioned earlier, my sister Hannah married Nathaniel Bird and they had one child, a daughter named Deborah Bird, who married Zebulon King and had a son, Charles Bird King. Hannah still lives in Newport, Rhode Island where she and Nathaniel moved after their wedding. Unfortunately, Nathaniel passed in 1796, but Deborah's son Charles continues to live near his mother and he continues to write me frequently. Hannah corresponds regularly, reminiscing about our early lives as young girls. Hannah sometimes likes to remind me about Mother and Father's conspiracy to marry me off, saying, "Mother would not relent in letting Nathaniel and I marry until you were wed." This was something else of which I was unaware. I mentioned in one letter, "Did everyone in the family know about the marry-off Mercy scheme?" She answered, "Everyone in the household knew about it, even though Mother and Father thought it was a secret." It is unfortunate that neither Mother nor Father are alive for me to tell them their secret was no secret except to me. I know Mother would have had a good laugh.

My youngest sibling, Samuel, married Elizabeth Gray Otis, and she gave birth to Harrison Gray Otis, who is still alive today; Elizabeth Otis, who died in 1788, and Jonathan Mayhew Otis, who was stillborn. Samuel was very accomplished, becoming the first Secretary of the United States Senate, serving twenty-five years in that capacity. Before that, he was speaker of the Massachusetts House of Representatives in 1784 and 1785, and delegate from Massachusetts to the Second Continental Congress in 1787 and 1788. I always enjoyed his correspondence about the happenings and gossip in the Massachusetts House and United States Senate. I wrote him once that even though I was an Anti-Federalist, I forgave his Federalist leanings. His response was he had never thought of me as anything other than a genuine American patriot. I appreciated the compliment and suspect he knew my authorship of the *Observations on the Constitution* which I will discuss in a forthcoming chapter. But if he did suspect or know, he never divulged it.

I am certain members of my extended family have been overlooked in this summary, but my omission does not minimize their contribution to our country. Many were present during the birth of our great nation and directly took part in the events leading to independence, the war, and the later events creating our republic. As I move forward with my journal, some family members will reappear as participants in and contributors to the establishment of this experiment in republican government.

Plymouth, Friday, 20 August 1813

Chapter 7
CATALYST FOR CHANGE

As noted earlier, the year of our marriage proved momentous for another less personal reason. The year 1754 marked the start of the French and Indian War, which pitted the colonies against the French with each side supported by Native American tribes. But the war became another one of those continuing hegemonic struggles between the great European powers. The conflict started in America, but spread to Europe when England, in 1756, declared war on France and her ally Spain. At this point, it took on the name as the Seven Years' War.

The main cause of the colonial struggle centered on which country, England or France, would control trade and settlement in the Upper Ohio River valley. At the beginning, I was less concerned about the war because we were starting our married life, giving birth to three of our five children, and it seemed far away on the frontiers of the colonies. Now in retrospect, and with my historian's eye, I came to realize there was another, less publicized reason leading to the war. Prior to the conflict, the colonies experienced an explosion in population moving to the Western Frontier.

From America's earliest settlement, the colonies had been a magnet for religious dissidents and political refugees seeking freedom from persecution, oppressive social traditions, and greater economic opportunity. I could not speak to the immigration numbers in the middle of the last century prior to the war, but if recent numbers are any indication, the last three censuses illustrate the desire of people to come to America. Between 1790 and 1810, America's population grew by sixteen million, of which unfortunately five million were slaves. I will discuss the slavery issue in a later chapter. The growing immigration begged the question: how did it influence events leading to the war in 1754?

In the last century, many immigrants came to America as indentured servants. Under English Common Law, indenture was a legal contract in which an immigrant entered an agreement with a ship owner or captain to pay for their transit. When the ship made port, the captain or owner advertised his indentured servants for sale in a local newspaper. When a buyer came forward, the city court recorded the sale. The indenture contract stipulated the number of years of servitude, typically four to seven years, and specified that the servant worked without pay and was not an apprentice. The latter was important because in English Common Law, apprentices had the same rights as ordinary workers while indentured persons were not considered employees.

In this legal relationship, the buyer was guaranteed compensation for the financial cost in entering the contract. Other contractual terms specified the individual could not marry without the permission of the owner, could be subject to physical punishment, and if a female servant became pregnant, the law allowed the buyer to extend the indenture contract term. From my perspective, this was a harsh system but unlike slaves, indentured servants would eventually be released from their legal bondage. I found this legal servitude, like slavery, a stain on our great nation. But how did indentured servitude become one of the causes for the war?

When released from their indenture, these people had little future in terms of mercantile skills, not having been apprentices. Most had worked as field hands, so they had some farming skills, but with little or no money, their prospects within the colony of their release were dim at best. The answer for these individuals was to move beyond the borders of colonies, like New York, Pennsylvania, and Virginia, to avoid regulations, laws, and social rules. The only uninhabited lands existed along the Upper Ohio River Valley, the western frontier of America at the time. This borderland was wild, dangerous, and unprotected, with native tribes who did not appreciate foreign interlopers invading their lands. But this was the only land available to the released indentured servants.

However, the problem with this population migration was twofold. First, the French considered the Ohio River Valley within their political and economic sphere of influence. The second was colonies like New York, Pennsylvania, and Virginia knew this wilderness offered economic opportunities, and they wanted to extend their influence into the region. These factors set the stage for the war, and the only requirement was a reaon. The justification came in the form of George Washington who, in 1754, led a surprise attack on a small French force at Jumonville Glen.

His later defeat and surrender to French forces at the Battle of Fort Necessity was the spark triggering the war. I remain convinced New York, Pennsylvania, and Virginia, for reasons of power and financial gain, needed to have the French driven from North America, so they appealed to the King for permission to raise an army and money on the spurious pretext they were defending themselves. Britain then took advantage of the colonial conflict in 1756 to declare war on France and Spain in Europe, making it a much wider conflict. The colonies took a narrower view; they wanted control of the Upper Ohio River Valley. On the other hand, England saw the war as an excuse to end long-standing territorial rivalries with France and Spain in North America, Canada, and the Caribbean. The war became another struggle for economic and political control among the European powers, which dated back centuries. The unintended consequences of the war fell on Britain. Their victory may have settled territorial claims on the North American continent, but the cost drained the privy purse, which forced the British government into a series of legislative actions, making their victory a Pyrrhic one.

Initially, the British victory in 1763 was great cause for celebration throughout the colonies. The peace ending the war opened a host of new opportunities for the colonists in the great Western Frontier, as the French ceded the contested territory of the Upper Ohio River Valley and Canada to the British. Then came the Royal Proclamation of 1763, which dampened the party. The proclamation effectively closed the frontier to colonial expansion to calm the fears of the native tribes, who believed the colonists would drive them from their lands as they expanded westward. The proclamation also forbade unspecified activities, created new laws to enforce the proclamation, and indicted unspecified persons for deceptive practices in getting native lands in times past, which meant nothing as "times past" was not defined by activity, claim, or individual.

The Parliament had no illusions about relations between the native tribes and colonists. They understood the colonists would not respect any boundary without an enforcement mechanism, and there was, as always, the underlying pecuniary goal. The English were interested in increasing the fur trade, which involved the native tribes and independent trappers who lived along and beyond the new frontier. To accommodate enforcement of the proclamation, Britain created a geographic line extending from Quebec in Canada to the new border of West Florida.

Along this boundary line, the British established military posts, claiming these forts defended the colonies. Of course, the cost of their upkeep fell on the colonies. This was duplicitous, for there were no adversaries from which the colonies required protection. From the viewpoint of the colonies, the burden of this act amounted to a tax and contrary to their interests. But the *Proclamation Act* proved to be the first of a series of actions taken by the British government that became the basis for dissent and revolution.

Plymouth, Monday, 13 September 1813

Chapter 8

SILENCE IS THE VIRTUE OF FOOLS

I would like to say my involvement in the fight for American independence was a conscious decision based on utopian ideals, but this would be an overstatement. My participation started innocently enough one Sunday at our Plymouth home. Mother and Father had come for the weekend, leaving Samuel to tend the estate, while my brother James and his wife Ruth had come down from Boston for the day. Dinner went well enough, but I noticed a tension in the air coming from Father. Normally social and talkative, he was quiet and circumspect. When dinner was finished, the children retired to the garden to play and Ruth, Mother, and me rose to retire to the kitchen. As I got to the door, Father called me to come back and sit down.

What happened next surprised my husband and me. Turning to James and me, Father told us that my brother, who was sitting across from me, had resigned his post as the Advocate General of the Admiralty Court because he had agreed, along with Mister Oxenbridge Thacher, to stand for a group of Boston merchants who were challenging the legality of the 1761 Writ of Assistance. I asked what could have driven him to do such a thing. James told us he had resigned from the Admiralty Court rather than argue for the customs officials because he believed the Writ was an illegal intrusion on colonial prerogatives.

As Uncle Jonathan would say, I here offer the context which motivated my brother. A Writ of Assistance was a general search warrant issued by superior provincial courts to help the British government in enforcing trade and navigation laws. This warrant authorized custom-house officers with the aid of a Sheriff, Justice of the Peace, or Constable to search a home suspected of having smuggled goods, without specifying neither the house nor the goods. Writs had existed since the reign of King Charles II in the seventeenth-century, and the current Writ had not aroused controversy until a renewal attempt was made in 1761 after George II died. Having described the context, let me turn to Jameses motivation. How I wished Uncle Jonathan were here to see this recitation. He would have been proud of his student.

James smugly said the petition before the Superior Court was not only a matter of law but a fight for the principle of individual, God-given natural rights, as established in English jurisprudence dating back to Saxon laws, the *Magna Carta*, and later precedents confirming the rights and principles enshrined in the Common Law. The Writ was contrary to basic English liberties and an instrument of arbitrary power. He argued the most essential maxim of English liberty was the freedom of one's home. A man's house was his castle and so long as he was peaceful, he was the prince in his castle. This Writ, if declared legal, would totally eradicate the privilege.

Father interrupted him, asking if he had won the case. James replied that the adjudication had been delayed to the next session of the court. Father sat back, with a sneer on his face, saying that he resigned his post on the Admiralty Court to argue for a principle and lost. James retorted, in an angry tone, that he had not lost. Father countered, in a sarcastic tone, "And who, by chance, was and will be the Chief Judge making the decision?" James, becoming angrier, said that Father knew darn well who it was. Father, raising his voice, replied, "Your much-disliked Thomas Hutchinson." Now we understood the reason for his foolish decision; there rested my brother's motivation. His arguments may have been sound in principle, but a personal grudge was equally in play.

Then, in a very haughty tone, Father continued by telling us that James was angry that Governor Bernard had not appointed him to Chief Justice of our highest court in favor of Jameses longtime rival, Mr. Hutchinson. At this point, Father uncharacteristically slammed his fist on the table and, looking directly at James, said after years of showing little regard for the family name, he decided to go off half-cocked and do something stupid. Father was clearly beside himself and so was I. This became the tinder box for James who exploded, saying that he would not condone such behavior from him or anyone. Father looked at him, his countenance becoming so red I thought he would have a fit and told all of us that James had done this because of a ridiculous feud with Thomas Hutchinson, calling him an "arse." I had never heard my father get angry, no less use a cuss word. To this day, I do not know who or what started the feud, which eventually led to tragic events.

Wanting to intercede to calm the situation, I realized nothing would cool their tempers, and looked toward my James, who sat silently, for help. He shook his head, saying without speaking, *Best to stay out of it*. James was correct, but I remembered my brother always telling me it was easier to effect change from within as opposed to banging your head against a stone wall from without. Of course, looking back, it was the Writ case that began the march toward independence, the war, the creation of a new nation, and the rapid mental decline of my brother.

Typical of his unpredictable personality, James exploded, telling Father that the colony was replete with political corruption, lackies, and intrigues designed to intimidate us into submission to the Crown and Parliament. Now I was angry and said, "Dammit, James, when are you going to think of the consequences before you act?" Everyone looked at me, never having heard me use an invective of any sort. I could not believe it myself. James became silent, but I could see he was truly angry and wanted to continue his tirade when Mother peered in and told us to keep our voices down, as we would wake the dead. In her own quiet fashion, she was calming the situation by warning us that children were around.

As early as I could remember, James had a contentious combative relationship with Father, and I thought to myself he was responding to Father from habit. One thing I knew about my beloved brother, he hated being challenged by anyone except me. I remember his last letter to me before he died when he said, "This you may depend on, no man ever loved a sister better, and among all my conflicts, I never forget that I am endeavoring to you and yours." Yes, he was unpredictable, but this was the first man in my recollection who argued that women were born as free as men, and it would be shameful to assert that they were all slaves by nature. He was one of the few, like my husband, to suggest females had the right to expect respectable suffrages, coming closest to supporting our right to exercise an active voice in government. But at this moment, my brother was hurt by my outburst. I suspect he thought my support was forthcoming. In all honesty, as much as I loved this volatile man, I could not; his decision had been a bad one.

Without comment, he rose from the table, apologized for his outburst, called to Ruth, and left the house without uttering a word. I had hurt him and felt bad for doing so. Turning to Father and in an unusually disparaging voice, I told him I was disappointed that he had managed the situation so badly, pointing out he knew Jameses confrontational personality when challenged. Father said nothing. James looked at me in astonishment and later that night, while we lay in bed, he simply turned to me, kissed my cheek, and uttered, "Damnit, my word, will wonders never cease." At which point, I smiled, kissed him, and poked him in the side with my elbow. He had said nothing at the table, but this simple utterance in bed told me he was on my side. I did suspect this was the night I conceived my third son, Charles. Odd, how certain situations excite the passion in one's heart. But it was from this day I took a greater interest in the political activities in the colonies while keeping a closer eye on my brother.

After the 1761 Writ, there came a flurry of enactments, making it appear that the Parliament and the King were purposely conspiring to create reasons for armed insurrection. In all honesty, however, these laws reflected the corruption and greed of the political class in England. In succession, after the *Proclamation Act of 1763*, there came the *Currency Act of 1764, Sugar Act of 1764, Quartering Act of 1765, Stamp Act of 1765, Townshend Act of 1767, The Indemnity Act of 1767*, and *The Tea Act of 1773*. Each was more egregious than the former, moving the colonies one step closer to war and independence. As mentioned earlier, *The Proclamation of 1763* closed colonial expansion into the newly won territories in the Ohio River Valley to appease the native tribes. This was done by checking the encroachment of settlers into their lands through a boundary separating the British colonies on the Atlantic coast from Native American lands west of the Appalachian Mountains.

The *Currency Act of 1764* prohibited the issue of any new paper bills and reissue of existing currency. Parliament favored a hard currency system based on the pound sterling and sought the abolishment of colonial paper money. By prohibiting the printing of new colonial paper bills, the act prevented the colonies from repaying future debts with paper bills. In my study of history, nothing angers people more than the impression of greedy and corrupt governments pilfering the individual's money regardless of the reason. Every colony protested vehemently against the act, noting the shortage of hard capital would further worsen the trade deficit with Britain. Interestingly enough, the issue of paper money versus hard currency arose again, causing Shays' Rebellion by Revolutionary War veterans in 1786 and 1787. But I digress.

The *Currency Act* also set up a superior Vice-Admiralty Court in Halifax, Nova Scotia, with authority from Florida to Newfoundland and judges appointed by the Crown. This court assured persons suspected of smuggling or other violations of the customs laws would receive a hearing favorable to the British. The problem was that Vice-Admiralty and Common Law court jurisdictions overlapped. To explain, customs officials and merchants could bring a legal action in whichever court they thought offered them the most favorable outcome. This appeared a clear injustice for those charged, declaring the lack of a jury trial was an infringement of their rights under English Common Law. The superior Vice-Admiralty Court could supersede the authority of local courts, if those charged believed they would receive unfavorable rulings.

The real problem was the court could not only prosecute but persecute those thought to be enemies of England. The court demanded anyone charged with a crime to travel to Nova Scotia and appear before an obviously biased court. The legal concept of these courts was a defendant was assumed guilty until proved innocent, and failure to appear as commanded resulted in an automatic guilty verdict. In the anger over the paper versus hard money issue, little regard was paid by the colonials to this clear breech of the Common Law. Money and greed have a way of justifying the more subtle but greater assaults on liberty.

The *Sugar or Revenue Act of 1764*, an amended version of the 1733 act, was enacted by Parliament to stop the smuggling of molasses into the colonies from the French and Dutch West Indies by cutting taxes on molasses. The act also imposed new taxes on other imported foreign goods, while further restricting the export of certain highly demanded commodities, such as lumber and iron, that could legally be shipped from the colonies under the *Navigation Acts*. The real purpose, however, was to raise revenue through the colonial customs service and give customs officials more latitude, with respect to executing seizures and enforcing customs law. And here was where protecting legal principles and financial considerations came into conflict.

The act came from Parliament rather than the colonial legislature. This alarmed some prominent Bostonians, most notably Samuel Adams and my brother, who believed the law violated the principle against taxation without representation by encroaching on the colony's charter rights to govern itself. Equally significant was the consequences for the colonial judicial system, which allowed British officers to try colonists who violated the new duties in the Vice-Admiralty Court in Halifax, thus depriving them of their right to a trial by a jury of their peers.

The *Quartering Act of 1765*, an amendment to the annually issued *Mutiny Act*, required colonial authorities to supply food, drink, quarters, fuel, and transportation to British forces quartered in their towns or villages. The impetus for the act was the British who had fought in the French and Indian War found it difficult to persuade colonial assemblies to pay for quartering and provisioning their troops. Thomas Gage, commander of British North American Forces, asked Parliament to do something to correct the problem. Once again, the colonies' opposition was motivated more by pecuniary considerations than legal principle, the latter being specious at best. The colonists disputed the legality of the law because it violated the *English Bill of Rights of 1689*, which forbid taxation without representation and the raising or keeping of a standing army without the consent of Parliament. In fact, the colonists were more agitated about being taxed to pay for the provisioning and quartering of a standing army they believed unnecessary during peacetime.

The *Stamp of Act 1765* passed by Parliament taxed all paper used for printed materials in the colonies. The purpose of the *Stamp Act* was to generate revenue to pay down Britain's French and Indian War debt, and pay for the British troops stationed in North America to protect the new lands won while preventing an uprising by the French colonists living there. The reaction to the *Stamp Act* outraged colonial leaders, who believed it was a blatant attempt to make money off the colonies. This act led to the creation of the colonial *Stamp Act Congress*, of which my brother and husband were participants, while political groups, most notably the Sons of Liberty, organized public and often violent protests.

In August of 1765, there were a series of damaging riots that took place in Boston, during which mobs threatened to tar and feather tax collectors, hung an effigy of a tax commissioner from the Liberty tree on the Boston Common, looted the commissioner's home and office, burned down his stable, and pillaged and damaged the governor's mansion, as well as the homes of other customs officials. American merchants joined the protest by organizing nonimportation associations to pressure British exporters to rally against the *Stamp Act*. The act, eventually repealed in 1766, made it clear to me that the Parliament and

Crown only responded to violent resistance or the threat of financial reprisals in the form of boycotts. But the need to pay for the late war forced the Parliament to pass more acts to find a way to collect revenue from the colonies.

The *Townshend Acts of 1767* was a series of five laws passed by Parliament, which restructured the administration of the colonies and placed duties on certain imports, such as glass, lead, paint, and paper, to raise revenue in the colonies to pay the salaries of governors and judges. The act gave local officials more power to deal with smugglers and those trying to evade paying royal taxes, and improve the collection of revenues from the colonies while strengthening the government's rule of law in America. More significantly, the act created the precedent that Parliament had the right to tax the colonies. This was only the second time in the history of the colonies that a direct tax was levied solely for the purpose of generating revenue for the Crown.

The other acts within the *Townshend Act* included the *New York Restraining Act of 1767*, preventing New York's colonial government from passing new laws until it complied with the *Quartering Act of 1765*; the *Indemnity Act of 1767*, which lowered taxes the British East India Company had to pay to import tea from England to make it cheaper and more competitive against smuggled Dutch tea; the Commissioners of *Customs Act of 1767*, which created a new customs board in Boston that was meant to improve the collection of taxes and import duties, and reduce smuggling and corruption. The *Customs Act* was a direct attempt to rein in the colonial government and place it back into the service of the British. The last, The *Vice-Admiralty Court Act of 1768*, changed legal procedures and venues, so smugglers were tried in royal naval courts without jury, not colonial ones, and by judges who collected five percent of whatever fine imposed.

The *Townshend Act* illustrated another of Parliament's attempts to raise revenues from the colonies to fill the depleted privy purse. But it was this act that began the march toward revolution because it convinced colonial leaders that Parliament, the King, and colonial administration were purposely enacting laws in violation of the *English Bill of Rights*, fostering the belief among our leadership that the British government had become a tyranny looking to dominate the colonies through threats, punishment, and violence.

The *Tea Act of 1773* sought to reduce the massive amount of tea held by the financially troubled and corrupt British East India Company in its London warehouses and help the struggling company survive by undercutting the price of the illegal Dutch tea smuggled into the colonies. The act granted the East India Company the right to directly ship tea into the colonies duty-free. All the colonies recognized the implications of the act's provisions, for what it did was set up a government monopoly through a private company, and a coalition mobilized to oppose the delivery and distribution of East India Company tea. In Boston, the resistance eventually culminated in the Boston Tea Party on 16 December 1773, but more about this episode later.

Rather than recognize their policies were alienating the colonials, Parliament enacted a series of punitive measures intended to stifle resistance. The final straw came in 1774 with passage of the *Intolerable Acts*, a series of laws meant to chastise Massachusetts by closing Boston Harbor until the losses incurred by the Boston Tea Party raid were paid. These ever-increasing, stern measures enacted by a government where its colonials had no voice made me more aware that no republic or state ever stood on a stable foundation without satisfying the common people.

On another note, keeping an eye on my brother proved an impossible task. Starting in the early 1760s, his attacks on the colonial administration and British government became more vociferous without regard for the consequences. In 1762, James had published *A Vindication of the Conduct of the House of Representatives of the Province of Massachusetts Bay*. The pamphlet defended the colonial Assembly's action of sending the governor a memorandum rebuking him for asking the assembly to pay for ships he had sent to protect New England fisheries against French privateers, considering the action a levying of a tax without the consent of Parliament. In 1764, he issued *The Rights of the British*

Colonies Asserted and Proved in response to the *Sugar Act* and the rumored *Stamp Act*. Using Locke's *Two Treatises of Government*, James explained why taxation without representation amounted to tyranny. James reminded readers individual rights were a gift of God and not governments. It was the duty of the government to acknowledge and protect the rights of its citizens, finally arguing the property of the American colonists could only be taxed by Parliament if they enjoyed representation in London. He also asserted all colonists, white and black alike, were by the law of nature freeborn, and slaves had inalienable rights, favoring the extending of freedoms of life, liberty, and property to them.

The subjects of his last two pamphlets published in 1765, *A Vindication of the British Colonies against the Aspersions of the Halifax Gentleman in his Letter to a Rhode Island Friend* and *Considerations on Behalf of the Colonists in a Letter to a Noble Lord*, furthered his argument that Parliament did not have the right to tax the colonies without representation. But it was his 1769 article in the Boston Gazette denouncing the customs commissioners who had charged him with treason, calling him a "malignant incendiary," that led to the violent altercation previously described with Thomas Hutchinson's supporters. This became my primary reason for beginning to write my satirical plays in support of American liberty. For me, unstable though he may have been, James was a real-life hero like the seventeenth-century English Whigs whom I had come to admire for their defense of liberty. But suffer not, reader, he has not yet left this journal's stage.

Looking back at the events leading to the Revolutionary War, I am reminded of Uncle Jonathan's maxim: define the context and seek the motivation. The context was the Parliamentary enactments, which were motivated by the need to pay down the debt from the French and Indian War. The context of the colonial leaders was the taxation, which affected their financial stability. The motivation of colonial leaders, however, was more complicated. There were those who cared only about personal, financial impact, while others were concerned about the principles outlined in English statutory and Common Law. Separately, each could not incite revolutionary fervor, but when the financial was wedded to the principle of no taxation without representation, the keg was filled with explosive powder, awaiting only the lighting of the fuse. And December 1773 was the month the fuse was set.

Plymouth, Thursday, 30 September 1813

Chapter 9

THE DIE IS CAST

Although the first Committee of Correspondence formed in Boston in 1764 to encourage opposition to Britain's increasing customs enforcement and prohibition on American paper money in the *Currency Act*, it was not until 1772 when Samuel Adams, the unrelated Dr. Joseph Warren, and myself formed a permanent committee in response to the British government's actions following the Gaspée Affair. In June 1772, the revenue schooner HMS Gaspée, charged with boarding suspicious ships to intercept smuggled goods and enforce the collection of customs taxes, was grounded in the shallow waters of Narragansett Bay while in pursuit of the small ship, Hannah. The crew of the Hannah escaped and landed in Providence, promptly notifying the citizens who then seized the Gaspée's crew and burned the ship to the waterline. To the British, this action was clearly an act of piracy, not to be ignored.

Parliament dispatched a royal commission to find the perpetrators and hang them. This proved a forlorn hope and after months of investigating, the commission gave up. The incident and lack of arrests led to the British decision to have the royal governor and judges' salaries paid by the Crown rather than the colonial assembly, removing the colony's means of holding public officials accountable to their constituents. But our committee's responsibilities soon expanded with the introduction of the *Tea Act* in May 1773. Our new mission was to develop a plan and recommend courses of action to the colonial leadership in response to this latest Parliamentary outrage.

Before moving on, the reader might note my husband, brother, and other colonial notables were not part of the permanent committee. We supplied updates to the nonpermanent actors when they periodically attended our meetings or through coded messages sent by post riders. The final decision for any course of action, however, rested with the permanent committee. The reason was secrecy; the colonial administration had spies everywhere, and prominent men were being watched. My husband had been outspoken during the *Stamp Act* crisis. He had been a member of the lower house of the Massachusetts General Court for twelve years and later became speaker in 1775. He was a covert member of the Sons of Liberty, supplying financial support. My brother had organized the first Committee of Correspondence in 1764, which opposed the stiffening customs enforcement and prohibition on American paper money. He was constantly under surveillance by the authorities because of his pamphlets and government accusations of treason. Besides, his problematic mental condition made him unreliable to the committee.

John Adams, along with the celebrated Jeremiah Gridley, the most prominent lawyer in Massachusetts, had openly opposed the *Stamp Act* but had defended the British soldiers involved in the Boston Massacre. They were excellent sources of clandestine intelligence, but any suspicion of active participation with the committee would have compromised their value. Other notables like Thomas Cushing, Samuel Phillips, and John Hancock were approached about joining the nonpermanent committee but had demurred, citing business obligations. Although they were quietly supportive of our cause, they were keeping their fingers in the wind to see which way the political winds blew.

As far as the permanent committee choices, Dr. Warren had shown no earlier political inclination or activism. Samuel Adams, a cousin to John Adams, was politically active, a merchant, and colonial newspaper publisher who had contacts throughout the colony. He was also the clandestine leader of the Sons of Liberty, the action arm of the anti-colonial government movement. He had covertly organized the protests and riots during the *Stamp Act* crisis. I was selected based on my relationship to my husband and brother, to whom I could pass information thought proper. I had also gained a reputation as a constitutional and English Common Law scholar and expert in political theory. Besides, who would believe a mere woman could be a revolutionary working against the government, being the perfect cover for our secret meetings? Yet, we needed to be extremely cautious. I cannot emphasize enough, there were administration spies everywhere.

Our committee's purpose was to alert residents of actions being considered or taken by the British and distribute exact intelligence reflecting our views to the proper groups in the cities, towns, and countryside. This was one of the duties for the non-permanent members of the committee who were members of colonial legislative assemblies, while others were active in the Sons of Liberty and 1765 Stamp Act Congress. We circulated information through coded hand-written notes carried by couriers like Paul Revere and William Dawes, who were two I recall. It was the former who later rode circuit announcing the pending arrival of the British army prior to the Battle of Lexington.

The fall of 1773 proved decisive to our cause when three East India Company ships, the Dartmouth, Eleanor, and Beaver, carrying tea anchored in Boston Harbor. Our committee was charged with the responsibility of managing the tea crisis and, more specifically, recommending a course of action. In November, we held a meeting to plan our response at my Plymouth home. If memory has not abandoned me, we discussed three workable options: a boycott, a port protest, or a raid to liberate the tea. We discounted the boycott and protest, as they took time to organize, and past attempts had brought a minimal impact on government policy. My position was simple. If we organized a boycott or protest, the ships would unload their cargo and regardless of how our fellow colonists might not like the heavy-handed British tactics, they would be hard-pressed in ignoring the cheaply priced East India tea, which would effectively injure the same people we wanted to help, our merchant community.

We agreed a more radical stroke was needed to send a message to the colonial administration, Parliament, and the Crown, so we selected the raid. We began by reviewing the options open to us. The first was to steal the tea but this proved impossible considering the chests were heavy and bulky and took too long to unload into the small boats, which might founder and take tea and raiders to the bottom of the bay. The second was to burn the ships, as in the *Gaspée Affair*. We rejected this choice because the ships had not foundered, and fires would quickly alert British army units ashore and British warships in the harbor, while endangering the raiders to capture and summary execution.

Furthermore, I pointed out that stealing the cargo, or firing or scuttling the ships, would be considered a violation of the 1698 *Act for the More Effectual Suppression of Piracy Act*. The act created the official legal definitions of piracy and allowed for pirates to be lawfully examined and adjudged in any place at sea, land, or in any of his majesty's islands, plantations, colonies, dominions, forts, or factories. This law expanded the Admiralty's authority to include the Caribbean and North American colonies by setting up overseas Admiralty Courts, which governed the process of pirates' executions who were considered guilty before trial. If one or more of our boarders were captured during or after the raid, they were legally subject to immediate execution.

On the other hand, I pointed out, if we destroyed the tea without damaging or destroying the vessels, the crime would be considered an act of vandalism. Under Common Law, the authorities' judicial options would be limited to jail time, fines, or restitution for the destroyed or damaged property. In the case of jail and fines, the length of the sentence or amount paid would depend on the monetary losses incurred by the East India Company. In the case of restitution, the convicted party or parties would repay the property owner for the financial losses, and a fine levied to the restitution amount. I then noted that the case would be decided in the Vice-Admiralty Court in Halifax because the crime was committed in the harbor. If, however, the vandalism took place on land, let us say in a warehouse, the adjudication would fall within the purview of the Massachusetts General Court. The latter case assumed the tea was unloaded in which event its destruction would be more difficult.

I then added that the *Sugar Act of 1763* and, later, the *Vice-Admiralty Court Act of 1768* had expanded the judicial powers of the Vice-Admiralty Court by changing legal procedures and venues, so crimes perceived to have been committed on the high seas or in ports were tried in Halifax and not colonial courts. Because of the special relationship between the British government and East India Company, which had spawned the current dispute, I was convinced the case, vandalism or not, would be referred to the Vice-Admiralty Court

Looking at Samuel and Dr. Warren, I emphasized that my opinion assumed no one, regardless of the type of action decided upon by the committee, would be captured. Without an individual or individuals to try and convict for the crime, the government, as in the case of the Gaspée incident, would have no choice but to seek restitution and fines by other means against the colony or the city of Boston. In either case, the authorities would only be adding to their existing woes with their recalcitrant colonists. Any enactment, which threatened the use of force, would be seen as the behavior of a tyrant.

I ended by offering the opinion that the government would seek restitution from the city and if none were forthcoming, they would issue further enactments chastising Boston or the colony. But exactly what these actions might entail, I could not say. As I looked at Samuel, I could see a broad grin lighting up his face. He had come to a decision, after listening to my exposition on the law and considering all options, and with our concurrence, decided to destroy the tea by throwing it into the bay.

Samuel's Sons of Liberty would conduct the raid. He believed about one hundred or more men would suffice for the action. He knew where to get the small row boats, but the quantity would depend on their size, sea worthiness, and number of raiders. He thought of the idea of dressing like Mohawk Indians to hide identities, even though there were few of these natives in Boston or its environs. I suggested we announce the raid as near the date as possible to preserve secrecy. We should only tell our avid supporters and non-permanent committee members when the raid was underway. I told them not even my husband would know until the last minute.

We then discussed the post-raid plan. With such a large raiding party, the participants would need to leave Boston. If the authorities captured even one of the raiders, they could compromise others who would be captured, tried, face long incarceration or even execution by the Admiralty Court. We agreed the raiders would disperse to the farms and estates of those who supported our cause. They would be employed as field hands or laborers until the uproar died down. We then began selecting dates for the action.

I remember sitting at our last meeting before the action, marveling at how Samuel and Dr. Warren approached the date and time for the raid. Starting with the week of 14 December, they chose the early evening of 16 December. According to the almanac calendar, there would be minimal or no moonlight and the tide at its lowest. Samuel would not be able to estimate the number of skiffs until he figured out the number of raiders, but he planned to distribute groups of boats to each ship.

After the raid, if it were successful, the boats would return to various locations along the harbor coast, and from these debarkation points, the raiders would disperse into the countryside to melt into the rural population. He would ensure transport was prepositioned for the escaping raiders, but the real problem was how to inform our supporters in the countryside that they were expected to supply sanctuary to the raiders without compromising the security of the operation. Samuel decided he would dispatch couriers just prior to the raid to ride predetermined circuits. They would carry coded messages in the event they were waylaid and, at each stop, inform our supporter in person and continue to the next farm. We knew this was risky, but we needed to ensure the raiders had places to go. We agreed it would serve no purpose to have men roaming the countryside like wondering vagabonds or gypsies. This would certainly alert the British and colonial administration, which would endanger everyone involved. All Samuel needed to do was recruit his Sons of Liberty.

I must say there was a surge in my breast knowing I was taking part in a revolutionary action, like my heroes and heroines in the histories I had read. I was exhilarated but frightened as well. There was a great deal at stake and keeping the operation from my husband only served to heighten my anxiety and fear of discovery by the authorities.

On the evening before the raid, I could not sleep. I tossed and turned like I had so many years ago after first meeting James. This feeling was different; it was not the passion of falling in love but a sense of foreboding. Caught up in the anticipation, my nerves were on edge, I could neither eat nor concentrate, except on questions about the raid. Would the raid succeed? Would the raiders face capture and death? Would our committee be discovered? Would my family be branded traitors and subject to incarceration or execution? I wanted to share my apprehensions and fears with James but could not until the raid was underway.

At six that evening, I was beyond anxious. I went outside and sat on the porch. It was cold but I did not feel it. James came out and, remembering it as though it were yesterday, said, "Dearest, what are you doing sitting in this cold without your shawl?" He wrapped the shawl around me, and, appreciating his loving tenderness, I felt now would be the time to tell him. I was about to inform him about the raid when I noticed a lone rider galloping up the path to the house. Alighting from his mount, he strode over to me, bowed, and gave me a note. The note said, "On our way. Will call again." This was the code phrase we agreed would announce the raid was underway, and I would receive another message when it was over. Samuel and Dr. Warren had recommended I stay in Plymouth in case the raid failed, as they did not want me in the city if things went badly. *Chivalry*, I thought, *was not dead*. The rider bowed again, remounted, and took off toward Boston.

James looked at me, "Bad news?" I crumpled the message and, turning to James, said, "My dear love, I have something to tell you." Needless to say, his look became one expecting unwelcome news and, in a way, it was. We went inside, and I sat him down in the parlor and told him about the raid, everything from the planning to the execution now underway. I explained, being sworn to secrecy, I could not tell even him. His face expressed surprise. I grasped his hand and apologized, telling him how bad I felt keeping this secret from him. He simply said I had made the right decision for the right reasons, and I need not apologize. Then he asked what the message said.

I told him the code meant the raid was underway and would receive another note when it ended. He nodded, saying, "Now we sit, wait, and pray for success, and that no one is injured or killed." I also told him we would have three Sons of Liberty staying with us as field hands as part of the post-raid dispersal plan. Typical of his calm demeanor, James simply nodded in agreement and said that we three had thought of everything and, smiling, added, "How does it feel to be an insurrectionist?" I said nothing, trying to restrain a smile of satisfaction because of my fear for the raiders. He rose and poured us two glasses of peach brandy, and we waited together. Around midnight, the same rider returned with the second message. All it said was "Success. No one injured. Dispersed. More tomorrow." I told James, who had waited up with me the whole time, the last part of the message, and that Samuel would have his publishing contacts prepare the story as soon as the printers got to work the next day.

The next day's news came not from a newspaper but carried by three riders who had taken part in the raid. They were still wet and out of breath as they alighted from their mounts. These Sons of Liberty would be staying with us until the furor over the raid died down. The riders were a Scot named Peter, a Portuguese named Cristobal, and an African named John. James took the lead and invited them into the house. They sat down, and I had the cook prepare a breakfast which, as luck would have it, included the last of my tea. The young men, who I estimated were in their early twenties, were grateful but refused the tea: Cristobal saying, in halting English, that he thought it would be a long time before we saw tea again. At this, we all laughed. Then I asked them to tell us about the raid.

John told us there were many boats of different sizes, occupied by six or eight oarsmen. There was no moon, so they steered by the lanterns of the anchored ships. Peter interrupted, saying they were so quiet you could only hear the breathing of the rowers. Even the oars striking the water were silent. I asked how many boats were in their small armada. Cristobal, obviously a seaman, said he thought there were at least eighteen to twenty skiffs, maybe more, with the six in their small flotilla, each manned by eight oarsmen and a helmsman. They were assigned to the Dartmouth while other groups steered to the Eleanor and Beaver. James then asked how much tea was dumped in the bay. Peter said the entire cargo of the Dartmouth was broken open and thrown overboard. He could not say how much, but the chests had been stowed on the upper deck, obviously waiting to be unloaded. What surprised them was that with all the secrecy surrounding the raid, when returning to shore, they could see a large crowd on the pier cheering. How the British army or navy did not react was beyond our collective comprehension.

I then asked how they had made their escape. Cristobal said they rowed to the south side of Dorchester Neck, just north of the Dorchester town, where three horses were waiting with directions to our estate. Three others in their boat and eight from another were supplied horses, mules, or carriages to take them to their assigned hideouts. He then added that he could not thank us enough for offering sanctuary, to which each in turn did the same. I then told them their chores would be light, mostly helping with minor construction and repair work, adding, "If any of our servants ask, I hired you on my last trip to Boston to do odd jobs around the estate." The fewer people who knew who they were and what they did, the better. I then showed them their lodgings in the stable's hay loft, mentioning if they needed anything, they should not hesitate to ask. Just see James or me. They rose, bowed, and thanked us for the breakfast and again for the safe haven.

The *Massachusetts Gazette* and *Boston Weekly Newsletter* finally published the account on 23 December 1773, but Samuel had sent a message previously on 18 December by a dispatch rider detailing the event, which he described as a tremendous victory for liberty and colonial rights. The raid ran from six p.m. to nine p.m., during which time an estimated 115 men of Scot, Irish, English, French, Portuguese, and African decent took part in the raid, slitting 342 tea chests and dumping approximately 90,000 pounds of tea leaves into the bay. The low tide created an unexpected morass on the mud flats. Samuel thought it an excellent object lesson, for the British would have to live with the slime and stench of rotting tea for a long time. Samuel then noted even though they had kept maximum secrecy until the very last hours before the raid, hundreds on the dock and surrounding areas saw the raid. As satisfied as he was, James and me were more sanguine, waiting for what the British would do. Their response was not long in coming.

In early 1774, Parliament issued the four-part *Coercive Acts*, or as we called them, the *Intolerable Acts*. I had partially guessed right about the government response. *The Boston Port Act* was the first enactment in response to the raid, where it closed the port of Boston until the colony paid for the destroyed tea and the King was satisfied civic order had been restored. The British were obviously viewing the destruction of the tea as an act of vandalism and not piracy. It was a small consolation because the next three enactments I had not predicted.

The *Massachusetts Government Act* unilaterally rescinded Massachusetts' Colony charter and brought it under the direct control of the British government, while limiting town meetings to one per year. The *Administration of Justice Act* allowed the royal governor to order trials of accused royal officials to take place in Great Britain, or elsewhere within the empire, if he decided the defendant could not get a fair trial in Massachusetts. The *Quartering Act* applied to all the colonies and created an effective method of housing British troops in

America by allowing a governor to house soldiers in other buildings if suitable quarters were not available.

I could not imagine why Prime Minister North, King George, and Parliament believed closing Boston's port, revoking our colonial charter, and restructuring the political and judicial systems would resolve the issues that had been brewing for a decade. The real problem was Parliament, and the royal governors had only two ways of enforcing the *Intolerable Acts*, either with cooperation or with force. The former had become impossible, making the use of force inevitable. The Parliament and the King had sowed the seeds of revolution and would reap the rewards with their own destruction.

Hosting the next meeting of the Committee of Correspondence, I noted these acts had only served to justify every claim we had made about the rampant corruption in the colonial administration and English government, which had thrust a dagger into the heart of our precious British freedoms, turning these institutions into tools of tyranny. If we did nothing, we would fall under the boot of the tyrant. I mused at the time that the Tea Party had succeeded in poking the British lion in the eye, but we had only managed to unleash blind fury. We agreed the colony needed to prepare for the coming deluge. I told the committee pointedly that I did not believe the British would lie back and wait for us to capitulate. They would use force instead.

It was at our second meeting, if I recall correctly, that our triumvirate of Dr. Warren, Samuel Adams, and myself grew with the addition of my brother, John Adams, Josiah Quincy, Thomas Young, John Hancock, Eldridge Gerry, Benjamin Church, and my husband. This was a significant gathering because twelve of the thirteen colonies, Georgia dissenting, were calling for a Continental Congress to meet in September and October 1774 in Philadelphia. The purpose was to discuss how to repair our frayed relationship with Britain while asserting the rights of the colonies. The meeting selected our representatives for the Congress, which included John and Samuel Adams, Thomas Cushing, and Robert Treat Paine; the latter not being a member of the committee, but who was a celebrated lawyer and member of the Massachusetts General Court.

Here, I interrupt my narrative to address what, for me, became an equally important event. Mr. Adams had brought his wife, Abigail, to the meeting. She was in her mid-twenties when we first met. She had a pleasing countenance with sharp features, brown hair, sparkling eyes, and a warm, engaging smile, all resting on a petite frame. I suspected her nervousness was due to the circumstance in which she found herself. She practically panicked when I introduced myself and took both her hands, asking her to sit with me and join the meeting. John, noticing her discomfort, told her that I was a member of the permanent committee that planned the Tea Party raid and was our much-admired English constitutional and Common Law scholar. I guided her to a seat next to me and whispered to not feel intimidated or bashful. If she had something to say, say it. I have interrupted my thoughts here because from that first meeting, we became the best of friends. But more on that subject later.

As the conversation progressed, I could see each man had a different opinion concerning the aim of the Continental Congress. We all agreed on the main point: we needed to try to resolve our problems with the mother country while asserting our rights. I remained silent, allowing the arguments to progress to the point where there was general agreement. Speaking finally, I remarked that I was less concerned about what we proposed and more about how the British government received the proposal. They would certainly agree to improve their strained relations but on what terms? They would demand recompense for the East India Company's losses, but there might be other conditions. I had no doubt they would try to place limits on our freedom and liberty, and they might not address the underlying issue of our representation in Parliament. Before continuing, my brother interjected that he believed I had touched the issue with the tip of the sword.

Continuing, I was convinced our effort at reconciliation would fail because the corruption within the British government could not abide democratic principles, which created an equality of condition. Their love of domination and uncontrolled lust for arbitrary power and money would prevail in their councils, so we needed a plan if our proposal failed. John Adams spoke eloquently on the possibility we might need to resort to force if Britain would not accommodate our proposal for equal rights, which he agreed must include representation in Parliament.

I noted cynically that the desire for power and wealth will naturally banish any sense of our general liberty, nourishing in the government the kind of dependence usually associated with aristocracy. Josiah, Thomas, and Benjamin agreed, but each pointed out, to one degree or another, that with the British navy and army in every colony and port, and units in the western forts, we would be hard-pressed to react effectively in case of a conflict. No one disagreed with this assessment, but my brother simply added that all men were, by the law of nature, free born, and if we did not obtain representation in Parliament, we would be no better than slaves. This we should not abide. Everyone concurred with this statement and before the meeting adjoined, we agreed to meet the following week to decide on our colony's strategy at the convention.

As we rose, I remember asking Abigail what she thought. She told me that she never thought so many men could disagree without coming to blows. I said they were behaving properly because women were present. Men always like to appear in control in front of women, thinking we see it as chivalrous and a sign of their strength; I see it as patronizing. Abigail noted that they were not patronizing when I spoke. She had watched her husband, saying he was no supporter of women in politics, but he was engrossed in my commentary, nodding agreement with everything I said. She added she saw the same respect on every man's face and then mused she could only wish to be as knowledgeable about these issues as me. I told her to speak with John and learn from him. He was an expert in his own right and if he demurred, she could come to me. I would be more than happy to discuss these matters with her. She smiled, saying she definitely would.

As she was leaving, she turned and said she would visit soon. I nodded, telling her anytime she wished, and that her company would be most welcome and appreciated, for being continually around men all the time was beginning to adversely affect my femininity. I then told her to call me Mercy, at which she simply smiled.

At the front door, as everyone was leaving, John approached me and, turning to Abigail, asked, "How did you like her first meeting as an enemy of the state?" Abigail smiled, coquettishly telling him she was certain he would explain all this to her on the ride home. Turning to me, he stated he sensed I had something to do with her comment. I replied that it was not me, but he and the others had piqued her interest. "Of course, with your permission, I hope she can visit again. I long for the simple companionship of a woman. Being around you men is making me cynical." He laughed and, with a nod, said, "She can visit anytime."

He then looked at me and said, "We all saw your hand in *The Adulateur* when it appeared in the *Massachusetts Spy* in March and April, and the committee hopes you might draft a poem celebrating the Tea Party episode." Before I could agree, he changed the subject and asked how I came to select the pseudonym, Marcia. I told him that I had always been fascinated by Roman history and recalled reading in Plutarch and Tacitus two references to a woman named Marcia. Plutarch's reference was to Cato the Younger's wife, whom he took with him when he fled Rome with Pompey at Caesar's approach. This did not seem right, considering I was not fleeing a battle. The second, by Tacitus, really hit the mark. His Marcia was the lover and one of the assassins of the tyrannical Emperor Commodus. Considering the subject of my satire, I thought this reference most proper, so Marcia it became. He chuckled and said he should have known I would have researched the name.

Returning to the focus of the conversation, John asked if I could do a satirical poem celebrating the Tea Party. Nodding, I said I would have something in short order, and he and the others could circulate it as they wished. With a bow, he and Abigail left. As they walked to their coach, Abigail turned and waved, saying, "I will be visiting soon."

Plymouth, Friday, 22 October 1813

Chapter 10

THE PEN IS
THE TONGUE OF THE MIND

The year 1774 was momentous in many ways. In April, my dear mother Mary passed away. The family was heartbroken, especially Father, who was inconsolable. I never saw him cry but he did so without embarrassment. His sadness reminded me of Uncle Jonathan's melancholy moods after Aunt Mercy's death. Mother had been his love and partner, sharing life's joys and tragedies while always projecting strength. I could only think how she guided me through life's challenges and supported my educational goals. I smiled, thinking of her homespun homilies, which I remember to this day; the conspiracy she hatched with Father to marry me off, and the way she always showed optimism in the face of adversity. We were a dwindling family by 1774: my sister Mary had passed away in 1763, Uncle Jonathan in 1759, Jameses father in 1757, and now Mother. I sat for days thinking about her, etching in my mind all the times we smiled and laughed together, the lessons learned, and the love she offered unconditionally. The other events shaping this momentous year were the Continental Congress and Abigail's extended visit with the family.

At our next committee meeting, I received compliments for the poem, *The Squabble of the Sea Nymphs*, which I learned had been sent to the other Continental Congress delegations, along with copies of the *Adulateur*. Some of the committee members especially enjoyed and quoted their favorite poem's lines:

> "Pour'd a profusion of delicious teas,
> Which, wafted by a soft favonian breeze,
> Supply'd the wat'ry deities, in spite
> Of all the rage of jealous Amphytrite.
> The fair Salacia, victory, victory, sings,
> In spite of heroes, demi-gods, or kings;
> She bids defiance to the servile train,
> The pimps and sycophants of George's reign."

The committee members also knew *The Adulateur* was a veiled attack on Thomas Hutchinson and his tyrannical colonial administration. Samuel Adams told me the play had caught the imagination of the public, who began substituting characters for actual political figures in their correspondence. I did not realize the play presaged the Revolution when I wrote the day might come when "murders, blood and carnage shall crimson all these streets." However, in the summer of 1774, there was still a sense of optimism about the success of the convention. I too wished for their success, but I knew hope was a poor substitute for raw power. My guarded confidence was based on the penchant in men's nature to tyrannize other men because in their natural state, men were disposed more to cruelty than courtesy.

Abigail had come along and sat beside me during the meeting, whispering that she had not realized how complicated the issues confronting the colonies and Britain were. After John explained all the intricacies, her woman's instinct told her the dispute with England and our demand for representation in Parliament was a risky undertaking that could end badly. I said a woman's instinct was often more correct than men's logic, and mine was telling me the same. The committee agreed on the points of contention we believed needed to be included in the official convention statement, and that the language should not be threatening but conciliatory.

Obviously, the issue of colonial representation in Parliament was the number one matter on the table. Without the British government acceding to this requirement, it would make reconciliation impossible. The committee participants also agreed, at my brother's insistence, that the official declaration include a statement calling for an end to the importation of slaves, beginning the first of December 1774. There was a brief discussion of what options were available if the British government rejected our proposal.

I voiced the opinion if the government rejected our demands, we should prepare for war. Their denial of our right to representation in Parliament would be a rejection of our British citizenship, making us no better than slaves. I reminded them that the primary goal of all governments was to protect the rights of its citizens and if they did not, then they were tyrants and abrogated their right to rule. With that, the meeting adjoined but, before separating, we toasted to the success of the mission.

As we sat informally chatting on different subjects, John came over to Abigail, James, and myself and thanked me for the opportunity to stand for our colony at the convention, remembering I had recommended him as a suitable councilor. I told him it was an honor to offer his name for consideration and pleased he had received the post. He then asked James and me if Abigail could stay with us while he was in Philadelphia. I said it would be wonderful to have her stay at Plymouth, but what about their children? If it were no inconvenience, Abigail said she would bring the two oldest, Abigail and John Quincy, and have her household staff look after the youngest, pointing out that Charles was only four and Thomas had just celebrated his first birthday.

Shaking my head, I told her to bring the entire family and would only feel comfortable if they all came, as we could easily make room. They were about to protest when James insisted there would be no further protestations. "You will all come, and we will enjoy the company," he said, adding that he knew I would be delighted to have two females to talk with; we men were driving me to distraction. Having resolved the matter, Abigail turned to me and said her daughter Abigail preferred the name Nabby. Abigail told me that nine-year-old Nabby preferred the nickname because it minimized confusion between mother and daughter.

On 1 September 1774, the Adams brood arrived at the estate. James looked at me and, shaking his head, said he had forgotten how much women could pack. It looked like an army train on the march. I gave him a light tap in the side with my elbow, telling him to hush. Abigail was carrying one-year-old Thomas, while Nabby was holding the hand of four-year-old Charles. Seven-year-old John Quincy was strolling with his head on a swivel, scanning the surroundings. I invited them inside and, turning to Abigail, said it must have been a trying trip. She nodded, again thanking us for opening our home to the family. I escorted her into the parlor. Little Thomas was fast asleep in her arms, and I directed our servant to bring my son George's old crib into the parlor. It was still in good condition so we could use it for the baby, and Abigail was happy to relieve herself of the tiny burden. I asked our cook to prepare a light meal for the children and warm milk for the baby. She at once turned to the children and waved them to follow her into the kitchen.

The first to scurry from the kitchen were John Quincy and my boys, Charles, Henry, and George, who were intent on getting outside to play games under the watchful eye of James. Then came Nabby, bounding into the parlor: smiling, eyes gleaming, and mouth smeared with powdered sugar from the half-eaten Apple Betty in her hand. Abigail gave a scowling look, but I smiled, remarking, "So child, you found the Betties. I hope you ate something else." With a look of pride, she replied, "A piece of ham, glass of milk, Blueberry Duff, and Betty in my hand." Then she said, "Mother, you must have one; they are delicious." I looked at Abigail but all she did was smile. Abigail told her to sit by my side and I promptly wiped her mouth, cheeks, nose, and chin of the powdered sugar, telling her that there was more sugar on her face than on the Betty. She giggled. Abigail looked at me and smiled. I had obviously made a friend.

Then Nabby turned to me and asked if she could call me Auntie Mercy. Before I could respond, she then asked if I had thrown any tea into the bay. Abigail and I looked at each other quizzically. Abigail asked where she heard this. Nabby sat up straight and proudly said she overheard Uncle Samuel telling Papa that Auntie Mercy was involved. Leaning forward, I told her my involvement was in planning the raid; I did not go to the harbor and throw tea into the water. She seemed disappointed but, thinking for a moment, retorted that planning was important. I said it was. She sat back, saying, "Then you took part in the Tea Party?" Abigail turned to me, whispering, "Out of the mouth of babes." She then turned to Nabby, saying, "Auntie's involvement was an important secret. You cannot tell anyone, or Auntie will get in trouble with bad men." She looked at both of us and promised she would keep my secret. Before I move on, I would be remiss if I did not speak about Nabby, with whom I forged a special bond.

When I first met Nabby during their visit, she was a bright, playful nine-year-old who grew into a beautiful woman with a pleasing countenance, sharp facial features, light brown hair, and big brown sparkling eyes, resting on a small frame with an appealing smile that at once captured one's attention. She was gracious, intelligent, curious, articulate, and always ready to engage in conversation. Over the years, as she spent time with me in Plymouth, I came to love this young girl as if she were my own. James often told me I doted on her as if she was my daughter. Nabby was the daughter I had always wished with each pregnancy but never had.

When she joined Abigail and John in England, and later when he was Vice President and President, and she married, I missed her winning smile, engaging personality, and conversations. When she and John Quincy left for England to join Abigail and John, I did not realize it would be the last time I would see her beautiful face. Writing to me while in England, Abigail divulged the reason for the trip, and it had to do with Nabby's choice of a man, something of which I was unaware.

According to Abigail, Nabby, who was eighteen by then, met and fell in love with Royall Tyler, a lawyer and playwright who had a disreputable reputation as a spendthrift who squandered his inheritance on parties, grog shops, and pursuit of women. I realized then why Nabby, who normally trusted my discretion and judgement, had not told me about this individual. Being concerned and knowing Nabby's stubborn nature, Abigail convinced John to allow Nabby and John Quincy to join them in England. She believed Nabby was too young to appreciate the mistake she was making and thought the trip would make her realize she was only infatuated with Mr. Tyler. As she wrote, out of sight, out of mind or something to that effect. I fully agreed with the decision, believing Nabby was too young to marry. Abigail read the situation correctly, and Nabby broke the engagement with Tyler shortly after arriving in England. However, she only succeeded in jumping from the Aesop's proverbial frying pan into the fire.

Shortly after breaking her engagement to Tyler, she met Colonel William Stephens Smith, who was serving as John's secretary and ten years her senior. Abigail informed me that even though she and John thought their courtship was too short, they were married in June 1786 at the American minister's residence in London. I could not understand why Abigail and John, who thought Nabby too young to marry Mr. Tyler, a man closer to her age, would agree to a marriage with a man ten years her senior. It made no sense, but I discovered later that their agreement to the marriage had to do with Colonel Smith's sister being married to their son Charles.

I came to know that while Colonel Smith was good to Nabby, he never settled into a comfortable lifestyle, continually seeking quick ways to make money, spending more than he earned, and eventually losing everything in real estate speculation in the early 1800s. In some ways, he reminded me of my son Winslow's undisciplined and wayward early lifestyle. The investment losses left them with a small farm along the Chenango River in central New York, but they later moved to New York City when his fortunes improved. To this day, I cannot understand why Nabby chose as she did, but as much as I guess, it did not answer my question. But back to a cheerier time.

For seven weeks, we were a happy little mob, if not a crowded one, at our estate. Our cook felt the chaos most. She had to feed eight children, three adults, and look after an infant. She barely finished cleaning up from breakfast when she had to prepare dinner, and the same held true for supper. By the end of the day, she was exhausted, and this was with Abigail, Nabby, and me helping as much as we could without adding to the chaos.

During the visit, Abigail and I became close friends, speaking about personal matters, politics, history, woman's issues, and how we had arrived at a breaking point with Britain. Abigail was smart and curious, with a quick and discerning mind. She at once grasped any point I made, but she also held radical positions on women's rights, especially when it came to education and political representation in government. She even dreamt of the day when women could enter the professions, vote, and hold public office. I told her she sounded like my brother, who had argued for women's political rights and better education. I also mentioned he was one of the first in the colonies to defend the natural rights of Africans and condemn slavery, believing they were, by the law of nature, free born.

I then broke my rule to never speak of family secrets. But in this brief visit, I had forged a strong bond with and affection for Abigail and wanted to share my concerns for my brother. I knew she would not divulge my secret to others, even her husband. I told her James had moments of mental lucidness but ever since the attack by the governor's supporters, he was becoming more unpredictable. She had not heard of the attack, so I briefly described the incident, telling her his mind had become addled with diminishing moments of mental clarity since the episode. I apologized for waxing melancholy, to which Abigail placed her hand over mine and said she understood. She said she hoped he would reclaim his mental capabilities because John thought he was the face of our movement. I thanked her for her kind words. It was one of the secrets we shared with each other.

My peaceful interlude ended in October when John returned from the convention to collect Abigail and the children. Their visit was all too brief, and I was sad to see them leave. Even with five of my own, the house seemed empty after they left, although Nabby promised to return. She was such a charming young lady whose presence lit up a room and my life. Abigail agreed to let her visit, and then invited us to their home, Braintree, for a visit, which I gladly accepted.

Before leaving with the family, John informed me that another meeting of the committee was scheduled for early 1775, with the location to be chosen in secret to avoid any official government scrutiny or interference. Although ominous in its connotation, neither James nor I were surprised. He then gave me a copy of *The Declaration and Resolves of the First Continental Congress,* which detailed the colonists' grievances in response to the *Intolerable Acts.* The *Resolves* was very much the legal document I had expected, concluding with plans to start a boycott of British trade until colonial grievances were redressed. Simple enough though it appeared, the next entry disturbed me.

The delegates had decided to draft a formal petition to King George III, which they believed offered an opportunity to de-escalate the conflict before taking more radical action. They had not drafted a similar letter to Parliament, considering them the aggressor behind the recent *Intolerable Acts*. I turned to my husband, giving him the letter and saying, "Read this. We need to talk." What the delegates had done with this letter to the King flew in the face of practical politics, and if they knew it, then the covention had been charade. Sitting together in the library, James, with a wary expression, took the document, sat at his desk, and began reading. Putting his spectacles down, he issued a low whistle and, thinking for a moment, looked to me and said that reading between the lines, there was more here than we predicted from the Congress. I added that I wished my brother was here, for he was more familiar with such political intrigues. James nodded his agreement, and we began speaking about the implications of the document.

I noted the letter to the King was like playing a weak hand in a game of Whist. James smiled, knowing how much I enjoyed Hoyle's games of chance and strategy. I remarked that the delegates could not be so naïve to believe the King wielded power over the Parliament. He might propose a law or action, but Parliament was the body to dispose and enact legislation. Ever since the Glorious Revolution, which deposed James II and installed Queen Mary, Parliamentary power has been on the ascendance. In fact, the adoption of the *English Bill of Rights of 1689*, following this bloodless revolution, gave Parliament more legal and legislative control over the authority of the King. The bill was supposed to usher in a new, more democratic government, but I fear all it did was exchange the despotism of monarchy with the tyranny of the legislature. Our delegates must have known this, so why send a letter to a man, king though he may be, who could not act without the legislature's authority?

James said nothing for a moment and then said the *Resolves* sounded like a legal brief a lawyer would send to a court. This was not wrong per se if you were arguing in front of a judge and jury, where a lawyer could use persuasive skills to convince the assembly of the gravity of the issue. This document was more of a Writ issued by a judicial authority, with an implied threat of action if ignored. I noted the document was designed to intimidate, not reconcile. James agreed, saying that the situation did not bode well for the colonies and believed that in ignoring Parliament, the delegates were issuing a challenge, which the British government would pick up and throw back into our collective faces. I then told him war was inevitable; Parliament would not back down, and I fear this will stiffen their resolve, excuse the pun. James smiled and thought we should wait until the next committee meeting to hear more about the delegate debates and their rationale for preparing the document as they had.

At our next meeting at John and Abigail's Braintree estate, I listened carefully as our delegates related the debates on the resolution.

John said there was tension from the outset. All believed Parliament had exceeded its authority with the *Intolerable Acts*, but our response of tossing East India tea into the Boston Harbor had not served to improve the problem, only worsened it. Now all the colonies were being expected to issue a proclamation with demands they believed the British government could not accept without appearing weak. In their assessment, Samuel Adams and Thomas Cushing saw sectionalism as an issue dividing the delegates. The delegates from the agricultural south, who relied on trade with Britain, wanted the *Resolves* to be less threatening. They also did not support the ending of the importation of slaves, which was a major part of their labor force. The colonies in the north understood this and, by consensus, agreed to drop the non-importation of slaves' demand.

Then John Adams declared that, at times, the delegates were speaking at cross purposes, adding, after a moment, that we were about one third Tory, one third timid, and one third blue. I sat thinking to myself, *Aristotle was correct, republics decline into democracies and democracies degenerate into despotisms. Factionalism would be death of our repnublican dream.* Waiting for the moment when all had expressed their viewpoints, and thinking the exposition was over, I was ready to speak when Mr. Paine, who had been silent, spoke.

He had been a party to the preparation of the document but noted his dissatisfaction with its tenor. He thought it less a legal document and more a threatening letter that offered no room for negotiation with Parliament. He disagreed with sending a private correspondence to the King while bypassing Parliament. In his judgement, you could not issue a threatening document on one hand and a conciliatory letter on the other. As I scanned the group, I could see discomfort with his assessment. Before I could interject, Samuel looked to me, saying I had been uncharacteristically silent and was there something wrong.

I stated to Samuel, and the committee, that quite a bit was amiss, but I wanted to understand the negotiating positions of the delegates, the dynamics leading to the preparation of the document, and collect my thoughts before speaking. I then began by noting my agreement with Mr. Paine by reiterating what James and I had spoken about previously. I told them the letter to the King was a mistake because the King wielded little power over Parliament since the enactment of the *English Bill of Rights*. Parliament, corrupt though we believed it was, exercises the real power. The King might propose legislation or action, but Parliament had the statutory authority. Sending a personal letter to the King while sending a non-negotiable quasi-legal instrument to the Parliament would not be received with equanimity. In fact, it would be considered a direct attack on the power of the legislative branch. I finished by saying the actions of the Congress did not bode well for the colonies and believed Parliament would view the *Resolves* as a threat to their power and would respond accordingly, as would I in their place. And then I declared, "Gentlemen, war with Britain is inevitable. Parliament will not back down."

There was absolute silence when I finished my invective. John Adams then spoke, saying the delegates could offer different solutions or soften the language at the next Congress. I then added that the idea of offering a different, less-threatening proposal might be perceived as a sign of our weakness, thereby making matters worse. I reminded them that the main issue facing us was colonial representation in Parliament. How would we achieve this goal by softening our language or proposing something different to win our argument? I reminded them that the mission when they left for Philadelphia was reconciliation, not surrender. If the *Resolves* were not accepted, and I figured they would not be, we could harbor no doubts about restoring peace with the mother country. Then, turning to Samuel, I simply said that I believed we would be needing the services of his Sons of Liberty for more than raids.

Looking toward me, Mr. Paine then spoke, and said, "Mrs. Warren, I have only known you by reputation, but I will say it here and now, I fully agree with your assessment of the situation and the conclusion that we are facing war. You have certainly confirmed your reputation as a political and legal expert." I bowed my head and thanked him for such an effusive compliment. Samuel looked to Mr. Paine and said, "I told you, Robert; she is the smartest and wisest of us all." With that, Samuel rose from his seat and, as I recall, said that we had much to think about, and we should start by sending correspondence to our peers in Congress, enlightening them of our, or more precisely Mrs. Warren's, assessment of the situation. It was this correspondence to the delegates that opened my dialogue with notable patriots like Messrs. Jay, Madison, Hamilton, Henry, Jefferson, and General Washington, to name a few.

Plymouth, Thursday, 4 November 1813

Chapter 11

FREEDOM IS WON, NEVER GIVEN

Having written about the war in the *History of the Rise, Progress, and Termination of the American Revolution*, I will not bore the reader with what was described in the work. I will instead narrate the pre-war intrigues and events leading to the conflict, and some thought-provoking facts about my involvement during the war. As I had predicted, the response from the Crown and Parliament was unavoidable. Our leaders' first problem was their belief in the outdated notion that the Whig party was supportive of the colonial position about taxation and representation. This proved not the case and, when speaking with John and Samuel Adams, I pointed out the celebrated Henry St. John, Lord Viscount Bolingbroke in his *Dissertation on Parties,* wrote that the Glorious Revolution had effectively destroyed the ideological differences between Whig and Tory factions, and they were now nothing more than nominal descriptions of political factions fighting for control of the government. In other words, the Whig belief in the ascendancy of Parliament and Tory support for the monarchy were no more than obsolete notions with no relevance to the reality of British politics.

I told them they should not expect support from either party. Both Whig and Tory focused on their control of policy and governance, and should the colonies jeopardize either one or both, they would react violently. Although they listened, I knew they did not hear me because they continued to insist the next Continental Congress, scheduled for May 1775, might be able to develop a more palpable solution for the Crown and Parliament. They simply did not realize the British government had changed. Ideological differences had fallen prey to practical politics, and as events unfolded, I was proved correct, although admittedly I did not expect the rapidity of the British response.

An article in a British journal, arriving in the colonies after the Continental Congress adjoined, and written before the publication of the *Declarations and Resolves*, declared that despite the tensions existing between Parliament, the Crown, and the colonies, the King was not wavering or conceding to colonial demands. The King meant to keep political unity between his colonies and Britain, regardless of how it affected the colonists, telling Prime Minister, Lord North, that the colonies must either surrender or triumph. There could have been no more a direct statement of purpose than this, and yet our leaders persisted in their belief that reconciliation was possible.

The same journal cited a quote from the celebrated literati, Samuel Johnson's pamphlet, *Taxation No Tyranny*, questioning the colonists' right to self-government, saying that we hear the loudest squeals for liberty from those who enslave others. It was clear the British had no intentions negotiating with people considered outlaws under Common Law, or persons who had defied the laws of the realm. As intelligent as our leaders were, they did not understand the nuance of political intrigues and exercise of power; and if they did, they were misreading or ignoring the temper of the King and Parliament.

In early March 1775, the committee met at our Plymouth home to discuss the strategies of the Second Continental Congress. The assemblage included John and Samuel Adams, Robert Treat Paine, Thomas Cushing, Dr. Joseph Warren, my husband James, and a new attendee, John Hancock. Abigail attended with Nabby, using the meeting as an excuse to visit. I found Mr. Hancock ingratiating, complimenting me on my involvement in the Tea Party raid and expert assessment of the overall situation. I reiterated for the group my earlier conversation with John and Samuel about how the Crown and Parliament would respond to the *Resolves*. To my surprise, every committee member knew about it, with John admitting he had briefed them prior to the meeting so we could discuss my appraisal.

Rather than repeat the narrative, I expanded on my position by asking the members if they had noticed any naval or army movements as of late. I did not know if any military movements were afoot but thought it sensible to ask if the British government was planning to use force to punish their wayward colonials. Dr. Warren commented that this seemed logical, based on recent statements by the British government about their unwillingness to negotiate with us and the simultaneous lack of action by the colonial administration. He suspected a flotilla with army units aboard were sailing from British ports.

Samuel mused that if he were the British, they would be preparing other units already quartered in the colonies to support any impending military action. My husband then added that we needed to consider the units stationed at the forts along the Upper Ohio Valley and, more importantly, the British military presence in Canada and the upper New York territory. The Canadian forces could also easily cross the border, link up with the upper New York garrisons, and sail down the Hudson to threaten Albany, New York City, Boston, and even Philadelphia, where they could bag the whole lot of us.

I interjected, pointing out that Governor Gage, in September of the previous year, had already begun reorganizing the garrisons in New York City, New Jersey, Philadelphia, Halifax, and Newfoundland, assuming overall command from Boston. I noted his aim might be to descend on our colony, thereby snuffing out the rebellion at its source in one swell swoop. Doing this would force the other colonies, especially our southern brethren, to capitulate and fall in line with British policy. Regardless of their strategy, Governor Gage's assumption of overall command meant he was positioned to order a concerted effort.

Uncharacteristically, Dr. Warren stood up, saying he was convinced we were correct in our assessment of the military situation and that we needed to prepare for an attack by the British. He also agreed with my position that the withdrawn garrisons from certain cities and other territories showed the main target for General Gage was Boston. To the British, this was where insurrection was born, and here it must die. New York City, Philadelphia, or even Charleston might also be targets of naval and army forces because they had expansive, deep harbors with critical road and inland waterway networks that could be easily invested and captured by British forces. He was most vociferous that we needed to communicate our concerns to the other colonies, especially those with harbors and navigable rivers. He then told Samuel that we needed his Sons of Liberty to spread the word. To this request, Samuel replied that it would be done at once. The conversation then turned to the Second Continental Congress agenda, even though I sensed the members were thinking more about an invasion than negotiating debates or positions.

An agenda was a moot point, I said. If the British had ignored the *Resolves* of the first Congress, I did not believe anything less than our total submission would satisfy the Crown and Parliament. Mr. Hancock looked at the group, with penetrating eyes, and said that we must be unanimous in our resolve. There must be no pulling in different directions with competing agendas; all the colonies must hang together or face the destruction of our liberty piece meal. Dr. Warren declared that he would appeal to heaven for the justice of our cause that we would die or prevail. These platitudes were born of the emotion of the moment. But on the objective side, it was best to be prepared for the worse. It had taken time, but the leaders now realized that reconciliation with the mother country was a lost cause.

James brought out decanters of East India Company-imported Arrack brandy and our domestic Apple Brandy with glasses. He invited everyone to toast to their success, regardless of the outcome. He then mused aloud that he was offering the Arrack, as it might be the last bottle we would see for some time. Anyway, it was better than salted tea from the Charles River, to which everyone chuckled and toasted to their success. As he rose to take his leave, Dr. Warren noticed I had risen as well. He bowed to me and politely asked where I was going. Looking at him and the rest of the group who had all risen to bow courteously, I offered my apologies, saying, I had to attend to my other guests and with a slight bow of my head to all, led Abigail and Nabby into the kitchen.

Abigail had said nothing during the meeting, so I asked what she thought. Before she could utter a word, Nabby queried why was everyone preparing for war. "Was this not a terrible thing?" Abigail interrupted, telling her that I was weary of talk about war and politics. I waved my hand, saying it was all right, and, then looking to Nabby, quoted from from the renowned Spanish author Miguel de Cervantes Saavedra's, *Don Quixote,* that "Forewarned, forearmed, preparation was half the victory." We were speaking about the worse that might happen in the hope it did not, but just in case, we should be prepared. I recall being mentally tired and emotionally drained. Talk of war always hits home with mothers with children of military age. My mind thought of my husband, James, my oldest, and Winslow, my second born. If it came to war, I knew they would join the fight, and this thought scared the life out of me.

Abigail caught my melancholy mood and changed the discussion, as she was a master at doing. She asked what I thought about teaching Nabby the game of Whist. I smiled, thinking to myself, *Leave it to Abigail to change to a happier subject.* I was relieved to have a new topic to take my mind off the crisis. Nabby said, "What is Whist?" I explained that Whist was a trick-taking card game where the rules were simple but required attention to the detail of the cards dealt.

I would need more time to teach her, but the game started with the cards shuffled by the player to the dealer's left. The dealer deals the cards, one at a time, face down, so that each player has thirteen cards. The final card, which belongs to the dealer, was turned face up to show that the suit was trump. The turned-up trump card remained face up on the table until it was the dealer's turn to play the first trick, at which point the dealer might pick up the card and place it in his or her hand. The dealing of the cards advanced clockwise. Then, the player to the dealer's left led by laying down any card in their hand. The other players, in clockwise order, played a card of the suit led, or a player with no card of the suit original laid down might play any card by either discarding or trumping. The trick was won by the highest card of the suit led, unless a trump was played, in which case the highest trump card won, and the winner of the trick led the next trick.

I could see Nabby was confused, so I told her we should wait until her next visit so I could show her the game by playing it with her mother. Nabby nodded in agreement. I then told her to go into the cupboard where she would find a Blueberry Duff or Apple Betty. She poured a glass of milk and returned with a Duff in hand, happily smiling with powdered sugar surrounding her mouth and a little on her button nose. Abigail smiled, saying that she feared I would run out of sweets if I did not keep an eye on her little imp. I said Nabby could have all she wanted; I was simply happy to have my mind off political intrigues and the specter of war.

John then peered around the corner, informing Abigail and Nabby it was time to leave. I walked them to the front door where the committee members were saying their goodbyes. Mr. Paine turned to me and, while thanking James and me for our hospitality, complimented me on the clarity of my arguments. He added that he only wished we had advocates like myself in the Congress, even better speaking to Parliament about their narrow-minded approach to our problems. His comment was exceedingly kind, but I was now mentally drained and could only reply, "Thank you." I wished him and the others good fortune on their trip to Philadelphia, and that I would pray for their safe arrival and success of their mission.

After everyone had left, I returned to the library, sat down, put my head in my hands, and wept. I had a bad feeling about everything that was about to happen, and when James saw my teary eyes, he came over, asking what was wrong. I replied that I was thinking about the coming war and what it would mean for our boys, and the other boys of other parents who would fight and die. I added that somehow, I felt partly responsible for it. James sat next to me and put my head on his shoulder and, in a soft voice, said, "Mrs. Warren, you cannot carry the world's problems on your shoulders. What will be will be, and we can do nothing about the unfolding events except live through the victories and defeats, joys and tragedies, and pray to our Lord our cause is righteous." James understood that it had been a long and trying day, and I needed to rest my mind. Then, as an aside, he said, everyone, especially Mr. Hancock, could not offer enough compliments on my legal and political acumen, and the clarity of my arguments. He and even Mr. Adams, among others, suggested you attend the convention, as it would be a shock to the other delegates. "Quite a compliment for my lady," James said and then kissed my forehead, and we sat in silence. I think he was as scared as me about the coming conflict.

Over the next few weeks, there was a flurry of activity, with messengers coming and going from our home on regular intervals as the crisis worsened. The first message came from Sam Adams, who informed us a merchant ship coming up from the West Indies had reported a large British flotilla heading west-southwest, presumably heading for Philadelphia or Charleston. The next messenger from Samuel, two days later, said that a large British fleet was sailing toward Boston to reinforce existing forces. The third message, from Dr. Warren, informed us British naval units had arrived in Boston, and another flotilla had split off and was heading south and west, presumably to Long Island Sound to threaten Providence or New York City, the latter being the most likely objective.

Although the intelligence was disjointed, coming from diverse sources, the information offered an insight into the overall British strategy. As we sat in the library and pieced together the disparate pieces of information, we could see a pattern forming. It was clear the

British were planning on laying siege or invading Boston, New York, and, most probably, Philadelphia. James and I asked ourselves, "Had Samuel and Dr. Warren shared these strands of information with other committee members? Did other committee members have more information and, if so, were they passing it on to Samuel or the other colonial delegates in the threatened cities?" We knew Samuel was secretive, but he was a thorough planner and would pass any relevant information to the other colonies' delegates.

I thought the British movements showed General Gage was setting a trap whereby he would move against the Massachusetts colonial militia, pushing it west while cutting off their retreat. This could be done with forces coming up from New York City and south from upper New York, Halifax, and Newfoundland. If he moved quickly, he would also cut the means of escape for our Continental Congress members, even capturing them. Looking at James with a wry smile, I said, "I must say the strategy is simple and reminds me of how you set me up for checkmate when we play chess." He countered that it certainly did appear that way but if memory served, I had seen through his ploys and beaten him the last two times. We could only hope that our peers saw the plan as we did. James then penned a note to Samuel, giving it to one of our field hands and telling him to deliver it directly to Mr. Samuel Adams and no one else.

Upon the field hand's return, he handed me a note from Samuel, thanking James for the information with which he agreed, noting he thought this was what Gage was planning. To that end, he had dispersed his militiamen and military stores to Lexington and Concord, continuing to keep a careful watch of Gage's activities. He expected the British to move once reinforcements arrived, and they had sufficient naval forces to lay siege to Boston and other cities along the coast. He also informed us that he had sent messengers to the other colonial militia leaders and delegations, warning of the expected British actions. He then asked that we send his three Sons of Liberty, who were still hiding with us, to Lexington.

Without saying so directly, he was telling us he needed every man for the impending battle. I called to the three young men and told them what Samuel wanted. After they had collected their belongings and saddled their mounts, I gave them three bags of food and three canteens of water for the journey. They thanked us for our hospitality and safe haven. I told them to be careful and that I would pray for their safety. I added that if they needed a place in the future, they were more than welcome to return, even if only for a visit. They bowed, mounted their horses, waved goodbye, and rode off. I never knew what happened to the Portuguese, Scotsman, and African who had shared our lives for a brief time; I only hoped they survived and were doing well.

The final message came in late March from John Adams, who informed us the delegates were leaving for Philadelphia. They were traveling separately and by different routes to avoid capture by the British. Like Samuel, he believed the British would move against our militia very soon and asked us to keep an eye on his family, as he feared retribution by the Loyalists in the colony. Their Braintree home was uncomfortably near Boston, so his fear was deserved. I turned to James, saying we needed to send a message to Abigail to tell her that she should pack up the family and come to Plymouth post-haste. I then went into the library, penned the letter, and sent it by messenger to Braintree. As I watched the messenger ride off, James turned to me and whispered that we would need to look after ourselves as well. What was coming would test us all; what I had predicted was happening.

Plymouth, Thursday, 25 November 1813

Chapter 12

THE PROPAGANDIST

On 19 April 1775, the battles in Lexington and Concord solved the problem of diplomacy, and yet I was torn, knowing, as the notable ancient Greek historian Herodotus in Isaac Littlebury's translation of the *Persian Wars* so eloquently said, "In peace sons bury their fathers and in war fathers bury their sons." I supported our struggle for liberty and equality, but there was also the realization we were embarking on a journey with unknown consequences. Furthermore, this was not a war against a foreign enemy or invader. This was a civil war and, as the renowned François Fénelon in *The Adventures of Telemachus* noted, "All wars are civil wars because all men are brothers." In this case, our brothers were Englishmen. Regardless of political disagreements and competing ideologies, we shared the same history, customs, language, and laws. Now I thought, we will be spilling the same blood.

I was at the same time emboldened in the justice of our cause and conversely fearful of the outcome. I dared not express my inner turmoil to my James, for he was four-square behind the war, and I did not want him to think my commitment was wavering. I was also scared for my husband and children, for I knew their fervor for the cause and would be hard-pressed to keep them from the fray.

Sitting alone at night, watching Charles, Henry, and George reading different Shakespearean plays, my mind turned to the events at Lexington and Concord. We had not heard much except the British failed to destroy our weapon stores. We had not surrendered but retired in good order. We had no major losses, and the British had sustained more casualties. However, it did not matter for I was having those conflicting thoughts again, yet now I knew why. I was rescued from my lethargy by Charles, who asked if he could stop reading. He was yawning, as were Henry and George. So, I bundled them off to bed, kissing each goodnight, and thinking to myself, *With the grace of God, we would build a better world for them.* Back in the parlor, I knew what must be done to focus my attention. I would use my pen in support of our fight for liberty.

I had been authoring poems for some time but not for publication. There were odes written to an individual, such as *To Mrs. Montague*, *To Torrismond*, *To a Young Lady*, and *To the Honorable J. Winthrop*. Others like *A Political Reverie* and *To Fidelio* were political in nature. My first published work, *The Adulateur: A Tragedy*, directed my invective against Governor Hutchinson, whom I blamed for my brother's worsening mental condition and his despotic behavior as our colony's British representative. The play had garnered wide attention and praise from our colonial leaders, who circulated it among the first Congressional Convention delegates. And although written under the pseudonym Marcia, notable revolutionary leaders guessed I was the author because they were familiar with my writing style and political position about our fight for liberty.

The theme of *The Adulateur* described the transgressions of the governor and other crown officials, personified in the character Rapatio (a play on the word "rape"), who was challenged and condemned in words and actions by the hero, Brutus, who stood for the colonists and suffered as a result of Rapatio's tyrannical leadership. Foreshadowing the coming revolution, I had my protagonist, Brutus, state, "Of Servia's virtuous sons, whose latest breath, shall execrate a wretch, who dare enslave, a generous free and independent people. If ye powers divine,

Ye mark the movements of this nether world, and bring them to account and crush these vipers."

Following its publication, at the request of John Adams and other colonial leaders, in early 1774, the Massachusetts Spy released *The Squabble of the Sea Nymphs, or the Sacrifice of the Tuscarora's*. James was enthusiastic, praising my genius, brilliant, and busy imagination as he put it, but I did not realize the poem's impact on the population until a meeting of the Committee of Correspondence. The success of *The Adulateur* and *Squabble of the Sea Nymphs* led me to write two more satirical plays, especially after Abigail encouraged me to continue, saying that the "Almighty has entrusted me with the power for good in the world."

Therefore, in 1774, *The Defeat* and, in 1775, *The Group* were published as sequels to *The Adulateur*, featuring a character based on Thomas Hutchinson, and like my first drama, the stories took place in the fictional nation of Upper Servia. In both *The Defeat* and *The Group*, a repressive government led by a tyrant was resisted by a small band of patriots, led by a passionate patriot who was symbolized by my brother. Although set in Upper Servia, each play drew on my study of ancient Rome and the conflict between republican and imperial factions during the first century. Satirical though they were, the plays were also propaganda devices aimed at bolstering our fledgling revolutionary movement, so I needed to develop an ideological foundation, and Rome was the best backdrop for setting the conflict between liberty and tyranny.

Knowing my audience was made up of educated men, I needed to define the philosophical basis of the ideological extremes. To this end, I used the principles of Locke and Newton. They described an ordered society as a balance between God, man, and nature. Only in this balance could we defeat tyranny and bring harmony to society. To reinforce the philosophical arguments of Locke and Newton, I cited the seventeenth-century English Whig activists and renowned authors like Machiavelli, James Harrington, and Robert Boyle, among others. Arrayed against the patriotic revolutionaries philosophically were the

Tory proponents of despotism and lawlessness, and their philosophical supporters, like Thomas Hobbes, Robert Filmer, Bernard Mandeville, and David Hume, among the most notable. I used this technique of developing philosophical foundations of ideological extremes because my readers would identify with the principles and authors. I knew this approach worked because I later learned these satiric dramas played a part in the removal of Governor Hutchinson, but I was not yet done skewering the British.

Unfortunately, in 1775, I realized one of my worst fears when, at the Battle of Bunker Hill, our dear friend and patriot Dr. Joseph Warren was killed. James then assumed the office of President of the Massachusetts Provincial Congress. Then, to add to my fear, in 1776, James joined General Washington as Paymaster General of the Army. In the same year, my oldest son, Lieutenant James Warren, joined our infant navy and, in 1777, I learned he was wounded in a sea battle and lost a leg. I was heartbroken but knew at least he was alive. When he returned to Plymouth, he had been fitted with a wooden leg, but he still needed crutches to get around while he learned to manage his movements.

I tried, as any mother would, to see to his comforts, but he was too proud and stubborn to accept what he thought was coddling. All the boys, to one degree or another, had a stubborn streak, which my husband attributed to my side of the family. He was probably correct; we Otises were a thick-headed clan. Then, in the same year, my husband James, claiming illness and having refused to accept a command in Rhode Island, resigned his commission in General Washington's army. Instead, he accepted another appointment as a Major General in the Massachusetts militia, again over my opposition. To my lasting relief, his duties were mostly ceremonial, as the British had withdrawn from the colony in March 1776. I thanked the Lord that he would take no part in any battles unless the British returned, which was unlikely, as the war had moved south.

As concerned as I was about my husband and son engaged in the war, in 1776, I read General Burgoyne's *The Blockhead of Boston*, a satirical play lampooning the colonists, portraying George Washington as an uncouth countryman who dressed shabbily with a large wig and a long, rusty sword. He lambasted us as prudes and tyrants to custom who he wished to see hanging from our liberty tree. I could not let these insults pass and at once published *The Blockheads or the Affrighted Officers: A Farce* in response to his play. I mocked the royal appointees, naming them Dapper, Dupe, Meagre, Paunch, Puff, Shallow, Simple, and Surly, comparing the differences between American and British values by satirizing social-climbing men and women. But the underlying theme was the conflict between American liberty and British despotism. I must say this play was fun to write, as it simply attacked the value system of an oppressor steeped in aristocratic haughtiness, greed, corruption, and uncontrolled power.

Then, in 1778, with all the chaos of the war around us, my dear father, James, passed away. He had been ailing for some time, so we were not surprised when he died. Yet, his loss hurt me deeply. He was the man who, besides loving his stubborn, little girl, fostered my education. To this day, I still remember hiding under his desk during hide-and-seek and knowing that James was sneaking books for me from the library. Even after I married and became a mother, he always called me his little girl, his rascal. His loss put me into a depression for a period of time, which was only relieved when James told me to pick up my pen and start writing again because the cause needed my satirical wit.

So, in 1779, I published *The Motley Assembly*, again comparing the differences between American and British values by satirizing social-climbing men and women and the results of their debased behavior. It also criticized those Bostonians who were still loyal to the Crown after the colonies declared independence. I was delighted with the reception among the prominent men of the age, receiving congratulations from George Washington and Alexander Hamilton, the latter remarking, "In the career of dramatic composition at least, female genius in the United States has outstripped the male." High praise indeed.

Then my son, the precocious Winslow, challenged me to write two plays in different historical contexts. He thought there was only so much that could be written about Thomas Hutchinson, the Revolution, Upper Servia, British tyranny, and America liberty. In his not-too-subtle way, he was telling me my plays were becoming predictable or, more directly, boring. This was a challenge I could not walk away from. So, in 1784, *The Sack of Rome* appeared in publication as a five-act tragic drama set in the crumbling Roman Empire of Emperor Valentinian III.

The play described the subversion of the western empire and the sack of Rome by the Vandal king, Genseric, which formed a revolutionary era in human affairs. I selected this subject because there were fewer periods in history corrupted by every type of luxury, tragedy, and barbarism. *The Sack of Rome* threw an impermeable cloud over the religious and political institutions of both the Roman and Gothic worlds, hastening the destruction of the former and the establishment of the latter.

The play received high praise in December 1787 from Mr. John Adams, who wrote that he was honored I had dedicated the play to him and wished to see it performed on the stage in London before audiences. He added that he had shown it to prominent British playwrights, Arthur Murphy, author of *The Grecian Daughter*, and Richard Cumberland, author of *The Carmelite,* both of whom offered favorable reviews, which he included with the correspondence. I later bought Arthur Murphy's play, learning that he was an Irish tragedian of notable recognition in his homeland. I also bought Richard Cumberland's play and discovered he was a politician, diplomat, novelist, poet, and playwright. But I was flattered by their reviews, praise, and belief the play was worthy of the British stage.

My last play, *The Ladies of Castille,* also published in 1784, was set in the Imperial Spain of Charles V and the tyranny of the Spanish Cortes by contrasting the different reactions of two noblewomen in support of liberty. Donna Marie, who despite the acknowledged "weakness of my sex," vowed to perpetuate her late husband's patriotic campaign at the risk of her own life after her liberty-loving husband's death. By contrast, her friend and liberty-loving compatriot, Donna Louisa, commits suicide in front of her husband, Don Francis, with her father's sword, agonized over her beloved husband's impending death. The theme offered the proposition that women could act as courageously as men, even in the face of defeat, hardship, and death. The drama was a guarded warning to my fellow citizens that we can only keep our independence by protecting those principles of liberty for which we had fought.

I personally consider this last play, along with *The Group*, my best because in it, I emphasized love and glory in the fight between liberty and tyranny by creating an emotional bond in which my heroines, Donna Maria and Donna Louisa, found their purpose as wives, mothers, and patriots. Each was willing to die for the cause in which they passionately believed. No one ever knew, even my beloved James, that I drew much of the theme from my own life. I saw myself in the role of Donna Maria and Donna Louisa, supporting my country's fight for liberty in the light of the sacrifices my loved ones endured for our country's freedom. This play was the answer to the inner turmoil in the months leading up to the war, concealed by my activities as a dramatist, satirist, and propagandist.

Then, my dearest James convinced me to shed the pseudonym and publish *The Ladies of Castille* and *The Sack of Rome*, and eighteen poems, under my real name. In 1790, *Poems, Dramatic and Miscellaneous* was published and sold by subscription whereby books were printed by a publisher based on orders received from individuals or groups. The work received complimentary reviews, but subscriptions were few, most coming from those who had been my enthusiasts before and during the war. The compliments included a lady who would become a close friend and celebrity unto herself, Judith Sargent Murray, but one review in particular was most rewarding.

In 1791, I received a charming letter from the celebrated Mr. Alexander Hamilton, declaring, "Madam, in making you, thus late, my acknowledgements for the honor you did me, by presenting me with a volume of your poems, I dare not try an apology for the delay. I can only throw myself upon your clemency for a pardon. I have not however been equally delinquent towards the work itself, which I have read, more than once, with great interest. It is certain that in the *Ladies of Castille*, the sex will find a new occasion of triumph. Not being a poet myself, I am in the less danger of feeling mortification at the idea, that in the career of dramatic composition at least, female genius in the United States has outstripped the Male. With great consideration and esteem, I have the honor to be, Madam, Your most obedient and humble Servant."

And still another laudatory review came from President Washington, who wrote, "From the reputation of its Author, from the parts I have read, and from a general idea of the pieces, I am persuaded of its gracious and distinguished reception by the friends of virtue and science." Such praise from the hero of our fight for freedom inspired and humbled me in the same breath. James simply said my genius was most deserving of such praise, to which I retorted that I could only hope these accolades translated into positions for him in our new government.

My first plays written anonymously prior to and during the war were propaganda devices in support of the Revolution. These plays and the last two solidified my reputation as a supporter of our cause and dramatist. But these assessments missed the other themes in my works: my disapproval of materialism; dependence on foreign manufactures; balance between Lockean and Newtonian principles about society's balance between God, nature, and man; and the debasing influence of fashionable amusements.

In each drama, I argued against the concentration of power in a central government because history was replete with examples of failed states and empires that fell into despotism because of the greed and desire for power of a ruling elite. My plays were not just attacks and warnings to the British Empire but to our fledging America as well. If we disregarded the liberty, freedom, and needs of the people, we would suffer the same fate as the great empires of history. And then

Shays' Rebellion exploded in 1786, and my worst fears seemed ready to be realized.

Here was an armed group of impoverished farmers, mostly Revolutionary War veterans, shutting down the courts to protest high property taxes and the scarcity of hard currency to pay them. In my judgement, the newly created federal government was behaving the same way the British had two decades before by enacting illegal laws that encroached on colonial rights and individual liberties. We had gone to war over those abhorrent laws and, from my perspective, these rebels were acting no differently when confronted by an uncaring and despotic government.

The revolt illustrated the difference between ideological clichés and the reality of governing. My opinion about Shay's Rebellion became known to some of the delegates to the Constitutional Convention, who agreed with my position. When approached by their representative to pen a response to the proposed Constitution being promoted by "Publius" in the *Federalist*, I initially demurred, candidly telling him that if my involvement became known, my family would suffer politically. My studies of history and politics had taught me what happens to those who fall into disfavor with the ruling elite and the three authors of the *Federalist*, who had been my enthusiasts, were now in power.

Plymouth, Friday, 3 December 1813

Chapter 13

THE COLUMBIAN PATRIOT

In late August 1788, Mr. Eldridge Gerry visited James and me at Plymouth to plead the case for me preparing a pamphlet responding to the proposed Constitution, which was being championed by the *Federalist* essays. I told him the proposed Constitution looked to create a government closely akin to the British model, and although I agreed with the concept of a federal and state partnership, there were few protections for state and individual rights and liberties. I noted that I believed the unbridled exercise of power by a federal government could lead to more Shays' Rebellions and tyranny because history has proven that those in power look to protect and perpetuate their self-interest.

Our conversation then turned to the practical problem of my name being associated with the pamphlet. I pointed out my dearly departed brother had taught me that political theory was different from practical politics. You could cite the theoretical concepts of a Locke or Montesquieu, but governance was best exercised using the pragmatic concepts of the renowned master of Italian politics, Machiavelli. Delegates endorsing the current version of the Constitution supported my works in the past and were now in positions of power, and I did not want my family to become the target of political retribution. We then arrived at an accommodation, meeting the needs of the Anti-Federalist faction while protecting my anonymity. I would write the pamphlet, and Mr. Gerry would take credit for its authorship; thus was born the "Columbian Patriot." Of course, he swore himself to absolute secrecy and, to this day, only my husband and a friend know of my authorship, but of the latter I will speak of later.

We then turned our attention to the pragmatic aspects of preparing the pamphlet. According to Mr. Gerry, "Publius," the authors of the *Federalist*, were focusing their arguments toward the people of New York State. They looked to influence the election of their delegates who, at their upcoming state convention, would vote to ratify the proposed Constitution. Mr. Gerry also intended on distributing the pamphlet to the other state delegations, believing Publius was subjecting their voters to the same propaganda campaign. Having read the essays, I agreed with his assessment that the *Federalist* essays were propaganda devices aimed at influencing the action of the various state delegations. This was done without necessarily divulging all the facts about the unforeseen consequences of their approval of the proposed Constitution.

Once completed, I would give Mr. Gerry the document for printing. To my amazement, he proposed printing sixteen hundred copies for the New York state and other state delegations. I thought the quantity excessive, but he pointed out he hoped it would gain in popularity and supply support for those delegates concerned about the direction of the convention. I told him it was premature to promise anyone anything until he read the pamphlet. He smiled and told me that he had every confidence in my ability as a constitutional and legal scholar, certain it would meet and exceed their expectations. We parted company, and I began reviewing the *Federalist* essays.

James had been unusually restrained during my discussions with Mr. Gerry and asked if anything was bothering him about the commitment. To my surprise, he commented that he thought I should publish under my name. He understood my concern about possible political reprisals, but he believed in my genius and the citizens of this country should know it as well. Then he asked how I would respond to the essays. I told him that I would pen the pamphlet as a political commentator, researching each point of the proposed Constitution in the *Federalist*, refuting or changing their positions while recommending alternatives in the form of amendments. The goal would be to convince readers it was a long-held republican principle that the majority should rule, and if a spirit of moderation could be accommodated on both sides of the debate, the voice of the people would be fairly heard. Admittedly, the treatise would be a subtle propaganda device, but based on practical application of political theory. In this way, I would use the same political theorists employed by "Publius" while inserting Machiavellian real politick. James simply nodded, saying he would leave me to my task, but if I needed anything, he was there for me.

Reading the *Federalist* essays, I noted five basic themes: federalism, checks and balances, separation of powers, pluralism, and representation. Although the essays were fairly consistent in support of these themes, there were inconsistencies among the authors. James Madison, a southerner, appeared to advocate for greater states' rights while Alexander Hamilton, a northerner, supported a stronger central government. Our family friend, John Jay, charted a middle ground, arguing in favor of a centralized but balanced system of government.

Although agreeing with the five themes in principle, I believed "Publius" and others through chicanery, intrigue, and false coloring were creating a system of government dangerously similar to the corrupt British model. Therefore, I decided not to focus on our concurring positions. Rather, as previously noted to Mr. Gerry, I would address points in their arguments with which I did not agree and offer amendments.

I chose to craft my arguments logically and objectively, using the essay style similarly employed by my brother in his pamphlets two decades before. I supported my positions by drawing on authors well known to the delegates, covering political theory, law, philosophy, and history. The choice included John Locke, Thomas Hobbes, Aristotle, Plato, Thomas Paine, Montesquieu, William Blackstone, Matthew Bacon, James Harrington, Nicolo Machiavelli, and Cicero, to cite the most notable. I knew the quantity and quality of authors cited or alluded to in the pamphlet would strengthen my arguments. I knew my readers; the delegates were educated men familiar with these authors and their ideas. The challenge was to use language that citizens who were not familiar with these authors could understand. They were the target audience who would vote on the proposed Constitution.

To summarize, I recommended annual elections, freedom of the press, judicial restraint, separation of legislative and executive powers, jury trial in civil cases, senatorial term limits, adequate popular representation, and individual and states' rights. I rejected a standing army, congressional budgetary power, Congress voting its own salaries, and the electoral college. I was proud to say several of my recommendations were included in the *Bill of Rights* while others were not. It has been twenty-five years since I penned the *Observations on the New Constitution and the Federal and State Conventions*, and will offer the reader my opinion on each of the amendments in light of where we were in America then and where we are now. In other words, I will do what I have rarely done; admit where I was wrong.

In the *Observations*, I argued the creation of a strong central government, as outlined in the proposed Constitution, lacked explicit protections for the people's liberties and individual rights. I contended the proposed *Constitution* without a *Bill of Rights* was politically and morally wrong, believing the new system would lead Americans into servitude to an aristocratic Congress and Chief Magistrate. Furthermore, the lack of a *Bill of Rights* would limit the people's ability to halt the growth of uncontrolled, centralized power, sinking the republic into a nightmare from which it might never recover. Rather than reiterate the recommended amendments for what a reader could review in the *Observations*, I outlined my rational for each.

With this in mind, I presented a listing of my recommendations, finishing with eighteen amendments to the proposed Constitution. Although my introduction covered political, philosophical, and moral imperatives the proposed Constitution needed to address, the most important theme was the responsibility of the governing to the governed. I declared all authors who professed support for republican government have agreed with the political axiom that man is born free and had certain unalienable rights. Governments were instituted for the protection, safety, and happiness of the people, and not for the profit, personal honor, or the private interest of any individual, family, or class of men. I noted the origin of all power rested with the people, and they had an incontestable right to check the creatures of their own creation invested with specific powers to guard the life, liberty, and property of the community. Others might point to other assertions in my introduction as more important than others, but this statement was the foundation for my arguments and amendments. To this day, I strongly agree with this notion because these maxims are the cornerstone of liberty, freedom, and equality.

Although the proposed Constitution included a statement protecting freedom of religion, speech, and the right of the people to peaceably assemble and petition the government for a redress of grievances, it did not do the same for the press. I found this odd, for without the freedom to disseminate information to our citizenry before the war of independence, the people would have remained ignorant of illegal actions of British government and colonial administration which led to the decision to rise up and fight. An ill-informed, ill-educated, and ill-read citizenry was the foundation for the rise of despotism. There could be no security for citizens or country without an amendment protecting freedom of the press. An unfettered free press is the guardian of individual rights against the exercise of arbitrary power and excesses of government by keeping the public informed. I continue to agree with this proposition, with the warning that the press owed the people honest reporting and evaluation of news while avoiding personal animus. To the credit of the delegates, they agreed with my recommendation, adding the phrase, "or of the press," to the First Amendment.

My next concern was the ambiguous language about the executive and legislative functions and responsibilities, which made me offer the recommendation that the convention delegates investigate what appeared to me a dangerous blending of the two branches. My rationale was people tend to think of despotism resident in an individual, but there were examples of the tyranny of political factions or parties. If the two branches of government were too closely aligned, a country could be subjected to the rule of a few. The English House of Lords, Commons, and King, the Spanish Cortes and emperor, and the Roman Senate, Plebian Assembly, and emperor came to mind.

Based on my reading, the separation of powers between executive, legislative, and judicial branches were present, guaranteeing the liberty and freedom of our citizens. But I proffered the the warning; to wit, citizens must guard against the specter of factionalism, combined in the legislative and executive branches, controlled by one party or faction. In this case, divided government was the best protection from the tyranny of the few or a cabal of like-minded corrupt politicians.

The abolition of trial by jury in civil causes was another cause for alarm. The celebrated and learned British jurist, William Blackstone, declared jury trials in civil cases a fundamental right and requirement of civil government in protecting property, liberty, and life. The proposed Constitution's ideal to promote a perfect union, establish justice, ensure domestic tranquility, provide for the common defense, promote the general welfare, and secure the blessings of liberty to ourselves and our posterity had to include the right of the individual to seek justice to redress wrongs from a jury of one's peers. This precept had a long history since first codified in Roman and English Common Law. The delegates accepted this concept and acted by proposing the Seventh Amendment to address civil trial by jury.

Although we are now engaged in a second war against the British, in 1788, I did not support the Second Amendment language that a well-regulated militia, being necessary to the security of a free state, the right of the people to keep and bear arms, shall not be infringed upon as necessary for the dignity and safety of America. Having been influenced by Shays' Rebellion, I feared such an organized militia, when controlled by the central government, could become a threat to the freedom and liberty of its people. A despot could call out the militia to suppress the murmurs of a group of people, community, or state.

Looking back in hindsight, and given our present situation, I am pleased the convention delegates thought better of my recommendation and rejected it. Nonetheless, the citizens of our great nation need to be vigilant that an army and navy did not gain so much power that they influenced government policy or actions. The responsibility of oversight of the army and navy must be the responsibility of the legislative and executive branches, and an unfettered press.

The next subject with which I took issue was the deceptive promise to guarantee a republican form of government to every state in the union, with no resources left for the support of internal government or the liquidation of the debts of the state. Every source of revenue in the proposed Constitution was a monopoly of the Congress. If state legislatures found themselves in an enfeebled financial state and, against their good judgement, wanted to tax their citizens to pay their debts or support of internal police, they would have to seek redress from the general government. I am proud to say that Article 1, Section 9 of the Constitution states that "No Tax or Duty shall be laid on Articles exported from any State," thereby nullifying my concerns about the powers of the purse. Before I leave this section, there are thoughts that have troubled me since authoring the original pamphlet, proving an unsettling omen for future generations of legislators and, on a broader level, America itself.

In Article I, Section 2, Clause 3 of the Constitution, to which the earlier paragraph refers, there existed a declaration, a part of which troubled me then and has continued to do so to this day. "Representatives and direct taxes shall be apportioned among the several States according to their respective numbers, which shall be determined by adding to the whole number of free persons, including those bound to service for a term of years, and excluding Indians not taxed, three fifths of all other persons." My problem was the vaguely worded "three fifths of all other persons," which forced me to beg the question, to whom was the phrase referring. Because of the deceptive wording, I did not realize at the time of my authorship that the phrase referred to enslaved Africans, and I suspected the vague wording was purposely intended to keep most of the delegates and citizenry in the dark as to the phrasing's real meaning and future implications.

In speaking with Mr. Gerry sometime later, he informed James and me this "three fifths of all other person," known as the three-fifths compromise, was a political intrigue hatched behind closed doors between a small cadre of the delegates to ensure the southern states would ratify the Constitution. This meant that three-fifths of a southern state's slave population would be counted toward congressional representation, even though the enslaved could not vote or exercise the liberty, freedom, and protections enshrined for other Americans in the Constitution. I told Mr. Gerry that we would rue the day our Founders allowed this abhorrent language and concept to infect our republic. He agreed totally, but without this unfortunate agreement, the Constitution would not have been enacted.

I told Mr. Gerry my brother, in his 1765 pamphlet, *The Rights of the British Colonies Asserted and Proved*, had declared that "Slavery is so vile and miserable an estate of man, and so directly opposite to the generous temper and courage of our nation that it is hard to be conceived that an Englishman, much less a gentleman, should plead for it." I then added that later in 1774, he recommended language to the *Declaration and Resolves of the First Continental Congress* demanding the British government cease the importation of slaves become effective 1 December of that year. This non-importations of slaves demand was excluded from the final draft to satisfy the southern delegates while the three-fifths compromise was included to garner support from the same aristocratic southern class. The result of including this odious language, regardless of the backroom mischief and rationale, served to legalize the institution of slavery in an America built on the notion of liberty and freedom for all.

It sickens me to know that fellow human beings, shackled in leg irons, were bought and sold like livestock. Looking at Mr. Gerry and

James, I asserted that slavery only illustrated my opinion that the human character offers at once a beautiful and a deformed picture of the soul, and flies in the face of my belief that true democratic principles are the result of equality of condition. We may amuse ourselves with theoretical systems of liberty, but we can only discern its true value by the practical and wretched effects of slavery. I can speak no more on this matter, as it continues to anger me. Let me return to the intent of this chapter.

Giving the Congress the power to decide their own salaries was preposterous. The ability of members to set their own pay would lead to the draining of the public purse and enrich the pockets of aristocrats. How would our citizens, suffering from economic depressions, view this government largesse when they were in financial distress? And what measures or factors would be employed to set up these salary increases? What controls would be put in place to ensure salary increases were not excessive? I recommended dropping this unwarranted inclusion in our Constitution as an insult to our glorious document. Even today, I continue to believe those representing their citizens should be more concerned about their constituents' needs than their selfish financial bounty.

I was profoundly concerned there was no provision in the Constitution for the rotation of lawmakers, leading to the potential corrupting influence of money, bribery, and other excesses while excluding men of proven abilities from seeking elective office. By this neglect, we lost the advantages of a check on the overbearing insolence of office which, by denying qualified men access to Congress, made that legislative body less accountable to the will of the people. To this day, I continue to believe congressional term limits empower the electorate by periodically selecting representatives of merit and avoiding the corrupting influence of special interests while opening representative government to more citizens. Finally, it lends strength to the republic by avoiding the despotism of a coterie of elected officials. As I expected, this provision was not withdrawn, thereby creating the foundation for a new class of men, the professional politician.

There were no specifically defined limits to judicial power or review by the Supreme Court of the land, which, when reading the original language in Article Six, Clause 2 of the Constitution, was so broad as to imply the highest court in the land could act as a legislative arm of government. The Constitution's original language did not protect citizens from being dragged from our county or state to answer to the litigious or unjust suits of an adversary in distant borders or between states. In short, the appellate authority of the supreme federal court included an unwarrantable sweep of power over the liberty, life, and property of a citizen.

But the Supreme Court's authority also extended to treaties, admiralty and maritime adjudication, and a host of controversies between the United States and other parties; disagreements between one or more states; between states and its citizens; between citizens of different states and citizens of the same state claiming land under grants of different states; and between a state or the citizens thereof and foreign states, citizens, or subjects. In my judgement, this unrestrained judicial power posed a threat because we hold law sacrosanct, but as with all human endeavors, man could be subject to corruption and despotism.

Although my recommendation arguing for judicial restraint was not considered in the original draft of the Constitution, the issue was resolved with the ruling by the Supreme Court in 1803 in the case of Marbury versus Madison, which established the principle of judicial review. In summary, this ruling gave American courts the power to strike down laws and statutes they found in violation of the Constitution. The real meaning for me was groundbreaking. I had always argued and believed the Constitution in total was a legal document whose articles, clauses, and amendments had the force of law, and not merely a statement of political principles or ideals. This decision proved the flexibility of the Constitution to change based on necessity.

During the debates to ratify the Constitution, a controversy arose over one provision of Article III, Section 2, allowing federal courts to hear disputes between a state and citizens of another state, or citizens or subjects of a foreign state. The Anti-Federalists feared this provision allowed individuals to sue states in federal court. Prominent Federalists assured their critics that Article III would not be interpreted to allow a state to be sued without its consent.

The Federalists were incorrect in their assumption, as later judicial action proved. A Supreme Court ruling in the Chisholm versus Georgia litigation, the very first made by that court, declared states were subject to the authority of the federal government. Recognizing the problem this ruling would cause, Senator Caleb Strong of Massachusetts quickly proposed the Eleventh Amendment, which changed the original language in Article 3, Section 2, in 1795. I say again, better late than never, and once again proving the inherent flexibility of our Constitution.

At the time I wrote the pamphlet, I argued the number of representatives not to exceed one for every thirty thousand was inadequate representation. To the credit of the delegates, the Constitution tied representation to a census conducted every ten years. This proved an important insertion. To illustrate the point, in the unofficial 1790 census, America's population was estimated at four million, but a more exact population count in 1800 showed 5.3 million. At that time, I mused to James, "Where were we going to put all these people?" Our country only extended from the Atlantic Ocean to the Ohio River Valley and Appalachian Mountains. How much land could be available to these new citizens?

Then, President Jefferson acquired the Louisiana Territory west of the Mississippi River from France in 1803, making America a truly continental country stretching from the Atlantic to Pacific Oceans. Then the census of 1810 showed our population at 7.2 million, excluding the enslaved. I continue to be amazed by how many people from all countries want to celebrate the freedom and liberty of our great republic. But I remain concerned for the native tribes who are in the path of these new settlers, who they consider trespassers and might not respect the borders of the tribal lands or their social and cultural values.

I recommended changing the ten voting electors per state to a system equal in number to each state's congressional and senatorial delegation. The original language in Article II, Section 1, Clause 3 of the Constitution defined which electors voted for president. Under the concept, each state's elector cast two votes for president. Whoever received the seventy vote majority from the electors became president, while the person receiving the second most electoral votes became vice president.

I wrote the failure to select the electors by popular vote was tantamount to the exclusion of the voice of the people in the choice of their first magistrate. Furthermore, the acceptance of the ten elector per state limit would be equivalent to investing the choice of our president solely in the hands of an aristocratic clique, who might combine in each state to place at the head of our union a despot. I agreed with Mr. Hamilton's assertion that electors should be chosen by state elections, while the original language had state legislatures selecting the electors. Unfortunately, the delegates did not see the wisdom of my and Mr. Hamilton's recommendation and did not amend the language, which presaged a future issue when, in the 1800 election, Messrs. Jefferson and Burr had an equal number of electors, forcing the House of Representatives to break the tie and chose our Chief Magistrate.

A senator chosen for six years by the state legislatures and governors would be, in most instances, a lifetime appointment, making the body indistinguishable from the British House of Lords or Roman Senate, and not subject to the will of the people. Such a term of office would also increase the opportunity for the corrupting influences at the governor and state legislature levels, whereby a powerful individual could buy his way into the Senate. I believed, and still do, that a six-year appointment would vest extensive powers in a senator, who could ignore their constituents because they were not directly involved in his elevation to the office. This was repugnant to every principle of free government but, alas, the delegates did not see the wisdom of my recommendation.

I noted there was no provision in the *Bill of Rights* to guard against the dangerous encroachments of power, more specifically the insecurity regarding warrants unsupported by evidence. The actions of granting Writs of Assistance in the former colonial administration of Mr. Hutchinson, the great champion of arbitrary power, subjected us to the insolence of any petty revenue officer to enter our houses, search, insult, and seize at will.

We were told with much rectitude the whole Constitution was a declaration of rights, but without specified protections stated in the Constitution, the rights of states and liberty of private citizens would be jeopardized by the deceptive activities of the federal government. But without enumerated protections for the rights of states and liberty of private citizens would be jeopardized. I further noted this has been the opinion of such notable writers like John Hampden, William Pym, the Earl of Clarendon, and other illustrious names who have stood forth in defense of English liberties and the Common Law. Even the master of Italian politics, the subtle and renown Machiavelli, acknowledged no republic ever yet stood on a stable foundation without satisfying the common people.

My concern was addressed by the delegates in the Fourth Amendment to the *Bill of Rights*, which stated, "the right of the people to be secure in their persons, houses, papers, and effects, against unreasonable searches and seizures, shall not be violated, and no warrants shall issue but upon probable cause, supported by oath or affirmation, and particularly describing the place to be searched, and the persons or things to be seized." Here, however, I must impose on the reader's patience and digress for a moment to explain how this particular issue, among others raised during the constitutional debates, became subject to the chicanery by a cabal of individuals led by Mr. James Wilson, leader of the Pennsylvania delegation of the Constitutional Convention.

As a member of the convention's Committee of Detail, Mr. James Wilson was responsible for issuing the first draft of the Constitution, which proposed the previously described three-fifths compromise and, after much debate and back room posturing, the first ten amendments. Mr. Gerry wrote me that Mr. Wilson addressed the convention on many occasions, acting like a fire-and- brimstone preacher extolling the virtues of the Constitution which, of course, represented his political and personal agenda. Even the renowned Dr. Benjamin Rush of Pennsylvania thought his performance during the convention exemplary. I found this accolade normal, as both men came from Pennsylvania and were of the same political persuasion. But there was more afoot than met the eye, and my suspicion proved correct when Mr. Gerry later wrote about a troubling action taken by a small group of convention delegates led by Mr. Wilson.

After reading his letter, I was dismayed to learn the manner in which the Constitution was being recommended to the people's judgement, without the advice and consent of the states' legislatures. This was a deliberate attempt to force the Constitution on the people before they could review and vote on the document. Equally disturbing to the independence and sovereignty of the states was shuttering the doors of the federal convention. This cabal resolved that no member could correspond with other delegates from different states on the subjects under discussion until the delegates agreed on the final amendments. This was contrary to the instructions given to the states' delegations when leaving on their mission.

The delegates were not authorized to consider amendments to a united federal union without the consent of their constituents. Without this permission, they would not be so bold as to approve alterations that might destroy their state's role in the new federal government. In other words, state delegations could not accept a Constitution that had not been ratified by state legislatures and the people. I apologize for the diversion, but the reader needed to know the internal political debates and trickery to understand the challenge in preparing the final draft of the Constitution. This was the primary reason I was asked to write the *Observations*. To the Federalists, there was no need for a *Bill of Rights*, as all specified or other non-specified rights existed in Article 1, Section 8 of the new Constitution.

It was this section to which I objected. The section enumerated the specified or expressed powers given to the Congress and included the power to declare war, print paper money and mint coinage, issue regulations to control foreign trade and the trade carried on between the states, run a postal service, promote of science and useful arts, constitute inferior tribunals to the Supreme Court, define and punish piracy, and control the granting of patents, to cite a few. There was no specific language detailing those rights and privileges left to the states and individuals.

To their credit, the convention delegates agreed with my recommendation and ratified the Ninth Amendment, which stated that the enumeration in the Constitution of certain rights shall not be construed to deny or disparage others retained by the people. In other words, the rights of the people are not limited to just the rights listed in the Constitution, which includes the presumption of innocence in criminal cases, the right to travel within the country, and the right to privacy. These rights, although not enumerated, found a home in the Ninth Amendment.

My next concern was that the proposed Constitution did not specify those rights and powers delegated to the states and individuals that were not covered in the Constitution. This concern was addressed by the Tenth Amendment, which declared that the federal government only had those powers delegated to it in the Constitution, and, if not listed therein, the powers belonged to the states or the people. In simple terms, this amendment set out the limits to the powers of the central government, saying any powers that the Constitution did not give to the federal government were the responsibility of the states themselves, such as calling and holding elections, organizing police, issuing licenses, and the responsibility of ratifying amendments proposed to the Constitution, to cite the most important. The Tenth Amendment left no doubt as to the separation between state and federal powers.

The declaration that the ratification of the Constitution required nine states for its establishment bothered me, as I believed this would sow the seeds of factional and sectional discord. I considered the nine-state ratification rule a subversion of the union of the confederated states, leading to the introduction of anarchy and civil convulsions, and could be the means of involving the whole country in a civil war. Of course, there was no way to change this requirement and, having not known of the three-fifths compromise at the time, it would not have mattered anyway. Once this hateful language became part of the Constitution, the southern states ratified the instrument, followed thereafter by all other states, Rhode Island being the last if memory serves me right.

Such was my contribution to the creation of the *Bill of Rights* to the Constitution of the United States. Although not perfect, for nothing ever is, the Constitution is the finest expression of individual liberties devised by imperfect men. I hope future amendments serve to strengthen this glorious expression of a nation's attempts to achieve greater rights for the individual citizen and guard against the unconstrained centralization of power. Once again, proving the flexibility of the Constitution, in 1804, the *Boston Gazette* noted the government had ratified the Twelfth Amendment.

This amendment revised presidential election procedures, whereby the president and vice president would be elected together as opposed to the vice president being the runner-up, as in earlier elections. After reading the article, I told James I suspected this had to do with the 1800 presidential election when Messrs. Jefferson and Burr had equal number of electors. To resolve the deadlock, the House of Representatives awarded Jefferson the presidency and Burr the vice presidency, with Mr. Hamilton being influential in brokering the agreement.

James noted that he recalled his surprise at the time when Hamilton threw his support to Jefferson, as they were political rivals stemming from their tenure in the Washington and Adams cabinets. I told James that I could only assume Mr. Hamilton had some unknown problem with Mr. Burr, and it must have been personal. Both men were Federalists, so there should have been no issue. James nodded in agreement, but the original idea of electing the president and vice president by who had the most electors was no way to select the Chief Magistrate of a great nation. We agreed with this amendment, even though I believed, and still do, that it would unleash political and sectional factionalism.

Interestingly enough, this amendment was ratified the month before the duel between Messrs. Hamilton and Burr, which led to the former's death. At the time, I told James his death was a great loss to our country. He was a clear-thinking, talented man who should have known better. A duel of all things, how medieval, how absurd! I learned later of Mr. Burr's arrest on charges of treason. Allegedly, he hatched a conspiracy during and after his term as vice president, using international connections and a cabal of American planters, politicians, and army officers to set up an independent country in the southwestern United States and parts of Mexico. Although acquitted of treason, it destroyed his reputation and political career. He truly exemplified my maxim, love of domination and uncontrolled lust for arbitrary power prevails in all people.

Plymouth, Monday, 20 December 1813

Chapter 14

THE HISTORY

I would like to take credit for the idea of publishing the history of our revolution, but this would be a mistake. The notion came from a dear friend, the noted historian and author Catharine Sawbridge Macaulay, of whom I will speak of in a later chapter. In 1787, she penned a letter relating how General Washington had offered materials for a history of the American Revolution when she visited America. However, due to health issues and concentration on a work about the education of the female sex, she recommended I undertake the task. She was very persuasive, telling me no one had a better perspective on the events and people than me. I wrote of my appreciation for her support and would do my best not to disappoint her or my country.

I had shared my thoughts about writing the history with Abigail and she must have spoken with John who, at the time, was in England on a diplomatic mission. In a very complimentary and supportive letter in 1787, he wrote, "Your annals or history, I hope you will continue, for there are few persons possessed of more facts, or who can record them in a more agreeable manner. Yet let me not deceive you. America must support the publication of it. No other Country will contribute much towards it." I began my research for the history in late-1787, interrupted only by my anonymous authorship of the *Observations* and personal health problems and tragedies.

Having read the great ancient and modern historians, and accustomed to writing satirical propaganda devices, I realized the history demanded a different approach. The events and people needed more objectivity, as there could be no room for subjective feelings or private opinions unsupported by evidence. I remembered Uncle Jonathan's axiom: "Do not ignore the context and motivation of the people in the study." I introduced the history by saying, "The historian has never laid aside the tenderness of the sex or the friends; at the same time, she has endeavored, on all occasions, that the strictest veracity should govern her heart, and the most exact impartiality be the guide of the pen." Unfortunately, I forgot Uncle Jonathan's maxim, always think in terms of context and motivation, and let my personal feelings enter my narrative.

Before engaging in my self-critique, a brief synopsis is in order. The context of the three-volume history covered the Revolutionary period from the *Stamp Act* crisis to the events leading to the ratification of the Constitution. At the time, I thought the timeline reasonable, covering about twenty-five years. What I did not consider was the degree of detail needed to present the context of the events and the motivations of the people involved, leading up to the war, the war itself, and the later constitutional debates in a comprehensive manner. Simply said, the subject matter of the book was too broad to do the period justice. The first problem was overlooking some of the early activities of our leaders.

I did not delve deep enough into the details of the pre-war planning activities of the Sons of Liberty, Committees of Correspondence, and the differing positions of the patriot leaders, especially the latter. For example, I described the Tea Party in volume one, but the success of the raid was based on detailed planning in which I took part and contributed. I excluded my involvement in the planning because, to put it simply, I did not want readers to think I was pursuing self-promotion. I knew Sam Adams had to enlist a sizeable force from his Sons of Liberty and needed to get the boats for the raid while keeping tight secrecy. Therefore, my narrative made it seem as if the raid was not a well-planned operation when, in fact, it was. I could have included a more detailed description of the planning phase without inserting myself into the narrative.

I did not include the fact that not all the leaders of the Revolution spoke with a common voice or purpose, especially with respect to the aims of the Massachusetts delegation to the first Continental Congress. There were committee members who, like me, believed preparing a letter to the King, while excluding Parliament, was a serious mistake, as it did not recognize the actual political power in England. Again, I did not consider the context and motivation of the debates among delegates and, as I came to know later, other delegations went to Philadelphia with their own agendas. This information might have been available if I had spoken with our delegates who had first-hand knowledge of the different strategies of the other delegations. Doing this, anecdotal though it may have been, would have added further context to the debates and the motivations of the various individuals and delegations.

The next error in my preparation of the book was relying on personal anecdotes from revolutionary leaders who, as it turned out, changed their political positions after the Revolution when they found themselves having to govern an independent nation. In this particular case, I must credit my friend Catharine Macaulay, who tried to open my eyes to the issue. In October 1788, while the debate was underway concerning the nation's Constitution, she offered a guarded warning which, at the time of its receipt, I gave only cursory attention. I later realized her cautionary note was a pointed warning. She noticed a change in Mr. Adamses political thinking and attitude concerning governance after returning from his failed mission to resolve treaty obligation issues between Britain and America. The issue had to do with our delinquent payment of debts to British merchants and refusal by the British to vacate forts in the northwest, as promised, until the debts were paid.

Buried at the end of her letter was the warning: "Mr. Adams, I see by the papers, has been long returned to his native Country. He is a very warm Federalist and by what I have discerned of your and Mr. Warren's political sentiments and opinions, you will not agree quite so well on public matters as you did formerly." I now realize this casual statement should have made me explore the changing political attitudes; not just of Mr. Adams, but of other former compatriots who had supplied what I now appreciate might have been unreliable or, more likely, dated information. I may be excused this lapse, but it still annoys me because during and after the constitutional debates, I saw the change in political attitudes and governing philosophy of former colleagues believing they still held similar views to those of my own. I should have included these viewpoints in the history, regardless of the political divisiveness they might have fomented. Again, I overlooked the context and motivation of the political players. Let me offer an added example.

The political factionalism came to the fore during President Washington's second term. There were two feuding parties: the Federalists, led by John Adams, Alexander Hamilton, John Jay, and John Marshall, who favored a strong central government. The other were the Democrat-Republicans, formerly the Anti-Federalist faction, led by Messrs. Thomas Jefferson, James Madison, and Eldridge Gerry, who supported restricting the powers of the federal government while emphasizing greater states' rights. Mrs. Macauley's words came back to me. The personages of both factions had been passionately united in their desire to separate from England, but once in power, their perspective on how to govern led to political acrimony.

I bore witness to this after the disastrous XYZ Affair, which led to President Adams signing a Federalist-introduced series of laws collectively known as the *Alien and Sedition Acts in 1798*. Within this law were four measures: *Naturalization Act, Alien Friends Act, Alien Enemies Act*, and *Sedition Act*. These anti-American and, in my judgement, unconstitutional enactments targeted immigrants, specifically the French, by giving the president greater deportation authority and more stringent citizenship requirements.

But the law that really angered me was the *Sedition Act*, which made it a crime to publish false, scandalous, and malicious statements against the government or its officials. It was clearly unconstitutional, but Mr. Adams signed the package into law, pressured as I later learned, by my friend, Abigail, and his cabinet. This was a man, like others in the government, who had fought for the freedom of the press, and here they were bending to political expediency. This event alone should have forced me to revise the history but missed doing so, forgetting Mrs. Macauley's pointed warning. Had I taken her words to heart, I would have realized these political intrigues presaged the political factionalism that marked President Washington's second term, later events in the Adams administration, and the very contentious and venal election of 1800, which he lost to Mr. Jefferson.

Finally, I declared earlier in the chapter the strictest veracity would govern my heart and exact impartiality would guide my pen. I only wish this were true. Interestingly, I had already been forewarned indirectly about becoming too emotional in my writings. In 1787, our family friend, James Winthrop, chided me for being too harsh in my condemnation of Mr. Hutchinson over the attack on my brother which hastened his mental decline. Heeding this advice might have helped avoid the more fundamental problem with my objectivity. He was right, because I let my emotions effect my context and motivation in another matter.

My lack of impartiality and subconscious political bias led to a confrontational exchange with Mr. Adams about my assertion that he favored a monarchy for the American colonies during our early Committee of Correspondence discussions. At an early meeting, he had asked my opinion on whether monarchy or republic was best for America. I replied, a republic, with which he agreed but my statement in the history was not merely an exaggeration; it was an untruth. I let personal feelings cloud my judgment and get in the way of reporting factual events. In the same way my dear friend Abigail had influenced John in signing the *Sedition Act*, I too was motivated by personal issues or, more so, my emotions. And I had a perfect example before my eyes and missed the message.

During the Adams administration as our Chief Magistrate, he was pilloried by Benjamin Franklin Bache, editor of the *Aurora*, an Anti-Federalist tabloid. Abigail's letters during this period were strident and emotional, to the point of a fanatical obsession in her condemnation of this Democrat-Republican periodical. From 1797 to 1800, this man, to quote my friend, "opined his batteries of abuse and scurrility" on John. Her blind anger made her influence John into signing the *Sedition Act*, which was clearly targeted at Bache and his publication. My friend was protecting the reputations of her husband and family. Given the circumstance, I might have done no different and, in my own way, I did so in my history.

When I accused Mr. Adams of preferring a monarchy, and that his passions and prejudices were sometimes too strong for his sagacity and judgment, it was a reaction to a series of events of what I believed were unprovoked attacks on my husband and sons. I was angry that during the Washington and Adamses administrations, my husband had not been offered a patronage position in the new federal government, and especially outraged with Mr. Adams who, as president, could have given James an appointment. To make matters worse, and even though knowing better about the falsehood of my statement, my anger was not mollified during our heated exchanges in 1807. I was so incensed and not being able to forget the disrespect shown to my husband, I wrote his letters were "marked with passion, absurdity, and inconsistency as to appear more like the ravings of a maniac than the cool critique of genius and science."

Even when he tried to soothe the situation by crediting me with teaching him to admire the British Constitution and Common Law, my anger over the treatment of my family was not pacified. From that year to 1812, neither John and Abigail nor I corresponded, but our healing will be covered in a later chapter. This episode was what led me to become self-critical of how I prepared the history.

Although Mr. Adams did not believe, as he told our friend Mr. Gerry, that "history is not the Province of the Ladies," President Jefferson wrote of my work, "The last thirty years will furnish a more instructive lesson to mankind than any equal period known in history." He thought enough of my history to order copies for his second-term cabinet, which included Vice President George Clinton, Secretary of State James Madison, Secretary of the Treasury Albert Gallatin, Secretary of War Henry Dearborn, Attorney General John Breckinridge, and Secretary of the Navy Robert Smith. Other notables who subscribed to the history included my compatriots from the Revolutionary period: Samuel Adams, Eldridge Gerry, John Hancock, George Washington, and my friend Judith Sargent Murray, to cite the most renown.

I also agreed with critics that the history offered controversial views about the Revolution, especially my opinion that Yorktown was a siege, not a battle; my stand against the institution of slavery, which banished a sense of general liberty; and the mistreatment of our native tribes who suffered throughout the Revolutionary and post-Revolutionary war periods. Notwithstanding my self-critique, I was proud to have done the history, regardless of the delays due to personal tragedies. I lost my sons, Captain Winslow Warren in 1791 and George in 1800. In the same year as Winslow's death, my mentor and dear friend Catharine Macaulay passed away. Finally, during this period, I began suffering health problems that persist to this day, but I managed to complete the book. However, it is now time to turn the attention to the friendships with three women who were important and influential in my personal and intellectual life.

Plymouth, Friday, 14 January 1814

Chapter 15

THE SAUCY LADY

Abigail Adams by Gilbert Charles Stuart National Gallery of Art, Washington, D.C.

How do I describe Abigail Adams who, for half a century, has been my dearest friend? She was sixteen years my junior when we first met, which made me feel like an older aunt. She had married at nineteen while I wed at the advanced age of twenty-six. At our first meeting, I saw a petite, attractive young woman who was reticent in the company of men but, at the same time, enjoyed their attention. I learned as time progressed, she was a complex woman who was caring, generous, honest, outspoken, and charming, with a well-timed puckishness who delighted in rumor and gossip. Conversely, she was controlling when it suited her need. She was very conscious of the family's social status, politically astute and designing, and extremely ambitious. She manipulated people while I manipulated words.

Even with our different personalities and intellectual interests, she became a good and trusted friend. We forged a friendship based on common interests and the important problems confronting America and women, both of us decrying the woeful state of women's education and lack of legal and political rights. But most important, we shared the chaos and confusion of the Revolutionary period and its aftermath.

When we began describing our experiences as young girls, there were similarities. We both learned the essential skills expected of a wife, mother, and household manager. Our early education was only comparable in learning to read and write. She had the opportunity to explore the family library, while I had to rely on my brother sneaking books from Father's intellectual, inner sanctum. Her minister father was an excellent and demanding mentor, while her grandparents instilled in her the values of discipline, justice, and a sense of public service. Although my parents taught me the same values, I had no such interaction with my grandparents; my grandfather, John Otis, having died the year before my birth and my grandmother, Mercy Bacon Otis, died in 1737 when I was nine years old.

Although her father directed her reading toward the classics, history, and theology, she preferred reading fiction, romantic novels, poetry, and drama that appealed to her emotions. Her favorite authors were Shakespeare, Swift, Sterne, Milton, Dryden, Richardson, Thomson, and Pope. While I enjoyed reading the same authors, my intellectual interests focused on history, political theory, philosophy, and law. Abigail, on the other hand, was striving to become a woman according to social norms of the day for a young lady from a prominent family. She studied French with Richard Cranch, a future brother-in-law, who also taught her an appreciation of Samuel Richardson's novels, James Thomson's poems, and other great romantic poets and novelists.

She especially enjoyed Thomson's *The Seasons,* which offered the promise that she could withstand life's turbulent forces by seeking strength in a wise and benevolent God. She delighted in Richardson's novels because they challenged her mind about the issues confronting young women, like personal identity, duty to family, sexuality, marriage, and the role of an educated woman in society. Important though these attributes were to me, I needed no such literary encouragement to define who I was and wanted to be as a woman.

Early in our friendship, when comparing notes, as woman do, we described our courtships, marital relationships, and husbands' personalities. I remember relating the conspiracy hatched by my father, mother, and brother to get me married. When she heard this, she laughed, asking me why I had not caught on. I attributed my ignorance to lack of feminine intuitiveness and inexperience in the ways of courtship. Regardless, I fell in love with James before even knowing it. I may have been naïve about the ways of courtship, but Abigail's experience was a different matter entirely and belied the problem of depending too much on romantic novels and poems.

She related meeting John and beginning their courtship when she was fifteen, while I was twenty-five when I met James. In my mind, her age was a significant factor in her decision-making, for maturity comes as we grow with experiences. I believed then, and still do, that fifteen was too young for a man or woman to understand what love is and the responsibilities that come with marriage. I was twenty-five and, without the marry-off Mercy conspiracy, would probably have been a spinster.

Abigail wondered if her meeting with John had been arranged by her sister's fiancé, Richard Cranch. In the spring of 1759, Richard arrived at our home with a lawyer friend, Mr. John Adams. She thought nothing of it because Richard often visited her eighteen-year-old sister,

Mary, who he was courting at the time. I told her that the meeting certainly sounded preplanned. It might well have been, noting that prearranged marriages were part of our inherited English tradition. I remarked sarcastically that parents did not want to take any chances with daughters: "Get us married and out of the house as quickly as possible." They cared less about the boys, although fathers occasionally tried to arrange a son's marriage for financial or political reasons. Abigail mused impishly, "What would happen if our spouses discovered we were arranging marriages for our sons?" Her off-handed comment illustrated the saucy nature and puckish side of her personality, which I found endearing if not downright hilarious. I never knew when her mischievous, sassy side would surface because it always occurred at the most inopportune moments.

Continuing with her courtship story, Abigail told me it was not love at first sight as in my case. John, who was twenty-four when they first met, thought her neither affectionate nor candid, and frumpy, if my memory has not forsaken me. This was not the most romantic way to introduce yourself as a potential suitor, especially for a young lady raised on the romance novels of Samuel Richardson and poems of James Thomson. Unlike my situation, where the arrangers were of one mind, her father approved the match while her mother was appalled. Her mother was horrified that she would be marrying a crude country lawyer, a demeaning proposition in her eyes. But her father wanted to get rid of Abigail while her mother wanted to wait so she could wed a rich Bostonian. In the end, getting Abigail out of the house prevailed and they were wed in October 1764, with her father, the Reverend William Smith, officiating.

Where James was a partner who enthusiastically supported my intellectual goals, Abigail's relationship was that of a traditional husband and wife, where he pursued his public life as a lawyer, and she managed the household and lives of the children. She had been raised to believe a woman sat quietly and spoke only when spoken to, and then only on matters of a domestic nature. Over time, however, this self-imposed viewpoint changed. As Abigail matured, she was not beyond challenging John, influencing him to achieve what she wanted, and her control of her children was absolute. Her marriage was not a partnership of equals, but one where each carved out their sphere of influence. But Abigail was the controlling force while John was the more submissive, often succumbing to her requests.

The best example of this was the Royall Tyler affair, of which I spoke earlier. Abigail controlled the situation and manipulated John and Nabby to meet her goal. If Abigail believed a person or event endangered the family's social, financial, or political status, she would respond by manipulating the situation to regain control. I did not find this behavior wrong or a weakness, but the normal response of a wife and mother who cared for her loved ones. And I might add, this trait applied to our relationship as well. In her fashion, she was as protective of me as she was of her family.

Although politically naïve when we first met, she grew into a self-confident, shrewd woman with the natural instincts of a seasoned politician. Her coyness with men was purposely disarming, hiding an uncanny talent for reading people, which helped John on his diplomatic missions to England and France, and later as Vice Presidnet and President. She claimed to be an expert in a new scientific method, whose name eludes me, which she described as the ability to judge a person's character from their facial characteristics. I am certain this method was used to judge the characters of Jefferson, Hamilton, and other of John's political opponents.

I once told her, in a light moment, she was more Machiavellian than the celebrated author, and Shakespeare must have had her in mind when he created the character Katherine in *Taming of the Shrew*. She responded with a smile and then, with an impish leer, told me that women have more power than they appreciate, and that men are easy to manipulate. As she pointed out, it took little talent to turn their heads and get what you wanted. I was more restrained and never thought of myself as manipulative, aggressive, or tempting, but this exemplified the side of her nature to control situations or individuals.

I remember Abigail telling me that it must be frustrating to know I was the recognized expert in English Constitutional and Common Law by the men to whom I lent counsel but could not practice law or hold public office because of my sex. I was hidden in the background, an afterthought by patronizing men who did not dare advertise my ability for fear it would make people, especially other women, know men were not the be-all and end-all of a fulfilling life. I never told her that the comment touched a nerve, but in her way, she was reminding me I was a woman in a man's world. It reminded me of my father's comment about to what end all the education was for when I could not practice a profession or hold public office?

But Abigail was always supportive of my intellectual efforts and, as I discovered that regardless of what people thought or might say, she was always there, cheering me on. I also learned she enjoyed rumors and gossip about the people she met, like Jefferson, Franklin, and others. In all the time we spent together, especially when John was away, there was one incident which was funny, and it had to do with Abigail choosing a pseudonym.

In the fall of 1776, she came to Plymouth with the brood of Nabby, John Quincy, and Charles, leaving young Thomas in the care of servants at Braintree. While the boys played with my sons, Henry and George, at horseshoes, jackstraws, and Rounders, Abigail and Nabby sat with me in the parlor discussing the previous year's outbreak of Black pox, which was not as widespread as earlier eruptions of this deadly disease. Even though we had both been skeptical of the idea of infecting ourselves with a deadly disease to cure it, we had been inoculated to confirm the theory before subjecting our children to it. But Abigail pointed out, the idea was not new.

She reminded me that in 1721, Dr. Zabdiel Boylston and Reverend Cotton Mather had introduced the procedure during the epidemic that year and had promising results among patients. Replying, I told her

Lady Mary Wortley Montagu, the renowned Shakespearean scholar in her *Turkish Embassy Letters,* the first written by a woman about the Moslem east, described how the Ottomans treated smallpox, as they termed it, by introducing the disease into healthy individuals in the hope they would contract a mild form of the illness, recover, and then be immune from further infections. It was her work that introduced the procedure into England, Europe, and America so Messrs. Boylston, Mather, and us had her to thank for this life-saving method. But the method of inoculation proved more complicated and frightening.

We compared notes on how we had been administered the pox inoculation and found that we had been subjected to the same procedure. The doctor administering our inoculations had bought secretions from the scabs of an individual suffering from natural pox. He then punctured our skin with a needle, which was contaminated with the diseased material. To say we were apprehensive would be an understatement. As Abigail put it, she was downright scared. However, we would not have our children inoculated until we had undergone the method. We both agreed that protection from the disease was more important than the side effects of sore arms, swelling armpits, slight fever, feeling of fatigue, and trouble sleeping, which we both suffered for days. But neither of us contracted the pox, and within the year, we had our children inoculated. Their younger bodies took the procedure better with fewer side effects.

I told Abigail, in speaking with our local midwife, that she told me in her fifty years in the profession, she had only heard of one person dying from the procedure. She also informed me that the practice of buying pox scabs was common. And when I inquired from our doctor about this practice, he informed me there were many methods used to introduce the pox disease into healthy children. In Scotland, he had read that wool contaminated with smallpox material was wrapped around a child's wrist. In another case, he had read about children holding smallpox scabs in their hand or wearing pox-infected clothes. Regardless of the method, the inoculation saved me and other parents sleepless nights when children contracted an ailment. At least they knew it was not the pox.

After our distracting recitations about the pox, Abigail got to the original purpose of the conversation. She was thinking of creating a pseudonym for herself and asked what I thought of the idea. Momentarily surprised by the abrupt change of topic, I asked if she had chosen one. She replied, "Portia, the wife of Brutus, the assassin of the tyrant Caesar." I replied teasingly, "You know Portia was also the brilliant and spirited lawyer in Shakespeare's *The Merchant of Venice*." I thought this Portia was more suitable.

When she asked why, I told her the story of how Portia, the heroine, had been bound by her father's will to marry the man who chose the correct of three caskets: one of gold, one of silver, and one of lead. However, being a recalcitrant lady, she favored a young, impoverished Venetian noble, Bassanio, a soldier and scholar, who, by chance, selected the right casket. This Portia, I believed, was more fitting for her. She thought for a moment and then declared, "Shakespeare's Portia it will be." When I asked why she needed a pseudonym, she simply replied that even though she would only need it for her personal correspondence, she liked the mystery in a pen name. I thought to myself, *She was trying to add a little spice to her life.*

Between 1776 and 1787, while the war raged and John and my James were away, Abigail and I spent a great deal of time together. Even after 1787, when she and John were in Europe on diplomatic missions and he became president, we stayed connected through correspondence and the occasional visits by Nabby before she joined them in England. Whenever I looked at Nabby, I saw the daughter for whom I had always wished. As I told James, after our fifth son was born, I gave up trying for a little girl. I was still deeply in love with James but was tired of producing only boys. Characteristically, he agreed, telling me that he too had hoped with each pregnancy that we would have a daughter. Nabby, who was very intuitive, sensed my longing for a little girl and responded by treating me like a second mother. She expressed genuine interest in my publishing career, political beliefs and activism, and education. But I digress, back to the narrative.

As I mentioned earlier, my friend Abigail had a mischievous side to her personality when speaking about serious issues and she loved to gossip, but her letters were also instructive. Having never traveled further than Boston, I found her insights into European culture, customs, and morals enlightening. In a series of letters, she wrote about Christmas celebrations in France and England, which were informative.

Christmas celebrations, like those in Europe, were rare in our colony. From the colony's earliest founding, the Puritans and Calvinists found no scriptural justification for celebrating a holiday tradition they considered examples of paganism and idolatry. Although other immigrant populations celebrated Christmas, most notably the Anglicans, Dutch, and French, my family did not and knew nothing of the different customs. I was therefore intrigued with her descriptions of this cultural tradition in other lands and, knowing this, she accommodated my interest.

In France on Christmas Eve, the holiday centered around a legendary gift-giver called *Père Noël* or Father Christmas. Before going to sleep, children would leave gifts in their small shoes left by the fireplace, filled with carrots and treats for *Père Noël's* donkey. Father Christmas would take the offerings and, if the child had been good, leave gifts of candy, money, or small toys in the tiny shoes. The Christmas Day feast included soups, assorted meats, mashed potatoes, beans, salad, peas, carrots, and bread, followed by a yule log cake, cupcakes, muffins, small sweets, and chocolate candies, as well as games, singing, and dancing.

Christmas festivities in England ran from the first week of December, Saint Nicholas Day, to the first week in January called Twelfth Night. On St. Nicholas Day, tradition held that friends exchanged gifts, marking the official start of the season. Christmas Day was a national holiday and people went to church and returned to a celebratory dinner, which included hot and cold food to accommodate the large gatherings of family and friends. On Christmas Eve, gentry and poor alike decorated their homes with holly, evergreens, ivy, mistletoe, and rosemary; these decorations were often adorned with spices, apples, oranges, candles, or ribbons.

One custom I found especially appealing occurred the day after Christmas, St. Stephen's Day, when people gave to charity, and the gentry presented servants and staff with Christmas boxes. The sixth of January signaled the end of the season and was marked by family gatherings, parties, dining, dancing, games, punch, mulled red wine with orange slices, spices, honey, and brandy served in a large bowl which dated to ancient Roman times. One game called Snapdragon intrigued Abigail and fascinated me, as it involved a wide, shallow bowl filled with brandy, to which raisins were added and then set afire. The participants quickly picked raisins from the burning brandy and extinguished them by closing their mouths and eating them. As I said, having never wandered further than Boston, her descriptions of these customs were captivating.

Another subject of interest were Abigail's descriptions of women's fashion in France and England. In this regard, Abigail seemed less impressed. According to her, the fashionable women of the French and English courts wore shorter length dresses with necklines more open, with the bodice cut so low that the slightest movement would expose more than should be seen in polite society. The ideal English or French woman had black, brown, or blonde wavy or curly hair. Her forehead was high with hair pushed back, her cheeks plump and rosy, and skin an ashen white. Her face featured black, brown, or blue eyes, with eyebrows slightly full, semicircular, and tapered at the ends in a half-moon shape. The lips were small, soft, and painted red. What she found most interesting, if not excessive, was the use of hired, professional hairdressers called *coiffeurs*, who colored or added false hair to natural hair. She noted that the ordinary city and rural folk dressed very much like us in America, nothing fancy. Although fascinated by these women's fashions, she ruefully wrote they would never be in style in America, as they were too revealing.

As I related earlier, Abigail loved her gossip. Her letters were sprinkled with tidbits of gossip, especially about the other commission delegates sent to France to garner support for our revolutionary cause. There was nothing Abigail enjoyed more than collecting rumors, especially about famous personages, and her attendance with John became for me a gold mine of unfounded gossip and scandal.

In 1784, Abigail informed me that she, Nabby, and John Quincy were joining John in Paris. She wrote that although she had dreaded the long sea voyage, she thought the journey interesting. At first, she found life in Paris difficult, overwhelmed by the novel experience of running a large house with a retinue of servants provided by the French. However, as the months passed, she began to enjoy herself, traveling through Paris, making friends, and discovering a fondness for French theatre and the opera.

But her snippets of gossip reminded me of Hannah Winthrop's letters on the rowdy behavior of the students at the Harvard campus where her husband, John, was teaching. Abigail wrote about Benjamin Franklin's dalliances with the ladies of the French court who thought him a charming, frontier gentleman. She once used the phrase, "lecherous old dog," in a letter describing his behavior. She wrote how Franklin had seen something called *Le Globe*, a balloon filled with air that soared into the sky with a small basket attached underneath for people to view Paris and the countryside. I tried imagining this object drifting into the air, wondering how it came back to earth. When I asked James and Winslow about it, they could not fathom this unique object. I thought, *Leave it to the French to invent such a toy.*

Abigail wrote how Silas Deane was covertly organizing shipments of arms and munitions to the colonies with the aid of Pierre de Beaumarchais, the playwright and outspoken supporter of American independence, and one of my favorite authors. She had also heard through her sources another unsubstantiated rumor, that Deane was somehow involved in a plot by a group of Scots to destroy Royal Navy stores and dockyards in Portsmouth and Plymouth on behalf of our

The Quality of Mercy

cause. Although I found this rumor interesting, it was no surprise. There were many plots afoot to hamper British attempts to subjugate her rebellious colonies. But the juiciest piece of gossip she saved for Thomas Jefferson.

Mr. Jefferson had lost his wife just before leaving for France and while there, he fell hopelessly in love, according to the rumors running rampant through the French court, with Madame Maria Cosway, a well-known and married Italian-English musician who was twenty-seven. Abigail wrote they saw each other often over a six-week period but when she returned to England with her husband, Jefferson was left pining for his lost love. *Juicy indeed*, I told myself. Just the personal snippet that would have excited Abigail, but my dear friend saved the best tidbit for last.

Jefferson sent for his youngest child, nine-year-old Polly, who was accompanied by a young sixteen-year-old slave girl from Monticello. Jefferson had previously taken this slave girl's older brother to Paris as part of his domestic retinue and was having him trained in the preparation of French cuisine. Mr. Jefferson, who obviously enjoyed French cooking and wines, wanted to ensure having a chef of his own to satisfy his epicurean taste. She noted how the southern plantation class seemed obsessed with the French language, manners, customs, fashion, and culture. For me, this snippet of information held no implications but for Abigail, she knew for sure why Jefferson was doting on this young man. According to the gossip in the French court, the forty-four-year-old Jefferson was having a torrid affair with the younger sister of his future French chef, the sixteen-year-old slave who had escorted his daughter to France. Of course, Abigail thought this absolutely scandalous and an affront to the American delegation, but the rumor fed her love of gossip.

When John was sent as our ambassador to England in 1785 to negotiate the peace ending the war, Abigail wrote that she hoped to meet Catharine Macaulay, who she said in a letter was a lady recognized as an eminent historian and wanted to inquire about her education and what first prompted her to study history. I found this curious because when Mrs. Macaulay Graham visited America in July 1784, and while spending time with us in Plymouth, I had penned a letter to John suggesting he meet our celebrated guest before she continued her trip to meet other revolutionary leaders and General Washington. I knew from Catharine's correspondence that she had met with both John and Abigail, so I could not fathom why, while in England, she wished to meet Mrs. Macaulay whom she had already met. But I suspected it had to do with her unhappy sojourn in that country and Catharine was the only person with whom she would feel comfortable, being a like-minded spirit.

Abigail disliked London immensely. She had few friends, being shunned by their so-called polite society, which is why she wanted to meet Mrs. Macaulay who was a vocal supporter of our cause. She found their theatre inferior to the French, and the haughty attitude of their aristocracy and gentry spoke to their misguided belief in their own self-importance. She wrote that my descriptions of our former English overlords in *The Blockheads* could not have been more correct. Referring to the characters in the play, she described how she had to tolerate the presence of a host of Dupes, Meagres, Paunches, Puffs, Shallows, Simples, and the lot. The only pleasant experience while in London was her temporary custody of Mr. Jefferson's daughter, Mary, for whom she came to feel a deep and lifelong affection. Writing later, she was ecstatic to leave England in 1788 when John came home from the mission. But let me now return to an earlier time in our relationship so I can narrate an example of her outspoken, controlling, and manipulative nature in pursuit of a goal, in this case the dismal state of the female rights in America.

After 1773, John was away more often as the situation with the British government deteriorated. Abigail, who knew of my poem *The Squabble of the Sea Nymphs* and plays attacking the British colonial administration and Parliament, began to address matters she believed would be important to the new republic if we won our independence. She spoke often about the difficulties women faced in American society, advocating for married women's property rights and more educational opportunities. She believed women should not submit to laws enacted against their self-interest, nor be satisfied with their roles as their husbands' homebound companions. Women should educate themselves and, thereby, become recognized for their intellectual abilities to better guide the lives of their children and husbands. She knew I agreed with her positions, so she continually discussed the matter with me.

We both believed slavery was an abhorrently evil institution. I remember a letter written in March 1776 where she declared that she suspected most Virginians could not have as much of a passion for liberty as they claimed since they deprived their fellow creatures of freedom. But she did not just theorize about the issue. In 1791, while in Philadelphia, she wrote that when a free African youth came to her house, asking to be taught how to read and write, she placed him in a local evening school. The explosion of objections from neighbors forced a stinging response that the young man was a free man as much as any other young man and merely because he was Black, should he be denied an education to obtain a livelihood? She did not think it any disgrace to invite him into her parlor and teach him both to read and write. My dear Abigail was not just a talker; she acted and suffer the fool who challenged her.

There was a depth and clarity in her opinions, having evolved from the young romantic who now read histories, philosophy, and political theory. Of course, she never ignored her favorites: Shakespeare, Swift, Richardson, Thomson, Dryden, and Pope. I joked one day that if she never signed her letters, I would know it was her hand because she often ended correspondence with a poem summarizing a line of reasoning or deeply felt sentiment. She continually remonstrated that her penmanship and spelling were horribly lacking from practice as a young lady. I told her what she wrote about was more important than the appeal of the hand. If people could read and understand her words, they would acknowledge her ideas. Then came the notable disagreement with John

The Saucy Lady

over women's status in our new republican experiment. And this episode best encapsulated my dear friend's personality traits.

As I said earlier, Abigail did not suffer fools, including John when she believed him wrong on an issue. I had travelled to Braintree in early March 1776 to find my friend in high feather. She had just received a draft of the *Declaration of Independence* from John in Philadelphia, and she was beside herself. She threw it on the library desk, telling me to read the document, which she thought insulting, abhorrent, and despicable. Having read the document, I asked what was the problem, as if I did not know. Knowing my friend, when she was this worked up, it was wise to keep your distance and let her get it out.

She declared with fire in her eyes that there was no mention of the rights of women. Half the country was being ignored, and were we not citizens of the same country? I let her go on, knowing full well she was beyond listening to anything anyone would say. She exhorted that she was not taking this lying down, the hubris of these men. I told her to not send a letter until you have calmed yourself. Think it out and attack the issue logically, objectively, and with historical examples. I could have been talking to a wild boar. Even Nabby looked at me, knowing full well her mother was going to launch into a diatribe. Thus was born Abigail's *Remember the Ladies* letter to John. She then asked me to join her in the petition. I nodded and diplomatically told her I needed to see the letter to know how to frame my response. Her letter was not an appeal; it was an out-and-out attack not just on the *Declaration of Independence*, but on all men.

On 31 March 1776, she sent the letter, which I can only describe as a salvo of siege guns, opening a contentious exchange with John about her expectations of the new American republic concerning women's equality. As I had suggested, she framed her position from a political and philosophical perspective, using Locke and Montesquieu among others, the same thinkers the framers of the *Declaration* were employing to develop the rationale for America's separation from England. When I read a copy sent with Nabby, who was spending a weekend with me, I found myself silently muttering, *So much for diplomacy.* Her argument was elegantly crafted, but this was as subtle as it got. In other circumstances, I could imagine my friend pounding the pulpit, preaching a fire-and-brimstone sermon to a congregation of sinners destined for Dante's hell.

Abigail's vitriol was classic. She condemned that all men would be tyrants, expressing her disdain for the social conventions keeping women as the vassals of men. She reminded John the cause for the American Revolution was no different in the bosoms of women, noting that we can foment a rebellion if women's lot in life was not considered by the new laws. She went as far as to threaten that we can extinguish the power of men who are vicious and lawless toward women. Being in a high lather, she widened her attack by describing how the passion for liberty in Virginia, the state that produced George Washington, could not be strong in the breasts of those who enslaved others, equating the servile status of women to that of slaves with neither legal rights nor educational opportunities. I remember clearly as if it were yesterday, Nabby looking at me and saying, "Mother has really opened Pandora's box." I replied, "Dearest, you have said a mouthful and an understatement in one brief statement, but you know Mother. I wonder how your father will reply." "Carefully, I suspect, if he values his life," intoned a smiling Nabby.

Nabby had extended her visit for a week, which I thoroughly enjoyed. To have another female in the home full of men was a delight. Even James noticed my happy mood. So, when Nabby and me traveled back to Braintree, I was confronted by Abigail, who was beyond angry. Giving her a kiss on the cheek to soften her obvious distress, I asked had she heard from John. This was wrong, wrong, wrong! When Abigail was angry, you could see it in her eyes. They flashed with fire. She gave me the letter, saying with a sneer that she could not believe she married this man. He was personally insulting her and all women for that matter, and who in the Lord's name did he think he was. Reading the letter, I too was offended by his language and his views of women.

Having lived with James and my sons, and corresponded with the men framing the *Declaration*, I was accustomed to being treated with respect and as an equal.

His letter made it clear women were just another tribe more numerous and powerful than all the rest, but we would receive no more consideration than natives, negroes, children, and apprentices. Whereas she believed women were slaves to men, John believed men were masters in name only, and should we enact her extraordinary code of laws, then women would subject men to the despotism of the petticoat. Abigail interrupted my reading, declaring that he must think we were all shrews, conspiring to control men when all we want was equality of condition. He thinks we were no better than slaves! She was pacing the floor and getting angrier with each step, and then declared, "How dare he compare our plight to that abhorrent institution?" Interestingly enough, John was correct in one way; he was subjected to the despotism of the petticoat. Unfortunately for him, it was Abigail's.

As I recall, the verbal jousting continued through May 1776, when I joined her in a petition to Congress to consider her list of female grievances and protect wives from the unlimited power of their husbands. Of course, my petition was more diplomatic but ignored, nonetheless. I may have been the revolutionary propagandist, "Conscience of the American Revolution," sister of the renowned James Otis, but I remained a woman and, as Abigail had previously pointed out, men found it easy to patronize women when we stepped outside our place in the social order.

In her next letter, she argued while Congress was declaring peace and goodwill to men, emancipating all nations, they insisted on keeping arbitrary and absolute power of husbands over wives. She was like a dog with a bone; she would not let it go. She warned John that despite all their wise laws and maxims, women had it in their power to not only free us but to subdue our masters, and, without violence, throw man's natural and legal authority at our feet. Reading the final draft, I said to her how did she propose overthrowing their power without armed insurrection. Thinking for a moment in the hope of defusing the situation, I continued with, "We could use the bedroom by denying them our wifely duties or let them cook for themselves." Starvation and lack of intimacy in the bed chamber were great equalizers. My comment did the trick, to which she frowned for a moment, then burst into laughter. Her ire spent, there was nothing more to say. Abigail smiled, saying she would teach him a thing or two when he returned from his all-male convention. This was my outspoken, controlling, and manipulative Abigail. But I knew my friend; this was not the end of the debate.

I knew Abigail was right about women's inferior social, legal, and political status, remembering how my brother, James, had argued for women's equality. I thought to myself it has been fifty years since he wrote those words. America fought a war for independence, wrote the *Declaration of Independence* and *Constitution* to establish liberty and equality, and the social, political, and legal status of our sex in American society had not changed. I asked myself, *What would it take for America to realize women had greater aspirations than marriage and motherhood, important as these institutions were to a civil society?* On a less happy note, during their contentious exchange, Abigail had been with child, but in 1777, the baby named Elizabeth was stillborn, sending my friend into a depression similar to what my mother had suffered after her personal losses. But Abigail was, no matter the tragedy, resilient, and, in 1779, she was once again showing the impish and manipulative side of her personality.

As previously noted, in 1779, I had sent a letter to my son Winslow, chiding him for believing Philip Stanhope's treatment of women was improper and immoral. Abigail read a copy of the letter and was curious, so she wrote to John, expressing her desire to read Lord Chesterfield's work. He demurred, believing this was not appropriate reading for a proper lady. Poor John, bless his heart. He always seemed to walk blindfolded into a problem of his own making, forgetting with whom he was dealing. How she manipulated John into allowing her to read the work was classic Abigail.

She told him if she could read James Thomson's character sketches and spirited and patriotic speeches in, *The Reign of George II* or William Congreve's plays, stained as they were with libertine morals and base principles, she was sufficiently sophisticated to read Lord Chesterfield. He finally relented, but this was not the end of her subterfuge. Having read a copy of my letter in 1780, without my knowledge, she sent a copy to the *Independent Chronicle* for publication. I believe she did this for two reasons: first, to show John she was mature enough to read Lord Chesterfield's work; and second and equally important, to express her independence as a woman. It seemed to me that John was always one step behind Abigail. And then there was her financial acumen, at which she excelled and John was less competent.

Abigail had a flair for financial matters, especially her choice of investments. She made investments through her uncle Cotton Tufts in debt instruments issued to finance the Revolutionary War. She told me it was wager the colonies would win the war and gain their freedom. She recommended James and me invest in these financial instruments, as they supported our fight for independence. Being neither a gambler nor dabbler in high finance, I was happy to do so because of the reason. As it turned out, we were both rewarded after Mr. Hamilton's "First Report on the Public Credit" approved full federal payment at face value to owners of government securities. Her financial talent provided well for the family and, to a lesser degree, mine. I cannot leave this topic without describing our small lace business, which we started to supplement our incomes during the war, and I would be remiss if I failed to mention the other reason for the business venture, which had less to do with lace and profits.

Both of us had been corresponding with our husbands: she with John in Philadelphia, and I with James, who was serving with General Washington. Although our letters described family matters, they also included the latest gossip about Loyalist and British military activities. Unfortunately, the gossip was unsubstantiated rumor and less than useful to our revolutionary political and military leaders in formulating tactics or strategies. The lace business became the perfect medium for us to gather real intelligence. Abigail naturally, with that puckish side of her personality, thought this an exciting foray into the world of spying. On the other hand, I was more interested in supplying real intelligence to my husband for use by General Washington. Either way, we became active participants in the dangerous game of gathering information for our cause.

Both of us had learned the art of needle lace work as young girls. I called it the needle and thread finger dexterity exercise. One particular style at which we both excelled was Hollie Point, which used inexpensive coarse lace worked in rows of stitches and looped into each other for decorating baby clothing, hat trim, bonnets, handkerchiefs, aprons, garters, and table linens. The raw cloth, imported from France, came through the Boston merchant community, who knew the shipping schedules, arrivals, departures, types of ships, cargoes, and the like. They were the perfect sources for gathering intelligence about British naval and troop movements.

Using our household staffs and sometimes my sons, we gathered information from local tradesmen, merchants, ship captains, and fishermen. Now, our letters included more precise intelligence on British movements. We obtained information from a Boston fisherman who had seen the arrival of a British fleet at Halifax and the lack of housing there, which obliged the British to pay six dollars per month for one room and scarce provisions. He told us that parents and children were often displaced from their homes and forced to live in the open. This action did not endear the British to the local population. We even knew when British warships or squadrons left Boston and to which ports they were destined.

Our informal spy network was not just dangerously exciting; it was empowering. To this point, my contribution to the cause had been with the quill or at the planning table, as in the case prior to the Tea Party raid. Now, I was an active participant, and it felt exhilarating. In the end, however, our lace business did poorly because of the shortage of French cloth and the inflated cost of the raw materials because of the war at sea. However, we continued the business charade to supply intelligence until another attempt to engage Abigail and myself as active participants came in the spring of 1776.

Abigail had sent a letter to John, describing how a group of Cambridge gentlemen recommended that I, Abigail, and our mutual friend, Hannah Winthrop, form a committee of ladies to examine Tory ladies. The aim was to decide the disposition of the property and rights of wives whose husbands were fighting for the British. John thought it an excellent idea, as New York was doing the same. Needless to say, nothing came of this proposal because Hannah and me refused to participate because, as I pointed out, it was illegal and morally wrong.

Before I continue, I would be remiss if I did not mention Mrs. Hannah Winthrop, wife of John Winthrop: noted professor of mathematics and natural history at Harvard College, renowned astronomer, and descendant of his namesake who founded the Massachusetts Bay Colony. Although she did not have the same influence as other female correspondents, I always enjoyed her letters because they shared the lively and raucous accounts of life in Cambridge. Her letters never failed to amuse with the latest gossip and sassy commentaries about the goings-on at Harvard. When she died in 1790, I lost a good friend.

Now back to my exposition about the confiscation laws. Although states enacted confiscation laws during the war, I did not believe these laws were morally or legally proper. How could we dispossess women of their rights and property without due process, especially when they had no property rights? Of course, there was always the insidious law of coverture, but the law only applied to debts incurred by a husband who had died or absconded the colony. Under the Common Law, property seizure applied to those convicted of treason but there was a loophole. Conviction implied a trial in front of one's peers, which was not the case with these confiscation laws. In my judgement, these forfeiture laws were designed to raise money for the Revolutionary War from the sale of property or to settle long-standing personal feuds. I applauded Mr. Hamilton's efforts in New York to successfully defend Loyalists from these illegal confiscation laws. After I explained the situation to Abigail and Hannah, they were less supportive of the action, and nothing came of it. Considering my sister-in-law, Ruth, was a Loyalist and Tory, I was doubly pleased with the decision. But every friendship must inevitably weather a period of anguish, and Abigail and I were no different.

Our estrangement began during the increasingly heated exchange of letters in August 1807 over John's critique of my history concerning my opinions of his performance prior to and during the Revolutionary War, diplomatic missions, and presidency. I wrote he was being vindictive in impugning my integrity and character, declaring I could not forgive his behavior. I knew John was stubborn and once his mind was set, he would defend the indefensible. Of course, I was no different, stubbornness being a part of my personality since my demands for an education as a young girl. I might add Abigail was even more stubborn than either of us. The breach lasted from 1807 to 1812 when our mutual friend, Eldridge Gerry, the former governor of our state and, as I pen this journal, Vice President of the United States under President Madison, brokered an *entente cordiale* reconciling John, Abigail, and me. The feud was over, but in the end, I lost more because I was not there for my friend when she confronted a tragedy that affected both our lives.

Tragically, I learned from Abigail my darling Nabby had contracted breast cancer in 1810, while we were not on speaking terms, and passed away in August 1813, after new tumors appeared in the scar tissue from the earlier cancer surgery. The time between our reconciliation and her death had been so short that Abigail did not have the time to inform me. What hurt most was that I did not see Nabby before she died to tell her how much I loved her, the daughter I always wanted. She was only forty-eight, and even though I had lost three sons, a husband, parents, siblings, and close friends, I could not hold back my tears. I could not imagine the pain and suffering Abigail was experiencing. She had been her mother's favorite, and I knew she would never recover from the loss. Like myself, she at least had the grandchildren, William, John, Thomas, and Caroline Amelia, to soften her loss; the latter being her favorite because she was so much like her beloved daughter.

When Abigail visited with me in Plymouth, she recounted Nabby's suffering. She first apologized for not informing me of her deteriorating condition, but everything happened so quickly, she had little time to do anything but mourn her loss. I knew she came because she needed to unburden herself and, over my protestations, went ahead to describe all the events leading to her death, staring with the surgery. What she recounted was horrific, leaving me speechless. In late 1811, Dr. John Warren (no relation) performed the surgery without anesthesia, strapping Nabby to a chair in an upstairs room of their home while Abigail, John, and Caroline Amelia helped. Abigail told me Nabby endured the pain of the surgery and cauterization without crying out which, Abigail noted, was so gruesome they had to turn away. By this time, we were both weeping uncontrollably, hugging each other for consolation.

After a moment, Abigail continued, both of us fighting back tears as she said that, after seven months, Nabby began feeling better, at which time she returned home to her New York home. But within a brief time, she began having abdominal and spinal pain and suffering from migraines. The local doctor diagnosed the pain as rheumatism, but in early 1813 new tumors began to appear in the surgical scar tissue. She returned to Braintree, where she died shortly thereafter. With that, Abigail sat back and let out a deep sigh. I said nothing, as I could not and did not want to. Her loss was my loss, a shared tragedy.

And then typical of the friend I had come to know, Abigail turned her attention to the ring of friendship, which she and John had crafted for me. Before continuing, she mused, "I only wish your James was here to see the ring. I felt so bad when I read of his passing and can only apologize for not reaching out to you sooner. He was a true gentleman and patriot who I knew was very much in love with you, as you were with him." At which point, she sighed and wiped tears from her eyes.

She then returned her attention to the beatiful ring on the gold chain drapped around my neck with its nineteen pearls surrounded by gold trim and a crystal enclosing entwined locks of their hair. I told her that it no longer fitted any of my fingers because of the swelling and pain in my joints, so I made it into a necklace. Grasping it in my hand, I told her that I liked it better this way because it rested near my heart, reminding me of our friendship and shared affection. Abigail smiled and said she liked it better there too.

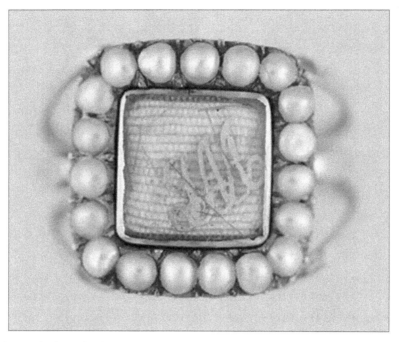

**John and Abigail Adams ring commissioned for Mercy Otis Warren (1812).
Gold, 19 pearls, crystal, gold foil, locks of hair.
Collection of the Massachusetts Historical Society**

She then pressed her fingers against the brooch I had commissioned for her as a token of my friendship, respect, and love. The pin had thirty-six pearls surrounding a gold foil trim with a crystal enclosing a lock of my hair. She said that she wore it every day in the same place, nearest her heart. Her granddaughter, Caroline Amelia, loved the trinket, as she called it, wanting one for herself with a lock of Nabby's hair, which she had. She planned to have a brooch crafted for her birthday.

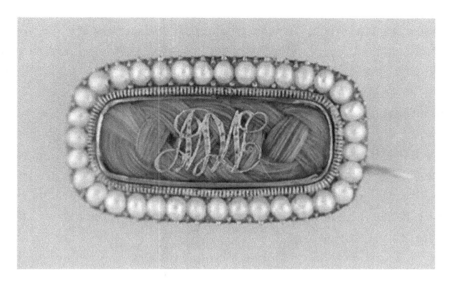

**Mercy Otis Warren brooch commissioned for Abigail Adams (1812).
Gold, 36 pearls with crystal, gold foil, and lock of hair.
Collection of the Massachusetts Historical Society**

I told her it would be a wonderful and thoughtful gift, noting that she and Caroline might consider visiting in the near future. I had so much to tell her about her mother. Pausing for a moment and then adding, I would have Henry drive me to visit Nabby at the Hancock Cemetery in Quincy. I needed to pay my respects. When Abigail left, she promised to visit again soon with Caroline Amelia. I nodded, telling her that I hoped she would visit soon and that I would miss her until she returned.

Two days later, Henry drove me to the cemetery in Quincy. I brought with me a bouquet of sawtooth sunflowers, orange butterfly milkweeds, and purple culver roots, Nabby's favorites, from my garden tied in a red ribbon and placed it on her grave. I also placed a small box with a wrapped spiced Apple Betty on her gravestone, remembering how she loved the sweet. It seemed so little to offer considering how I loved this young lady who called me Auntie Mercy. Sitting by the grave, I could see her smiling and giggling through the powdered sugar surrounding her mouth from a Blueberry Duff or spiced Apple Betty. I said a silent prayer and promised to return. On the carriage ride back,

I murmured to myself, "How many more loved ones must I bury before I die?" Henry turned and asked if I had said something. I replied no and sat in silence for the rest of the trip home.

Two weeks later, Abigail returned with Caroline Amelia, whom I found affable, intelligent, inquisitive, and the mirror image of her mother. Inadvertently, I called her Nabby a couple of times and when I apologized, she smiled, saying that no apology was necessary. "Grandmother often made the same mistake," she said. During their visit, she inquired about my education, revolutionary plays and poems, political activism, and history. She was so much like her dear mother, genuinely interested in learning about me.

The entire day was dreamlike. Caroline insisted Abigail and I speak about our friendship, and how we came to exchange locks of hair, saying that she hoped someone, someday would do the same for her. Abigail only offered a side glance, knowing full well she was planning on presenting Caroline with a brooch containing a locket of her mother's hair.

The oddest thing happened when my cook entered the parlor with coffee and a platter of Blueberry Duffs and spiced Apple Betties. Caroline, grinning, declared that they were her favorites. I had to hold back my tears, saying only that they were her mother's favorite as well. When it was time to leave, I told Caroline she could visit anytime but I felt despondent, seeing this beautiful young lady and my friend leave.

I began this chapter with the question, how do I describe my friendship with the Abigail? Simple, we were different people in many ways, but we had shared personal successes and tragedies, weathered the pressures any friendship endures over fifty years, and in the end came out stronger. I do not know how much longer I will be here to share my life with Abigail and the family, but I know our friendship will endure beyond the grave. And if there is a heaven, I know we will meet again. But for now, I will cherish every moment with my dear friend.

Plymouth, Monday, 31 January 1814

Chapter 16

THE CELEBRATED LADY

Catharine Sawbridge Macaulay
by Robert Edge Pine circa 1775 National Portrait Gallery, London, England

My friendship with the celebrated Catharine Sawbridge Macaulay was different from my relationship with Abigail. Even though we met only once, no woman had a more profound influence on me. She was my Clio, the eminent English historian, political and women's rights activist, and supporter of our revolutionary cause. She first came to my attention when corresponding with my brother James in 1769, presenting him a copy of her *History of England from the Accession of James I to that of the Brunswick Line*, and assuring him British liberals supported colonial actions against Parliament, the King, and colonial administration.

We began corresponding in September 1774, when she sent a letter complimenting me on *The Adulateur* and *The Squabble of the Sea Nymphs*. How she knew my authorship was beyond my knowing but assumed my brother had informed her in their correspondence. I only discovered later that both works had found their way to England. So much for my vaunted anonymity. While we corresponded, I came to appreciate her subtlety as a thinker, divulging only information she thought relevant but presenting her arguments with great clarity and passion. When I wrote earlier about the only other person who knew of my anonymous authorship of the *Observations on the New Constitution*, it was Catharine. Other than the normal social amenities and courtesies attendant in correspondences, our letters dealt with the ongoing dispute between the colonies and the colonial administration, Parliament, and the King. But letters were no replacement for face-to-face dialogue, and our chance came in 1784.

In July 1784, Mrs. Catharine Sawbridge Macaulay Graham and her husband, William, visited our home in Plymouth at the beginning of a journey to meet our revolutionary leaders that lasted a year. As the Grahams walked up the path, I took note of Mrs. Graham. She was about my height with light complexion, chestnut brown hair, brown eyes, sharp facial features, and a thin frame. Mr. Graham was a little taller with brown hair, brown eyes, thin face, and a small frame. My other impression was how young Mr. Graham appeared. He could not have been older than thirty while I knew Catharine was in her early fifties.

When they reached the door, she took my hand, thanking us for the invitation. William did the same, and then he turned to James, grasping his hand and saying that he hoped to learn about his time with General Washington's army. There was no formality, and we quickly fell into using first names.

Our servant collected their luggage and deposited it in the guest room, which I selected with its northern exposure and morning breeze coming from the bay, offering a panoramic view of the farm. We went into the parlor to share a decanter of peach brandy and flagon of ale, compliments of Samuel Adams, who had opened a brewery in 1783. As Catharine and I sipped our cordial, James and William their ale, I said they must be hungry after the long trip, so I had a colonial dinner being prepared of fish soup, roast turkey, cranberry sauce, sausages, vegetables, corn bread, pudding, coffee, and tea, hoping this would suffice.

Catharine smiled and said they were famished. The food aboard the ship was not very appetizing, so she was looking forward to a continental meal. Smiling, William agreed, saying that I had read his mind and agreed with his beloved lady about the shipboard food. Tapping his stomach and pulling as his shirt, he said he had lost at least ten pounds, noting his clothes were at least two sizes too large and he looked like a London street urchin, begging for alms. We could not help but chuckle at this description, and after toasting to their visit, we went into the kitchen. While we dined, and being curious, I asked them to describe their sea voyage.

Catharine began by telling us the trip was twelve weeks of misery. The stench from the vomit was overwhelming and below deck, the smell was worse, permeating the air to the point one could not breath. There were moments when she was gasping for air, making her seasickness, headaches, and dizziness worse, and then there were cases of the flux, diarrhea, passengers with unknown fevers, and the heat, my Lord, the heat was unbearable. The food was so highly salted, she was not sure whether it was meat or fish. At least there were ample supplies of fruit to fight the scurvy. And these miseries did not include the lice and rats, which abounded everywhere.

Her sufferings reached a climax when the ship ran into a gale, which raged two days and nights. The ship violently pitched back and forth and up and down to the point she believed it would founder. She prayed to the Lord to take her life. Looking in a mirror one day, she was appalled at how ashen her complexion had become. Then looking at William, she asked if he could add anything she may have forgotten.

William replied that her description captured the voyage perfectly but added that the only one that fed well was the cat who dined on the rats. Chuckling, he said the cat ate better than they did, and that was a certainty. Continuing in serious tone, William did remember one evening when on deck, he heard the suffering wails of a woman giving birth. The ship's wild pitching made her seasickness worse while she tried to push the infant out. He recalled how her screams blended into the wind whistling through the sails and rigging, making the episode eerie. He summed up by saying that giving birth was difficult enough on land, but he could not imagine what this poor woman was experiencing.

Catharine turned to him, asking why he had not told her about the incident. He rejoined that she was in enough distress and did not want to upset her further. James commented that they could count on regaining their strength with us and, turning to William, said the lost weight would return quickly. Our cook would make sure of that and if there was anything they needed, they only needed to ask. Catharine nodded, thanking James for his thoughtfulness and then, changing the conversation, said that she was distressed to hear of my brother's death the year before. She had only heard of the tragedy before they left London. She so much wanted to meet the man who had written against slavery and so eloquently about women's rights. I nodded, telling her that my brother would have been honored to make her acquaintance and speak about the issues confronting women in England and America and the evil institution of slavery.

The Grahams spent two weeks with us, visiting Boston to see where the spark of liberty and revolution had been lit. We toured Bunker Hill and the Lexington and Concord battlefields. In the meantime, however, most of their stay involved short trips to the shore and strolling the estate. Catherine especially enjoyed an early sunrise walk, explaining how she appreciated the salt air scent drifting on the morning breeze. We would walk arm-in-arm like old friends, speaking of the issues confronting America and England in these times of radical change for both countries. James and William, on the other hand, took horseback rides every morning.

James told me William was an excellent equestrian, always looking for a stone wall or rail fence to jump. Following him was an adventure said James, adding, "He got my blood up and it was invigorating." He told me that William was madly in love with Catharine and although she was much older, he thought her as half her age. However, he believed the voyage had not only sapped her strength physically but also emotionally. She would not admit it, but she was in terror the entire trip and when they arrived in Boston, her steps onshore were so unsteady, he thought she would have toppled over if he had not been holding her arm.

One morning sitting on the porch, Catharine and I spoke about Edmund Burke's *Thoughts on the Cause of the Present Discontents*. Catharine noted that the book was so pessimistic, it would destroy the little virtue and understanding of sound policy left in the English nation. She added Burke was influenced by the corrupt principle of self-interest, hoping the aristocracy would return to power. He did not understand the problem was political corruption and desire for power, which had its origins in the Glorious Revolution. The revolution may have ended absolute monarchy but replaced it with parliamentary rule of the few, and now our government representatives had become a corrupt cabal only caring about money, power, and the next election. The notion of the Parliament and the King sharing power was a myth, and the proclamation of our *English Bill of Rights,* which was supposed to become the pillars of British society, was nothing more than high sounding words on paper.

While James and William listened, Catherine described how the Whigs and Tories had become mere political factions seeking only to perpetuate their power. She noted that originally, Whigs conceived power as residing in the people or in the people's representatives, viewing rulers as serving the will and welfare of the people, as embodied in Parliament. Conversely, she remarked, Tories conceived sovereignty as residing in the King, regarding the people as subjects whose duty was to obey their monarch and established church. Now, however, the ideological differences were no longer relevant, each faction preaching nonexistent political differences to a population kept in perpetual ignorance. Parliament, all their blustering aside about the *English Bill of Rights*, were now a rubber stamp of the King and Privy Council, each only interested in perpetuating their power. This was why she advocated for a system of the annual rotation of members of Parliament, believing this would mitigate the corrupting influence of greed and desire for power. This statement influenced me later when, in the *Observations*, I argued for congressional term limits. If I had thought their visit would be relaxing, I was wrong. Catharine was a very inquisitive person, and no subject was sacrosanct as I soon discovered.

One morning, James was driving the four of us to the shore. For a July day, the morning breeze was cooler than normal. James turned to Catharine and asked how she came by her education. Replying enthusiastically, she informed us she was educated by a governess in the traditional readings of the day: religion, poetry, romantic novels, and books on domestic affairs. She admitted being a foolish young girl until twenty, when she developed a fondness for the history books in her father's library. She was especially drawn to the ideals of liberty extolled in the annals of the Greek and Roman republics. Interrupting, I said, "Then you were self-educated?" She replied that I was correct, adding that her father was incredibly supportive and demanding, recommending books that she devoured. Then, looking at me, she asked how I came by my learning.

I related the story about how my brother, James, and I cajoled my parents and uncle into allowing me to study in his university tutorial. Interjecting before I could continue, she stated she was not surprised that my brother supported my goal, noting he was one of the first of his sex to advocate for women's political and educational equality. Sighing, she said how she wished to have met this unique man. I then described how his mental deterioration had accelerated after the attack by Governor Hutchinson's supporters, saying, "I think of him each day and know if he were here with you and William, he would be honored to meet a person he considered a friend and like-minded spirit."

William then commented that the attack on my brother exemplified that despotism knows no law, only the caprice of the powerful, noting Locke said it best in the *Two Treatises of Government,* "where law ends, tyranny begins." Mr. Hutchinson's behavior was lawless but as Dante has described, the treacherous and traitors populate the ninth ring of hell along with Cain, Ptolemy, and Judas. He certainly deserved to be there with the others of his ilk, William stated. Then he remarked, with a smile of pleasure, that my plays were, in part, the reason for his recall to England. I nodded, telling him I had heard rumors to that effect.

Catharine was gazing toward the sea, musing that there were individuals who influenced our futures as mentors and supporters. I had my parents, brother, and James to bolster my desire for an education. She had her father and Miss Elizabeth Carter, England's famous Latin and Greek scholar, whom she met in Canterbury. After offering her opinions to this renowned intellectual on history, philosophy, and politics, she told Catharine that she had developed an extraordinary intellectual method, which blended the philosophy of St. Evremond, renowned wit, hedonist, essayist, and literary critic because of her interpretations of Spartan law, Roman politics, and Epicurean philosophy. Epicureans believed the greatest good was to seek modest pleasures in order to attain a state of tranquility and absence from bodily pain. This gracious comment led her to author her first history and began her questioning why all women did not have the same opportunity for an education like Miss Carter and herself. I was not surprised that Catharine was an adherent of Epicurean philosophy. Others might have believed she was a radical, but I knew different. She was a moderate, practical person.

Every day was a new learning experience with Catharine. One day, while James and William were horseback riding to Barnstable, we had a conversation about our personal lives. She was more open-minded about intimacy than expected, and about which I was more circumspect.

While strolling the estate, she related how she had married the Scottish physician George Macaulay in 1760, who was fifteen years her senior. He was an incredibly special man, a perfect match for her personality, especially concerning her intellectual goals. She pointed out that we lived in a time and society where male sexism rules, but George empathized with women's plight, discouraging sexism in the Lying-in Hospital in London where he worked. He contributed his spare time to training midwives and worked tirelessly on medical innovations, especially those associated with women's birthing problems. Like my James, he was an enthusiastic supporter of her writing, further saying she started her history in large measure because of his support and encouragement. He was always there, helping in any way he could. He even agreed with her radical political views, although he thought she should be more cautious, for empowered men would look to demean her efforts if she became too bold or outspoken.

Catherine was happy for six years and gave birth to her only child, Catharine Sophia, born in February 1765. Sighing, she said, "But happiness was often an illusion," and within a year of her daughter's birth, she lost George, this very special man, in 1766. At the time, she never thought of marrying again. I thought to myself, *For all the joys of love and loving, there were the tragedies that left us with only memories and feelings of emptiness.*

I told her we had been lucky in our choice of men. James encouraged me to get involved in the 1773 Committee of Correspondence with Samuel Adams and Dr. Joseph Warren, no relation by-the-by, which planned the Boston Tea Party. She interrupted and, with a surprised

The Celebrated Lady

look, said she did not know I was so intimately involved. I told her very few knew of my participation. She thought my role amazing. A woman, no less, actively taking part in lighting the fuse in the powder keg of liberty. She then queried why I had avoided recognition for this singular contribution. I told her that mine was one of many others and no more special than any other, including my son Samuel, who lost a leg in our fight for freedom.

Still, Catharine countered that I deserved acknowledgement, a woman at the center of planning a revolution. This male sexist world would have had convulsions. What next, women in Parliament or Congress? Oh, she could see it now, tongue-twisted men tripping over themselves to leave the chambers. I could only laugh at her recital, but she knew how to circle back to the main point of a discussion.

Catherine pointed out that fame and celebrity had drawbacks if a woman did not conform to society's norms, and she was no different. I noted that she was the celebrated Mrs. Macaulay, a woman recognized for her intellectual gifts and contributions to English history. Who would dare to attack her? She then related when she married Mr. Macaulay at the advanced age of twenty-nine, she was inexperienced in matters of the heart. Coming close to me, she whispered that she loved George, but they were missing the passion of lovers like that of Romeo and Juliet or Antony and Cleopatra. He was enthusiastic about his work while she was enthusiastic about her writing. She told me how surprised they were when she became pregnant, so little did they share the intimacy of the bed chamber. When he passed, she thought her life would involve raising their daughter and publishing her histories.

Then she met William and fell passionately in love at the tender age of forty-seven no less. She did not believe it. Interrupting, I said that there was no age limit to falling in love, but I knew the feeling: the ache not knowing why, the sleep that eludes, and the continual thoughts of the man. She smiled, nodding her agreement. But, she continued, William was twenty-one, nearer her daughter's age than her own. I was not surprised by the revelation, having noticed the age difference when they arrived. "So what," I retorted, "Age was a number, a state of physical being while the state of mind was how she thought of herself. If she thought herself young, then she was, regardless of a date and year on a calendar or a birth certificate."

Catherine agreed but our sexist society did not. She pointed to the fact that a man of fifty could marry a child of eighteen with no personal or public embarrassment. But God forbid a woman did the same; she was personally and publicly ridiculed as a cradle-robber. When they married, she became the object of scorn and abandoned by many of her friends and supporters. She became a social pariah, the object of gossip; the scandalous woman author who married the younger brother of the sexologist James Graham. Oh, how the tongues wagged, she forlornly mused. William told her the criticism of their marriage was only an excuse to hide the real reason, which were her radical views of women's role in society, political opinions about factionalism and government corruption, and support for the American cause. She realized that he was trying to make her feel better, but she did believe he was partially correct. Stopping for a moment to organize her thoughts, I realized she wanted to unburden herself, having few friends to whom she could turn.

Catherine began by noting that throughout her history of England, she showed an overriding concern for the protagonists' moral character and conduct, believing only a virtuous people created a republic. She explained that self-interest was the worst fault of which a king or political leader could be guilty of, criticizing their obvious devotion to politics for personal gain rather than the advancement of liberty and protection of the people's rights. Initially, she said, the Whig community welcomed her history as an answer to Hume's Tory, *History of England*, but in 1768, all changed when she published the fourth volume of the history.

Dealing with the trial and execution of King Charles I, Catharine expressed the view that his execution was justified, praising the Commonwealth of England for the action. In doing so, however, she revealed her republican sympathies, and Whig supporters of her work, like Thomas Hollis, Horace Walpole, and Thomas Gray, condemned her. She was no longer the celebrated Mrs. Macauley, who Mr. Gray had once extolled that her work was the most sensible, unaffected, and best history of England that he had read. She was now treated like a political pariah. William Pitt, Joseph Priestley, John Wilkes, Lord Lyttelton, and James Burgh continued to be supportive, but their voices were drowned out by their enemies. I then told her that she had stood by her principles, reminding her that critics were most often self-absorbed individuals with selfish motives and agendas. I also added that activists, like ourselves, who believed in freedom and liberty were, "In for the penny, in for the pound," so the saying went. Before I could continue, she raised her hand to stop me, saying, "There was more."

She was then derided because of her association with the colonial cause. She believed it unjust to tax the colonies while they had no representation in Parliament. Then she published, *Address to the people of England, Scotland, and Ireland on the Present Crisis of Affairs* in 1775, a copy of which she promised to send me upon her return to England. The essay sealed her political fate and squandered what little support remained. In the pamphlet, she called on the British people to support the rights of the American colonists, warning them that what the government was doing to their American colonists could easily happen to them. She knew full well that the English populace believed their tax burden would be less onerous if the levies fell on the colonies. She argued that by supporting the colonial cause, they would protect themselves from the encroachment on their own liberties and protect their own rights. For her pains, the *Westminster Magazine* caricatured her as a dagger-wielding mix of a Roman matron and Indian chief about to plunge her weapon into Britannia's breast.

Exhaling, Catherine said that she did not consider herself or her works all that radical. She was a Whig in the traditional sense, opposed to absolute monarchy, supporter of constitutional monarchy and the parliamentary system. But she mused regretfully, England had strayed from the ideals of the Glorious Revolution, which installed George I and defeated the Jacobite uprising. The Whig reforms of the last century had purged Tories from important positions in the government, army and navy, Church of England, legal profession, and local political offices, but they had lost their way ideologically. Now both parties relied more on the support of a small cadre of wealthy businessmen and aristocrats than on the citizens they were chosen to represent. Control of the elections to the House of Commons were now in the hands of a few power brokers who acted as puppet masters, pulling the strings of members of Parliament for their personal gain. She had argued against this evolution but to no avail. And yet, I replied, she had not been silenced in her protestations by these powerful interests.

Catherine thought me correct but believed her support of our cause had only served to increase their attacks. The Whigs of old fought against tyranny but now, she feared, they exemplified the corrupting influence of power and money. Then, of course, she was harshly criticized for her support of the *Wilkites* and *Society for the Supporters of the Bill of Rights*, both of whom sought reforms of Parliament. She was interested in the substance of an argument, the political theorist, but theory was not the reality of politics. She lowered her head and whispered to me the renowned Machiavelli would be disappointed with her. Even the great James Harrington would furrow his brow and narrow his eyes at her political naiveté. Adding with a grunt of disgust, she always seemed on the losing side of an argument, whether it was her position regarding Catholic emancipation; vocal support for the exiled Corsican, Pasquale Paoli; Edmund Burke's advocacy of the colonial cause, or criticism of Dr. Samuel Johnson, England's revered writer and moralist.

I looked at her distressed countenance and, unable to control my anger, pointed out that she should ignore Johnson, who was a committed Tory and would naturally attack anyone who did not subscribe with his opinions. He was no supporter of political equality because he feared change. He did not want to anger his rich patrons. So much for being a renowned intellectual and moralist. He was a hypocrite who should concentrate on his poetry and playwrighting. He might believe himself the arbiter of English morality, but he was committed to supporting the status quo for his benefit. I knew nothing of Mr. Paoli or the issue concerning Catholic emancipation, but wholeheartedly agreed with her about Mr. Burke who supported our fight against the tyranny of the English government. I told her that she was on the right side of history with regards to our revolution, and her support had been most welcome and influenced me to greater contributions in support of our fight for freedom. I told her, "No insult intended, you were more like a rude colonial revolutionary than a celebrated English historian and political theorist."

Taking her hand in mine, I said that we in the colonies knew the English thought of us as crude and unsophisticated, almost barbaric, but here she was the celebrated Mrs. Macaulay, and I would not stand by and hear people speak ill of her. There were always gossips; people who had nothing better to do to fill their empty lives but chatter on, impugning a person's integrity just to feel good about themselves. My prediction regarding her celebrity in the colonies was proven correct as later events demonstrated when she discovered a very warm and friendly reception among those she met. I applauded her candor and individuality, ending with my personal opinion that she had found her passion in William, and they should seek pleasure in the feeling. She broke out laughing and planted a kiss on my cheek, saying, thank you, and then adding my brother's description of me did not do me justice.

Then just as quickly, Catharine changed the focus of the conversation by commenting on how James doted on me as a lover who had never lost his passion. Caught off guard for the moment and recapturing my presence of mind, I told her that we fell in love at our first meeting, although we did not know it at the time. Every day we fell in love all over again. When he left General Washington's army, his reason was me, not the spurious gossip about his disagreements with the professional army officers. I was lonely, scared for his safety, and simply longed for his presence by my side. He gave up much to come home to be with me. This was what being in love versus simply loving was about. I remarked that being in love is one thing, staying in love demands work every day.

Besides these specific topics, which led to her ostracization by many in English society, we had more detailed discussions, especially on politics, best forms of government, and the challenge of governance. She noted, with which I concurred, that any form of government became corrupted if those in charge did not know how to govern or lost their focus on the people. One of our first discussions, in which William and James took part, concerned the best form of government for the colonies. This became a spirited discussion into Catharine's views on the issues confronting the ideals of the republican form of government versus the reality of governing. I found it fascinating and instructive. We agreed regardless of the form of government, even one benignly organized became corrupt when the empowered sought to perpetuate their power and wealth. The crucial limiting factor was the ability of the people to exercise control over their government through voting and awareness of what their magistrates were doing.

I declared that even though the Roman republic, which had evolved into a government with a Senate, two consuls, and Tribunes of the People elected annually, the examples of the Gracchi, Marius, Sulla, and Caesar showed they had failed in curbing the desire for money and power. When the Imperium began under Augustus, the republican system existed in name only. The institutions of government bent to the will of the emperor and the emperor in turn controlled the people with *panem et circenses* (bread and circuses). As time progressed, the political corruption, greed, and desire for power eventually brought down this great empire to whom we still owed a great deal.

William noted cynically that government was reliant on the people, but it was the people who placed their despots in power. He thought they should be more aware of the potential for corruption, but peoples' self-interest always seemed to win out. James interjected that the problem was the people who put their own in power were no less corrupt than those corrupting the government. It did not matter who was selected to rule, he feared the end result would be the same: corruption and greed eventually leading to tyranny and the collapse of the social order. He also agreed with me that Rome was a perfect example of this.

Catharine offered that to one degree or another, and with some modifications, European nations followed the Roman model. Each had upper and lower legislative chambers, monarch or emperor, and advisory council, but power rested with the monarch and the council. The system bred the potential for corruption and tyranny. Changing this model was daunting. The legislative chambers needed the authority to curb the monarch and council by enacting laws protecting the liberty and rights of the people from the corrupting influences of the empowered. The power and influence of the aristocracy had to be weakened, and this could only be achieved by an independent judiciary, armed with laws aimed at controlling the excesses of government. Free annual elections was another method for controlling the corrupting influence of money. In the end, however, the powers of the monarch, chief magistrate, and even the legislature must be restricted to the point that they must, by law, bow to the will of the people. She pointed that our *Declaration of Independence* and *Articles of Confederation* were starting points.

I noted that the *Articles* had serious flaws that restricted the people's rights and ability of the government to govern. Each state only had one vote in Congress, while Congress had no power to tax or regulate foreign and national commerce. There was no executive branch to enforce acts passed by Congress. There was no national court system, amendments required a unanimous vote, and laws required nine of the thirteen states to pass in Congress. America could not govern in this fashion; we needed a constitution to correct these weaknesses. Catharine replied, "Exactly," at which point James interrupted saying there was talk among our states' leaders that we needed to empanel a constitutional convention to address these issues. William declared that this was sound in theory, but how did you keep corruption out of the constitutional convention debates? You were still dealing with people with differing opinions, motives, and goals. There was silence when he finished. I remarked that Plutarch observed the disparity between rich and poor was the oldest and most fatal ailment of republics, while the famous moralist, Aesop, noted we hang petty thieves and appoint the great ones to public office. James offered that the great lawgiver, Solon, had stated, societies are well governed when the people obey the magistrates and the magistrates obey the law.

These were the discussions and friendly debates we had during their visit, but not every day was a conversation about serious matters. As long as she was not riding on the ocean, Catharine and William enjoyed visiting the coast and strolling the beach, picking up the odd seashell or simply looking out at the fishing boats bobbing in the bay. She especially enjoyed the salt air mingling with the sea grass, scrub pines, and wildflowers dotting the shore. As she said one day, there was a serenity here that calmed her soul and relaxed her mind. She could not remember when she had slept so well. What I found most endearing was that whenever we strolled the estate or beach, we always did so arm-in-arm.

During the last days of their visit, Catharine spoke less about her past life or politics and more about the future. She seemed preoccupied with her health and legacy. One day while William and James were visiting Boston, having left early by horseback, we were strolling and Catharine stooped over, collected yellow sawtooth sunflowers, orange butterfly milkweeds, and purple culver roots, bundling them into a bouquet, and commenting that these would make a nice centerpiece for the dinner and supper table. I noticed, however, a sadness in her eyes, as she was worried about something she was keeping to herself. But before I could inquire if there was a problem, she turned and said that she had been thinking about what to write next, maybe a history of the American Revolution or something specific to women's education or political rights.

Although she was not asking for my opinion, I told her a history of our revolution would be perfect. This trip was ideal because she would be meeting the leading participants, especially General Washington, who could supply material as well as other luminaries who were there from the beginning. The trip could be a fount of information for her. Catharine nodded that she had been thinking the same thing but did not want to appear too aggressive, being a woman and an English one no less. People might be suspicious of her motives. I replied that she was speaking nonsense. We in the colonies considered her a supporter of our cause who had suffered at home because of it. Adding to this, I said I would not be surprised if she were not asked to make her home here in America.

But as I had learned those past two weeks, she was quick to move on to another subject. She paused for a moment, then said she was really thinking of publishing a piece on woman's education and political equality, and what did I think of the project. I smiled, telling her that a work of that nature coming from the pen of the celebrated Mrs. Macaulay would give comfort to all women and would set men on their collective, male-domineering "arses". Before I could continue, she burst into laughter. I thought she would choke and asked what was so funny. She replied, "You, my dear, well-educated and proper friend, using the common word arses. I did not know you had it in you." "Catharine," I shot back, "Having been around you, I seem to have acquired some rude habits, my dear scandalous friend." At this point, we were both laughing.

When William and James returned that evening, Catharine could not help but recount the conversation and my use of the word "arses." James nearly choked on his sausage and William nearly spat out his ale from laughing. James declared through his laughing fit that we had been married near thirty years, and had never heard me utter a cuss word. This was truly a momentous event to be noted in the annals of history. I replied that I knew when I was being made the butt of a joke, at which point the laughter turned into howls. I had not realized my use of the word butt had only worsened my embarrassment. But their laughter over my verbal faux pas became infectious and I could not help but start laughing, and it was nice to see Catharine enjoying a moment of mirth even if it was at my expense.

The last day of their visit, while we went to the shore and Catharine and James were conversing, William pulled me aside and spoke in muffled tones, saying he was concerned about Catharine's health and had I noticed anything wrong, or had she said something to me. Caught off guard, I cautiously replied that asking about his lady's health could never be construed as impolite. But yes, I had noticed that she seemed at times melancholy and preoccupied with a matter about which she had not spoken. She told me, however, that she had regained her health visiting here after the horrific sea voyage, which obviously had drained her strength. I also thought she was worried about the reception here, but I had told her this was not a problem. She was much admired and beloved here. In fact, I had drafted an introductory letter to the people she would meet which, I believed, would ease her concern.

William nodded that a letter of introduction from the renowned Mrs. Warren was most gracious, but he had a nagging feeling there was something else bothering her. I told him to ask Catharine directly. I did my best to allay his fears but was certain I had not. Here was a man deeply in love with his lady, and I saw the consternation in his countenance over her health. In the end, he said he would but not until they had left. He did not want to spoil Catharine's enjoyment of being with us, and wanted her to think of these two weeks as a joy. With that, we returned to Catharine and James, who were still enjoying a laugh at my expense over my use of "arse" and butt. I just shook my head, knowing full well that James would never let me live it down.

The rest of the last day Catharine and William spent packing. They were traveling by coach to New York City, passing through Rhode Island and Connecticut, stopping along the way to stay at inns overnight. In New York, I told them of the correspondence sent to John and Abigail who were expecting her, telling them that she was a lady of extraordinary talent and commanding genius with a brilliance of thought who had supported our cause. I told Catharine that John would be a fountain of information about the people and events leading to the war. She could not thank me enough, grasping my hand tightly and saying that she would miss me very much.

I made certain our last supper would be a meal to remember and our cook did not disappoint. We had wild green soup, seafood casserole with cream sauce and bread crumb topping, sausage, mashed potatoes, corn bread, pudding, apple pie, and coffee surrounding the beautiful bouquet of flowers picked by Catharine. At our table talk, we reminisced about the last two weeks, etching every memory into our minds, however minor, lest we forgot as time passed. I kept my own counsel that I was sad they were leaving. I knew James caught my mood. He had enjoyed William's company, feeling like a young man again, riding his horse, jumping stone walls and picket fences, and the enlightening conversations. Catharine and William caught our mood, but they continued to speak of the memories they would take with them.

The next morning, the carriage arrived and while the driver loaded their luggage, we hugged for so long that William had to remind us that the coach was waiting. I slipped a letter of introduction to General Washington into Catharine's hand. She looked at it and gave me a kiss on the cheek, saying she would miss me terribly and promised to write. William went to James and, while shaking his hand, thanked him for a wonderful time. He then smiled, saying he was going to miss their spirited rides and conversations. He then turned to me, gave me a hug and kiss on the cheek, thanking me for the hospitality of our home and endearing friendship. And with that, they climbed into the coach, waved, and were off. As the carriage rolled into the distance, I stood on the porch and placed my head on Jameses shoulder, telling him that I would miss her presence. James whispered, "I will miss them both; we were blessed by their presence."

I received a letter from Catharine on 15 July 1785, from New York City, thanking me for the letter of introduction and her friendly reception in New York City, Philadelphia, Mount Vernon, and other places where they stopped. She met many of our revolutionary war leaders who came to see her and thank her for supporting our cause. They spent ten days at Mount Vernon in the company of the Washingtons and was not surprised when she noted there were discussions to which she was privy about developing an American constitution, but no details were available. She offered a final comment that many of our notable leaders asked her to take up residence in our country where she would be most welcomed. To this, I could only smile. She may have disagreed with the direction of her country, but England was the home of her birth, and it was the place where she could be of most value.

Two days later, on 17 July, they left for France. I learned later from a copy of *Jackson's Oxford Journal* James had bought in Boston that, "After having visited several parts of America, and received many tokens of esteem from the principal characters in the United States, she has now retired, on account of her health, to the south of France and lives with her husband, William, at a beautiful villa in the environs of Marseilles." James looked at me, handing the journal to me and as I read it, he said, "You know, William asked me if either of us knew of any health issues with Catharine." I told him that I did not and that he might speak with you. I replied that William had, and I told him she seemed melancholy at times but had not confided in me. I told him to speak with her directly to learn what was troubling her. I told James, I was worried for my friend's health. I knew how she disliked sea travel and was not surprised if her ill health was not due in part to the long and harrowing ocean voyages. James nodded his agreement, saying simply, "I just hope she will be well."

Finally, in September 1786, I received a letter from Catharine. They were back in her beloved England where my letter was waiting. They had weathered another long and hazardous voyage across the Atlantic to France where she had become fatigued traveling through the country. I sympathized with her. After experiencing the sea voyage to our country, then journeying throughout the greater part of America, and then back on another harrowing voyage to France and then back to England, it was no wonder she was exhausted and in ill health. In my letter, I made it known her celebrity among Americans had only increased since her visit. I wrote she was our idol, equal to past political and philosophical authors who stood forward for liberty and freedom. And the feeling here was that should she ever decide to visit again, it was hoped it would be as a permanent resident.

In March 1787, I received a correspondence informing me Catherine had journeyed to the south of France again where she lived for a time, telling me of her alarm, expressed in a letter from Mr. Washington, for the safety of our infant government because of Shays' Rebellion and the corruption surfacing in some of the states, which she compared to the Parliament's interest in party business only. There was a pessimistic tone in the letter. Worried about her health and hoping to lift her sprits, in September 1787, I sent a guardedly optimistic letter, informing her a federal convention had met in Philadelphia to consider a constitution for our infant republic. Her reply offered a more hopeful tone than her earlier letter. She believed the adoption of the Constitution would elevate our people in a brief time to the happiest and greatest of nations. I may have been overreacting, but I still had this nagging and bad feeling about my friend's health.

Then in 1787, I sent a letter informing her of the voting for the new Constitution, in which only five states had adopted the proposed system. Two states, Massachusetts and Maryland, wanted amendments added to the proposed document before adoption, while other state populations had rejected the Constitution out-of-hand, although they did declare they would accede to the document with certain amendments. Then in 1788, I sent a copy of the *Observations on the New Constitution by a Columbian Patriot* for her review and comment.

I found it odd she did not reply so in July 1789, I sent another letter, voicing my apprehensions about the new Constitution and the emerging factionalism among my former revolutionary associates. Their squabbling was jeopardizing the security of liberty and the inherent rights we fought so hard to achieve. I wrote to Catharine, "It was true we now had a government organized with Washington at its head, but we are too poor for monarchy, too wise for despotism, and too dissipated, selfish, and extravagant for republicanism." Sitting with James, I could not hold back my concern for Catharine's health, recalling our conversations with William that last day of their visit. I still had a feeling there was something else wrong, and it had nothing to do with sea voyages. James thought I was worrying too much, telling me that I was acting like an overprotective mother. Yet, I could not shake the feeling.

Again, receiving no correspondence from her, and becoming increasingly worried about my friend's health, I wrote again in September 1789, expressing my concern about our nation's stability. We were living in an age of violent revolution, and after hearing reports of the excesses in France and the instability in that great nation, I feared it would spread to America and Britain. I was worried that a constitution creating a powerful central government might jeopardize the liberties for which we had struggled. Still, I received no response, which only served to increase my apprehensions about her health.

Finally, and to my great relief, I received a letter in the spring of 1790. Having read the *Observations*, Catherine thought my pamphlet offered a practical approach to governing, agreeing that the legislature must be a separate and independent branch of government from that of the Chief Magistrate. If anything, Catharine was intuitive. As she noted in her letter, the pamphlet had Mercy Warren written all over it, but she would keep my secret, which she did to the grave. She agreed with my position that a third separate branch of government with lower courts and a supreme court would insure the protection of the peoples' rights. The three arms of government, legislative, executive, and judicial, with the proposed amendments, would control the undue influence and personal motivation of the ambitions of the Chief Magistrate and the Congress and Senate.

She specifically commented on the term limits for Congress and Senate, which reiterated her notion that the best safeguard against corruption was representative rotation in office through periodic elections. This way the rights of the people would be protected from the tyrannical actions of the legislative or executive branches. She also compared the new French government with that of the American system, declaring because of their geographic proximity to England, the French were offered the opportunity to observe the deformities of our government.

In her letter in March 1791, she informed me that a parcel awaited her attention at her bookseller with a volume of my *Poems, Dramatic and Miscellaneous*. My letter included a note that I had bought a copy of her book, *Letters on Education with Observations on Religions and Metaphysical Subjects*. As expected, her next letter included a complimentary review of my plays and poems, and her critique of Burke's work, *Observations on the Reflections of the Rt. Hon. Edmund Burke, on the Revolution in France,* in which he vehemently attacked the French Constitution and legislature. He noted the people of England looked very malignantly on the prospects which our enlightened neighbors were making toward political perfection.

On 31 May 1791, I wrote what would be my last letter to my friend. I agreed with her criticism of Burke's work, saying even misguided Americans who fought for their country and had been instrumental in her emancipation from a foreign yoke had now become advocates of monarchy. I pronounced that from age to age were the people cajoled, cheated, or bullied until the hood-winked multitude set their own seal to a renunciation of their privileges and, with their own hand, riveted the chains of servitude on their posterity. It was my opinion the commotions in France would check the designs of certain characters and, for a time, keep them within the bounds of moderation. As I look back now, both of us could not have been more incorrect about the outcome of the French Revolution and its system of government.

Then James came home one day from Boston in a very melancholy mood. Under his arm, he carried a copy of *Gentleman's Magazine*. He opened it up to a page and gave it to me without saying a word. I nearly fainted from shock, needing to sit down, and read that my friend had passed away after a painful illness on 22 June 1791. James sat next to me. I was crying and he nestled my head on his shoulder, saying that she was a singular woman with an intellect far in advance of our current society and time, saying he would miss her but no more so than me. I could not respond. I just rose, walked out the door, and strolled the same path we had taken when she visited, thinking the whole time about our conversations, walking arm-in-arm, and weeping for my loss.

A week later, I contacted the publishers, Thomas and Andrews, in Boston. I told them of my decision to honor the memory of my friend by having an American edition of her last work, *Observations on the Reflections of the Rt. Hon. Edmund Burke, on the Revolution in France*, published complete with the introduction written by me. As I wrote in the introduction, "The celebrity of the author precludes the necessity of an introduction to any of her works, and the truths contained in her observations might be their best recommendation, even though they had thought proper to prefix her name."

James and I penned a letter of condolence to William and her daughter, Catharine Sophia, expressing our deep sorrow over their loss and ours. We received a warm reply from William who told us that Catharine thought the height of her American visit was the time she spent with us. Thus, my friend and mentor, my personal Clio, the muse of history, and intellectual giant, passed into history but not in the memory of this author who remembers her warmly each day.

Plymouth, Monday, 14 February 1814

Chapter 17
LADY CONSTANTIA

Judith Sargent Murray by John Singleton Copley (circa 1769-72)
Smithsonian American Art Museum. Washington, DC.

Judith Sargent Murray first came to my attention in August 1784 after Mrs. Macaulay Graham's visit. I received a copy of *The Gentleman and Lady's Town and Country Magazine* and read an excellently written essay, *Desultory Thoughts on the Utility of Encouraging a Degree of Self-Complacency, Especially in Female Bosoms* by a lady using the pseudonym Constantia. I thought the article offered a compelling argument extolling the benefits of well-educated young girls and women. The author reasoned educated young ladies would gain greater self-respect and self-confidence, thereby preventing them from marrying for social status, financial security, or to avoid the dreaded label of spinster. The latter caught my attention, having heard Mother incessantly lecturing my sisters and me on the tribulations of being a spinster. Constantia was arguing for the independence of young girls and women from subservience to outdated social traditions.

In the same year, the *Massachusetts Magazine* published *On the Equality of the Sexes*, another well-crafted essay in which Constantia argued the notion that women were the mental equals of men in all areas, but constrained from exercising their minds because of limited, educational opportunities. She pointed out women's intellectual energies were directed toward fashion, slander, and gossip, contending that traditional female domestic activities only served to limit their creative potential, while discouraging their intellectual growth in other avenues of learning and expression. I was more than curious about this author's identity. I wanted to offer my congratulations for such well-written and thoughtful essays, the themes with which I fully agreed. I asked James to do all in his power to discover her identity, but his queries came to naught.

But this anonymous writer's work resurfaced in my mind after reading Catharine's *Letters on Education*, and two years later, *A Vindication of the Rights of Woman* by the English author and activist Mary Wollstonecraft. The similarity of their arguments about women's political and social status in American and English societies did not seem coincidental. I recognized there was a movement afoot with which I agreed, but of which I was ignorant. All three argued women should have an education equal with their growing position and importance in society. They were redefining a woman's role, claiming they were essential to a nation because they educated children and were more partners in marriage than mere wives and domestics.

Their arguments sounded somewhat similar to the notion of the Republican Mother, wherein the survival of our American republic rested with mothers who nurtured public-spirited male citizens. Women, including my friend Abigail, supported this idea while I disagreed. My opposition was more nuanced. I saw this as another way for men keeping women in their traditional domestic roles by defining a new quasi civic responsibility. We now became receptacles of future, public-spirited male citizens, and I never thought of myself as a vessel for birthing males, especially having given birth to five boys and lost all but two before their time. So much for populating America with civic-minded male heirs.

How intelligent women, including my friend Abigail, could not see through this travesty confused me. They most probably believed this was as near to a public role as women would ever achieve in America, and I had greater hopes for our sex and our country. The three essays offered another underlying message, with which I also agreed: women should have equal political rights with men. It reminded me of my brother who had argued the same message. I asked myself, *Had I missed a new cause or movement for women's liberty and equality? Like those supporting Republican Motherhood, had I come to accept the status quo in women's position in society? Was I getting too old to appreciate the activism of a new generation of women?* When I told this to James, he laughed, saying that I was not too old to learn something new, and the fact I asked the question told him I was still sharp of mind and wit. He then added that he had every confidence I would catch up with these new ideas. Besides, he remarked, my life and achievements were what these women were writing about. However, I still did not know Constantia's identity, but that changed quite accidentally.

In early 1792, I received a charming letter from a Mrs. Judith Sargent Murray, whose name was a mystery to me. As I read, I blurted out to James that the letter was from my mystery woman, Constantia.

James said it was a wish come true and after all his failed investigations to uncover her identity, the fates had seen fit to complete his quest. I read the letter aloud. Mrs. Murray explained she had wanted to write sooner but personal matters and travels with her husband on his ministry did not allow time. She did not know I was the Marcia whose plays and poems had influenced her work. She had read my five plays and *Squabbles of Sea Nymphs* when they were published by the magazines, but she did not know who I was until she met the Adamses in New York City.

By chance, she had seen a copy of the *Poems, Dramatic and Miscellaneous* on the parlor table and asked about it. Mrs. Adams told her I was the author: the celebrated Marcia, Mrs. Warren of Plymouth, sister of the equally famous James Otis, and her dearest friend in the world. Stunned into silence, she wrote that she caught her breath and informed Abigail she had wanted to meet me for years but did not know my name. Abigail told her to write to me.

Her letter could not have been more effusive with compliments, noting I was her personal Calliope, the muse of eloquence and poetry. She said her essays and writing style were inspired by my works, and she was now engaged in preparing a novel titled *The Gleaner* and a play, *The Medium, or Happy Tea-Party,* which she hoped to stage at Boston's Federal Street Theatre. I could not have gotten to the library desk fast enough to pen a reply. James, following me into the library looked at me sitting at our desk and said, "Too old, disconnected, dated. How wrong you were. This was a young woman whom you have influenced." Answering, I said that she also sent her apology to James for keeping her identity secret. Had she known who he was, she would have told her editors to supply her name.

Returning to my response, I offered the normal social courtesies and wrote how her two essays on women's education and equal political rights impressed me. I noted the essays had the same themes as those of my friend, the renowned Mrs. Macaulay, and the equally notable Mary Wollstonecraft. I wrote that it was to her lasting credit and honor that an American woman was taking the lead in changing our status in society and invited her and the Reverend Murray to visit with us in Plymouth for a weekend or a week, their traveling schedule allowing. In the last line, I asked which name she preferred, telling her she could call me Mercy but not Mrs. Warren. The latter made me feel old, and I still had my prideful side.

Her next correspondence arrived just after the holidays in 1793. She apologized for not responding sooner but she and the family had moved from Gloucester to Boston, where the Reverend Murray had founded a Universalist church. The other reason for the delay intrigued me. The city had recently lifted the ban on theatre performances, and she wanted to concentrate on staging her dramas and defending the cultural benefits of the theatre. Unlike the religious zealots in our state, she believed the theatre was not a corrupting influence on audiences. She wanted to transform the American theatre experience, believing the stage could be a powerful force in forming the opinion and manners of the people, and that we needed an American stage with American scenes and actors. She then asked for my opinion on the matter, which I found ingratiating because my knowledge of the intricacies of dramatic productions was limited to writing satirical plays, which were not performed, or attending theatre performances with James before the Revolutionary War.

Surprisingly, Judith also offered personal tidbits of information about the family. She related her first marriage had ended with the death of her husband in the West Indies where he had fled to avoid debtor's prison. This left her deeply in debt to a host of creditors that forced her to start publishing to make a living. She had also adopted two of her first husband's orphaned nieces, Anna and Mary Plummer, and young orphan, Polly Odell, a distant relation, and was supervising the education of her daughter, two nieces, Polly, and the children of her brothers and some family friends. I thought this was an exceptional woman with a self-confidence rare in so many of our sex. Finally, she offered to visit in the spring after the winter chill abated and icy roads were less hazardous. I mused, *This is a lady who spoke her mind without apology, not a woman to dismiss, ignore, or challenge.*

My response complimented her focus on children's education, and wanted to know her schooling as a young girl. I also inquired about the subjects she taught and expressed a desire to know the topics she considered important. I did not inquire about her first husband or their financial difficulties, believing this was inappropriate in a letter. I then expressed my elation that she and the Reverend Murray would visit, telling her anytime in the spring would be fine. Her next letter was brief but did say early May would be a suitable time to visit. However, she could not be certain Reverend Murray could attend because he was deeply engaged in setting up his Boston church and ministry.

The letter included a brief description of her teaching program, which emphasized the classics, ancient and modern philosophy, history, political theory, and female authors, especially the latter which she believed offered real-life examples of women who succeeded in the male-dominated world. She was mostly self-educated, having attended a penmanship school at her father's insistence and sharing a tutor, Reverend John Rogers, with her brother, Winthrop, as he prepared for entry into Harvard College. After he left for college, she relied on him to guide her reading on his vacations. This last sounded all too familiar to my journey.

I wrote anytime she wished to visit, we would welcome her company. If she wanted to bring children, she could do so, as we had five bedrooms and more than enough outdoor space to accommodate play. I told her if she could set a date, I would have James pick her up in Boston, as he spent time traveling there on business and it would be no inconvenience. I ended by stating her educational experience was similar to my own and hoped we could discuss the specifics when she visited. In her next letter, she declined the offer to have James drive her, choosing to hire a coach. She planned to arrive on Saturday, 3 May, and hoped to stay three days, if this was not inconvenient. I replied she could stay as long as she wished, but I insisted James drive her back to

Boston, dropping the need to schedule a return trip and thereby saving money. Again, her reply was brief, saying she would see me on the third and accepted the offer to have James drive her back.

On the day of her scheduled arrival, I paced the porch to the point that James declared he had never seen me so nervous, while adding that I was wearing out the flooring. He also mentioned looking at my watch every couple of minutes was not going to make the time move any faster, or the coach arrive earlier, saying she would be here soon enough. Scanning the horizon, there appeared a rising grayish-black cloud, which I at once knew was the dust kicked up by horses, a carriage. The coach skidded to a halt and the coachman alighted, taking the luggage from the upper rack and then, opening the door, offering his hand to a diminutive lady stepping out and fixing her dress. He picked up the luggage and deposited the two bags on the porch.

Behind him stood a petite, slim woman with finely sculpted facial features, delicate hands with brown hair, and penetrating brown eyes. Mrs. Murray looked like a woman in her twenties, which I knew was not the case. Before I could welcome her, the coachman excused himself and asked if he could care for his horses, as the lady told him to not spare the whip. They were sweating and needed to be walked and groomed, adding if he could feed and water them, it would be appreciated. I told him to take them to the groom; he would see to their well-being and return to have some food and drink while he waited. He thanked me and led his team and coach to the stable.

Stepping forward, I offered my hand to welcome Mrs. Murray to our home. Before I could utter a word, she clutched my proffered hand, saying she could not thank me enough for the invitation and how honored she was to have the opportunity to meet me. She also added that she preferred being called Judith. Responding, I too was looking forward to meeting her, saying I had many questions but first, let us get inside. I offered her the opportunity to freshen up after the long ride, saying we could speak after she refreshed herself. I then introduced her to James, who moved forward from where he was standing and, grasping her hand, said he was honored by her visit, adding that he had not seen me this excited since the late Mrs. Macauley visited with us. Judith flashed a look of surprise at his statement. As I later learned, she idolized the celebrated author and activist.

I escorted Judith to the guest bedroom, which had been Winslow's. As we entered, I told her the room was spartan but had an expansive view of the estate, and the northern exposure allowed a refreshing sea breeze to fill the room. Thinking to myself, I could see Winslow at the desk reading; he once told me it was his special hideaway. Returning to the present, I pointed to the table with water ewer, rose-scented soap and oil, towels, and a desk with pen, inkwell, and paper under a window, with simple curtains framing the cut glass panes. I told her there was a bath next door with a soap plate, lavender-scented water, towels, and a fireplace to heat water.

As Judith thanked me with a beautiful smile, I could not help but notice those penetrating eyes and thought this was a lady who knew who she was and proud of it. Turning at the door, I informed her dinner would be ready in an hour or so, but to take her time and join me in the library where we could speak. She nodded and, closing the door behind me, I could barely withhold my excitement. But my thoughts lingered on those eyes: bright, expressive, and penetrating. I was definitely looking forward to speaking with her.

When she entered the library, her eyes first fell on my John Singleton Copley portrait commissioned by James. She smiled, saying Mr. Copley had painted her portrait, a gift from her husband John. Scanning the room, she commented on how beautiful the library was decorated. She had a look I recognized from five decades before when I first walked into Uncle Jonathan's library. Her eyes danced across the shelves, her fingers gently running along the volumes in the same way I had done that first day of the tutorial. Her soft voice brought me back to the present when she turned and simply said, "Unbelievable, magnificent." She then added, while her fingers came to rest on a volume of

Shakespeare, that she had expected no less from an American icon. I replied she was most gracious, but I was no icon.

Then, smiling, I gestured toward my portrait and said, "I should have looked that good in person when it was painted. Mr. Copley was a master of his art and should be complimented." Judith rejoined that I still presented a graceful countenance and regal manner. Thanking her, I noted she was truly a vision of beauty and gentility, and such wisdom in one so young. Judith turned to me and said she was forty-three years young. I was surprised, saying she looked twenty-five, adding with a grin that everyone appeared younger to my failing eyes at the tender age of sixty-four. We both laughed and, again, I was captured by those eyes.

At this point, the cook announced dinner was ready, saying she had prepared a cod and clam chowder soup, potted baked salmon flavored with cloves, mace, and nutmeg, and vegetables, corn bread, Apple pie, and coffee. I noticed Judith ate sparingly, reminding me of the late Mrs. Macaulay Graham. After dinner, we retired to the parlor to share a glass of peach brandy, at which point James declared that he was going for a ride to work off the meal, and he might try jumping a fence or two. When Judith protested for him to stay, he said he knew we had much to talk about. This was our time. As he turned, I told him to be careful and not to damage himself or the horse. He was not young anymore.

As we sipped our brandy, I asked Judith how she came by her education, telling her there were similarities in our experiences. She told me that being born into a prominent merchant family, her father provided her with an excellent education for a young lady, even sending her to a school for penmanship to improve her hand. I complimented her beautiful hand, the same graceful Italian *cancellaresca* script I learned. I told her as a young girl, I selected it because it was pretty. Smiling, she nodded in agreement, saying that it was a beautiful, elegant, and refined hand.

Continuing her recitation, as a young girl, she remembered spending sleepless nights, weeping over the fanciful embarrassments and distresses of some hero or heroine who had blazed away in the pages of a romance. She owed her interest in philosophy, history, and politics to her brother's tutor, Reverend John Rogers, with whom she studied for a brief time while he prepared her brother for Harvard College. After the tutorial, her brother Winthrop continued guiding her reading on his vacations from school, concentrating on history, philosophy, geography, and literature. She believed women could only succeed in life if they were educated, and her reading of history proved the point.

There were many examples of women from ancient to modern times who were as intelligent and accomplished as men. She looked at me and said that I exemplified exactly what she was saying. I became her real-life heroine, a woman with celebrated accomplishments who forged an independent, intellectual life, respected by men and women alike. She offered that Mrs. Adams could not praise me enough for my accomplishments and involvement in our country's creation.

I thanked her for the compliment, and then related my educational experience with the Reverend Russell and my brother when he was preparing for entry into Harvard. I too decried the dismal state of women's education, noting even in our new republic, old prejudices about women's intellectual abilities prevailed. I declared that it annoyed me I could not practice law by men who would dash my dream based on outdated social traditions, but then used my expertise in constitutional and English Common Law and skill as an author to elicit my support. They were more than happy to offer encouragement and extol the virtues of liberty and freedom in my satirical poems and plays, but when the clouds of war cleared, they conveniently forgot my contribution. So, I very much understood her frustration.

Changing subjects, I asked how many children she supervised, mentioning that her letter said she tutored her daughter, nieces, an orphan, family members, and friends, and what was her teaching method. Judith followed the traditional recitation and memorization method for learning to read and write, followed by penmanship instruction. She instructed fifteen children of different ages, so each were studying subjects commensurate with their age, ranging from the

Bible and theological tracts to history, philosophy, political theory, and literature. For the older students, she concentrated on women authors because they were inspirational examples of women taking part and contributing to their societies. She even encouraged her young boys to read about successful women in history, in the hopes they would learn and appreciate the intellectual equality of the sexes.

Observing her countenance, I noticed her enthusiasm was reflected in her eyes, which became brighter when she spoke about a topic about which she was passionate. I had never given it much thought, but eyes were the window into a person's soul. I then recalled how Abigail's eyes glowed with fire when she was enthusiastic or angry about a topic or Catharine's which became serious or somber when doing the same. I made it a point from then on to observe Judith's eyes.

She hoped someday to open a female academy, where young girls attending the school could learn more than religious texts and domestic skills. This way they could rise above the stifling social traditions that trapped them in the home as wives and mothers. She wanted young girls to learn subjects that improved their self-confidence so they could make independent decisions about their futures. I added that I too dreamt of the day when we would have female lawyers, doctors, and ministers. I truly hoped so because this would be the realization of my vision for our republic.

I then suggested to Judith that we stroll the estate, the weather being delightful. As we walked arm-in-arm, I could not help notice how delicate she looked and asked that I was not aware, until mentioned in an earlier letter, that she had previously been married. She then went ahead with total candor to relate her story, her eyes taking on a more serious stare. The sparkle I had just noticed disappeared.

She married John Stevens, a successful ship captain and merchant when she was eighteen. When we went to war with England, she initially supported our cause, despite her family's financial ties with the mother country. But as the war dragged on, her support became lukewarm as she began questioning the conventional social attitudes in a nation being founded on egalitarian principles, which applied to men but not women. Adding to her dilemma, she was angry with the Gloucester's Committee of Safety, who looked to banish John, at that time her pastor, for his religious convictions on the morality of war. His spirited defense of civil and religious liberty deeply influenced her, and she often had taken the opportunity to defend the rights of all dissenters, including Loyalists, Quakers, and others censured for merely having different opinions. And then there was the multi-headed hydra of factionalism.

She admitted being a Federalist by political persuasion, believing a strong central government was the best chance for women to realize the equality denied them by social traditions. Regardless, she would still defend the rights of others to dissent without recrimination. She said, with deep conviction reflected in her eyes, who were any of us to deny anyone the right to their opinion or life choices. She considered herself a citizen of the world related to every son and daughter of humanity. She paused, waiting for my response, and for a brief moment, I thought she seemed to harbor some Anti-Federalist sentiments. However, I chose to avoid a discussion of politics until we had become better acquainted. I then mused, *Publishing the Observations anonymously was a wise decision.*

Replying, I said I thought it interesting she should mention the civil liberties of Quakers and Loyalists and told her about the request to particpate in a committee with Mrs. Adams and Mrs. Hannah Winthrop, widow of the late John Winthrop, to investigate and decide the disposition of Loyalist wives' property. I thought the idea, prevalent in other states like New York, both legally and morally wrong and convinced Abigail and Hannah not to take part. As it turned out, Mr. Hamilton, to his credit, successfully argued against this abuse of power by New York, and the entire program was dropped.

I said her defense of those who were vulnerable in times of crisis and war laudable, as they were most likely to face discrimination and abuse. I too believed the Quakers have been unduly persecuted because they were a different religious persuasion and believed in pacifism.

How hypocritical of the religious martinets who condemned Quakers, while forgetting they escaped from England and elsewhere for the same reason: religious persecution. Like her, I thought all people, no matter where they lived on this good earth, had the same dreams and aspirations in common. In that regard, we were all citizens of the world. Her eyes brightened when I ended my commentary.

She then added that there was also a personal reason for her tepid support of the Revolution, and the problem concerned the welfare of her brother Winthrop, who was serving in Washington's army. In the beginning, she believed his experience would earn him financial advantages and the admiration of Americans. Nevertheless, she had insisted that he, like all soldiers, adhere to high principles of morality. While shaking my head in despair, I told her I knew how she felt for as the war approached and knew there was no turning back; my greatest fear was for my husband and sons. I knew they would want to enter the fight, facing harm or death. My fear proved an omen, as my older son James lost his leg in a naval battle early in the war, and my other son, Captain Winslow, died in the recent Indian War in the Ohio Valley. I abhorred war. We mothers buried husbands and sons and were left to mourn, with only the memories of what was or could have been if they had lived.

Judith pressed my arm with those delicate fingers, saying she was so sorry for my losses, but that the only consolation was the righteousness of the causes for which they fought. She noted as the war dragged on, her essays, letters, and poetry became increasingly preoccupied with images of death. The rewards she had envisioned for her brother were now steeped in blood. It also troubled her that the Revolution ignored women like herself, and the more she thought about this issue, the more she came to appreciate traditional feminine values. For her, those values were the strength needed by America to insure the survival of our egalitarian message. She wanted both sexes to recognize that women were an equal part of the republican ideal, with an equal voice in their destinies and that of society.

Silent for a moment, Judith added that she tended to ramble on, forgetting others were around but she was so passionate about certain subjects she could not stop. Smiling, I said it was better to hear someone speak with passion than simply parrot platitudes. She was a doer, not a talker, and I applauded her for it, adding that she never stop speaking her mind, regardless of who might or might not be listening. But I reminded her that we were speaking about your first marriage before we distracted ourselves.

Distractions were often more enlightening, she noted and resumed. "The war destroyed my husband's business and in 1786, he was forced to flee to the West Indies to escape debtors' prison where he soon died. Two years later, I married Reverend John Murray in Gloucester and thereafter moved to Boston, when he founded the city's first Universalist church." Interjecting, I asked how she came by so many children. She replied that during her first marriage, she adopted two of Mr. Stevens's orphaned nieces and, briefly, a family relation who had been orphaned. The orphaned niece's parents had died of the pox while the other orphan's parents succumbed to the bloody flux. She halted for a moment, as if pondering what she wanted to say next, and then continued that she learned a great deal about life after her husband's death. I recalled asking her what she meant.

Judith believed she was too young when she married and, looking back, realized she was immature and not ready for the responsibilities of a wife and mother. What did any young girl of eighteen know about life, no less love? Bred on the romantic themes in novels and poetry where the heroine always succeeded in finding happiness with her Prince Charming, she discovered after her husband's death, there was a harsh reality to marriage.

I replied that she should not be so hard on herself. When I met James at twenty-five, I did not know if I was ready. She stopped and, looking at me, said, "Have you ever questioned your decision to marry?" She had and said so candidly, and that was not the worst of her problems.

Before I could speak, she continued, saying that being an expert in the law I would understand.

"After my husband's death, emotionally difficult though it was, I found myself being pursued by a host of creditors, seeking payment for the debts that had forced him to flee. I learned to my disbelief and chagrin that under the law of coverture when we married, we became a single entity legally. I had no separate legal status when it came to property and other rights. Under this law, I could not have controlled my property unless provided for prior to our marriage, which it had not. I was defenseless against these vultures."

I recall pressing her arm closer, saying I knew of the law. William Blackstone wrote on the subject which, if memory served, had been part of the Common Law since the Middle Ages. It was an archaic law that had no place in the American legal system. To his credit, James planned for this eventuality when we married. He did not want me straddled with creditors if he died first. I apologized for the interruption and asked her to continue her story.

In order to generate an income to pay creditors, she was forced to publish a few poems in the *Gentlemen and Ladies Town and Country* magazine, followed in 1784 with *Desultory Thoughts* and *On the Equality of the Sexes*. Despite her efforts, the line of creditors kept growing, and after Mr. Stevens died, she tried to eke out a living while being pursued by creditors. But she was honest, noting during these tough times, her father, Winthrop, was always there to keep the creditors at bay. If not for him, she did not know how she would have survived. He had always been influential in her life and the first to embrace Universalism, introducing her to Reverend John Murray. Reverend Murray encouraged her writing, and she, in turn, became an ardent supporter of his efforts to sow the seeds of Universalism in our nation.

She accompanied him on his preaching trips to New York, New Jersey, and Pennsylvania, meeting prominent citizens like the Adamses and Washingtons. It was through Mrs. Adams that she had found me. Now she was financially comfortable but during those first years, life was challenging and humiliating. I replied that like herself, my parents, brother James, and husband always encouraged and supported my education and writing efforts, noting that we were fortunate to be married to men who treated us as equals. I commented that a marriage based on equality made it easier to deal with the tribulations of life. I then noted my ignorance of Universalism and asked if she could describe its doctrines.

With eyes brightening, she began by saying the established Puritan and Calvinist churches emphasized predestination, austerity, literal adherence to the commandments, and belief all men were sinners and must be saved from themselves. Conversely, Universalism preached that God was a rational being whom humans could understand and whose nature would never condemn the majority of his creatures to eternal damnation. Universalists believed all humans formed a single family under God's loving fatherhood, and salvation was attainable to those who performed acts of benevolence, lived virtuous lives, and believed in Christ the Redeemer.

Their message was democratic, challenging the despotism of religious, outdated social traditions, and prejudices against women's education. Before I could comment, one of our young lads came running to announce supper was ready. So engrossed in our conversations, we had lost track of time. We walked back at a leisurely pace and turning to Judith, I said that she could tell me more about Universalism over supper.

Over supper, Judith described Universalism's democratic message and how it differed from other established churches. Universalists abhorred slavery, believed in the separation of church and state, and supported women's education. James interrupted, declaring that he recalled a lawsuit brought by the Gloucester Universalists against the First Calvinist Congregational Parish who demanded they pay taxes to their established church. The case was appealed to the Massachusetts Supreme Judicial Court, and the petitioners won the case, which set a precedent under the Constitution's freedom of religion clause, meaning anyone had the right to support their own church, have their own minister, and not pay taxes to an established church.

Judith proudly told us that this was her congregation. They did not believe the government should be engaged in setting up a state religion or showing favoritism to others. I nodded in agreement, but as I glanced toward Judith, I could see she was tired. It had been a long day, and I suggested she take a bath and retire for the evening. We could resume our conversation in the morning. She thanked me, saying it had been a long day but extremely rewarding. As she retired to the bathing room, James said she was quite the woman, just like me.

After breakfast the next morning, while we sat sipping our coffee, I remarked that she must tell me more about the Universalist views on female education. At this, her eyes brightened, and I noted to myself that those expressive eyes always sparkled when she was enthusiastic about a topic. Universalists believed young girls and women should have the same opportunities to pursue learning as men. By creating female academies or co-educational institutions, they believed women, like those in the Quaker community, could pursue the ministry and preach the gospel. Interrupting, I replied that a female academy would go a long way in creating the equality of the sexes about which she so eloquently had written. James entered the parlor, saying, "Ladies, let me drive you to the shore. Why waste this beautiful morning indoors?"

On the ride, I asked about the planned projects she wrote about in her letters. If I thought she was enthusiastic about Universalism and women's education, I was mistaken. Her enthusiasm was unbounded, again seen in those eyes, and at once launched into a description of her first project. As we sat by the shore, enjoying the soft breeze, Judith described her play, *The Medium or Virtue Triumphant*. The play's theme supported her view of marriage as a woman's choice based on mutual respect and admiration, not only love.

She believed that our country would only realize the promise of the egalitarian words in the *Declaration of Independence* and *Constitution* if society moved beyond traditional social hierarchies, when women were considered citizens with same rights as men, had access to an education, choose their futures, practiced the professions, voted, and held public office. I had questions but did not interrupt, hearing the passion in her voice. This was a subject touching her very being. James interrupted our musings and announced that it was coming on the dinner hour, and we needed to ride back or our cook would be put out if we were tardy. Once again, we had lost track of time.

On the ride back, she continued, the plot focused on Ralph Maitland, a member of the elite and the older generation who opposed his son's choice of a woman, Eliza Clairville, a lady not from an upper class or prominent family. His opposition was based on outdated notions of social hierarchy, believing our revolution's democratic promises would lead to disruptive changes in the social order and new attitudes about women's role in society. Virtue was triumphant when he met Eliza, who through the force of her principles, independence, and sound judgment changed his mind and, in the end, she was rewarded with social status and wealth. She stopped for a moment and asked what I thought of the play. Before I could answer, we were home.

Over dinner, I said the play's theme and plot were especially relevant, for it offered a fresh view for American women who were demanding equal rights and opportunities. The play avoided the notion of Republican Motherhood, which I personally found repugnant. This notion continued the view that women were merely educators of future, civic-minded male citizens with few legal rights and no access to the male-dominated education system. It sounded nice but did not deliver on our revolution's promise of liberty, equality, and freedom.

Her plot showed women could achieve success if given the opportunity to express their moral beliefs and expand their intellects. Her antagonist projected a self-confidence and self-discipline, born of a good education beginning as a young girl. I told her that in some ways, her story was autobiographical, to which she agreed. She also added that what she learned as a child lasted a lifetime, and that her education formed the foundation of her belief that any young girl or woman could realize their aspirations and overcome patriarchal traditions and antiquated arguments about proper social roles. She said that women could be wives, mothers, and intellectuals, and this scared men who did not want the competition and feared their loss of control over us. The play would touch a nerve, and I hoped to have the opportunity to see it performed. I then asked what her plans were to have it staged.

She said that my critique was on point, and I saw in the play what she hoped others would. Pausing for a moment, she then surprised me by saying, "I wish your plays could be performed. Having read them, I found your satirical style, mocking people's politics, personal behavior, and foibles, wonderfully entertaining. The themes were as pertinent today as they were during those tumultuous times of the Revolution. Liberty, equality, and freedom were universal precepts and never out of fashion." I thanked her but noted I doubted the current generation would understand or appreciate my sardonic humor in support of our cause. On the other hand, her cause was a worthy one, important today and for future generations of the female sex.

I then inquired as to the difficulty of staging the production. I thought it would be a challenge considering the best performers returned to England when the war broke out, leaving few experienced actors in America. And what about the belief among our Puritan and Calvinist brethren that the theatre was a corrupting influence on people's religious values and morals? Finally, would the Federal Street Theatre even reopen, given the need for financing?

She responded that she had thought about the same problems, saying, "Having spoken to the theatre management, I was especially concerned about the lack of trained or professional acting talent in Boston, and that production might also be a problem because there were even fewer people familiar with backstage tasks." She recognized the risk, but the reward was greater. One thing was certain: the Federal Street Theatre wanted to stage the production. Replying, I declared that with her determination, I had no doubt the production would be a success. Then I changed the focus of our conversation to her book project but before we started, I suggested we take the afternoon to rest, as I found a short nap in the afternoon revitalized my strength. She agreed that she could use some rest to refresh herself, noting that she was amazed how our conversations tired her out. I recalled Uncle Jonathan's statement that intellectual pursuits were sometimes more tiring than some physical labor.

At supper, we kept the conversation relaxed, speaking about our favorite authors. We agreed Shakespeare, Cervantes, Chaucer, Dante, Locke, Machiavelli, Pope, Dryden, Gibbon, and Swift and ancient authors like Homer, Tacitus, Herodotus, and Caesar were necessary for a true education. In literature, we debated the differences between dramatists like William Congreve, the Corneille brothers, Prosper Crebillon, Jean Racine, and Moliere. Judith asked me who were my favorite dramatists.

Thinking for a moment, I said I especially enjoyed Corneille's early comedies and *Le Cid*, his five-act tragedy set in Seville, Spain during the Middle Ages. I used this play as the historical foundation for the *Ladies of Castille*. Congreve appealed to me because he satirized fashionable English society's affectations and manners in the same way my plays lampooned the Tories and Loyalists. Shakespeare's tragedies were insightful for examining how personality flaws in characters inevitably led to tragic outcomes, and the historical plays depicted the struggle between individuals for power. Racine's tragedies depicted how men fall from prosperity to disaster; the higher the status from which the hero falls, the greater the tragedy. Crébillon's tragedies were melodramatic, notably his use of horror, which aimed to move audiences to pity through terror. Although Moliere's portrayals of human nature I found odious and Borgian, he was a superior dramatist. His themes, plots, characterizations, and use of language sounded to me like the solemn strains of the tragic muse, which had been more to my taste than the lighter representations in his plays. Yet, the follies and absurdities of human nature exposed to the ridicule in his masterful manner often had a greater tendency to reform humankind than some graver lessons of morality. I returned the favor by asking Judith who her favorite authors were.

She enjoyed the same dramatists as me, especially Moliere, the Corneille brothers, and Shakespeare. Beside dramatists, she was partial to female authors like Anne Bradstreet, Marie deGournay, Catharine Macaulay, May Montagu, Hannah More, Mary Wollstonecraft, Mary Astell, Stéphanie Félicité, Countess de Genlis, and me. When I protested being included with such renowned authors, she adamantly declared that I had earned the honor. Besides, how could she not include the woman who had the greatest influence on her writing and publishing career. Smiling at her gracious accolade, I noted my familiarity with Bradstreet, Macaulay, Montagu, and Wollstonecraft, but only had a passing acquaintance of the others. I asked her to describe their works so James could buy them when next he was in Boston. I was certain Thomas and Andrews would have them.

Marie deGournay, a seventeenth-century French author, was known as an early women's rights activist for her views on female education. She described the great women of the past who proved the ability of women to learn. She published *The Equality of Men and Women*, *The Ladies' Grievance*, and, after Michel de Montaigne's death, the third edition of his *Essays*. Caroline-Stéphanie-Félicité, Madame de Genlis, was well-known for her books about children's education, which used Rousseau's methods while criticizing his philosophical principles. Her works were notable for avoiding libertine and Roman Catholic concepts often associated with the French by the British, who welcomed her inventive, educational methods, particularly in her morality plays like *Adèle et Théodore*, which she had only recently read.

The English author Mary Astell wrote that women were just as rational as men, and just as deserving of education, and proposed a plan for an all-female college where women could pursue intellectual lives. She attacked Locke's deism and skepticism, arguing the soul and body distinction embedded within his larger argument was contrary to his doctrine of thinking matter. She viewed herself as a self-reliant woman and took immense pride in rescuing the female sex without the help of male authority, whom she believed kept women in a place of subjugation.

Meanwhile, poor James was trying to keep pace with our conversation, trying and failing to add his choices to the authors we were going on about. Having failed, he threw his hands in the air, saying that it was true when two women engaged in their favorite topic, they were deaf to everyone else. Turning, I asked if he had said something. He looked at both of us. "Nothing dearest," he said and returned to his coffee, still inaudibly muttering something to himself. Poor man appeared addled.

By the time we finished going through our mental libraries, it was time for a bath and bed. It had been a full day and speaking about our favorite authors was a revelation because in doing so, we were also describing our intellectual identities. Equally significant, we were defining the parameters of our relationship. Before retiring, I turned to James and asked if he could pick up any books by Marie deGournay, Madame de Genlis, and Mary Astell for me. Replying with a smirk, he said, "So now I am here." Judith and I looked quizzically at each other. James shaking and lowering his head in dismay, simply stated, "Of course." To this day, I have no idea what he was about that day.

The next morning at breakfast, we picked up our conversation about Judith's planned projects and my history of the Revolution. Judith began by telling us she had been writing a series of essays for her literary column in the *Massachusetts Magazine* under the pseudonym, "Gleaner." The essays would focus on politics in America, religious and moral themes, women's political equality, education, and financial independence. The plan was to compile current and future essays into a collection titled *The Gleaner*.

Margaretta, the novel's protagonist, was an intelligent young woman who fell prey to a sinister lover, rejected him, and forged an independent life for herself. The essays in the book would address issues with which Judith had experience, such as the sudden loss of fortune, imprisonment of debtors, suffering of lonely wives, and unexpected death of spouses. Other topics would include the principles of true religion, debtor's responsibilities, philanthropy, the Constitution, and partisan politics. She knew the work sounded broad but asked my opinion about it. While she concluded her narrative, I mused that her choice of preferred female authors had not been wasted. She was continuing their fight for female emancipation from our male-centered society.

Broad and encompassing indeed, I noted. However, the essay format offers great flexibility in moving from topic to topic. On another note, I told her to choose a different pseudonym, preferably a male one. She could not use the "Gleaner," as it gave away authorship to anyone who had read her essays in the *Massachusetts Magazine*. The other reason was as a woman, she would still be operating on the margins of a society that showed indifference, not to say outright contempt, for female productions. I described my experience when publishing my plays and poems in my name. It did not matter that I was the celebrated satirical propagandist who had supported the Revolution. I was a woman author, and this convinced me the book subscriptions suffered because of this social attitude.

Judith replied that I was correct about the pseudonym, but she suspected there would be those who figured it out regardless of what alias she selected. That was true, I replied, but if she believed this might be the case, she should be careful about crossing the line between her public, private, and secret life. She looked confused, obviously not understanding my statement. Reflecting in my mind about my secret authorship of the *Observations*, I noted that Catharine Macaulay, Mary Wollstonecraft, and other notable women authors had public personae. When we spoke yesterday about the women authors we preferred, I told her we were defining their public personae. And her published writings and themes defined her public image in the same way my writings and themes defined mine.

I explained that for good or bad, women authors were defined by the topics they wrote about. This was obvious, and we were critiqued accordingly by those who agreed or disagreed with our themes and philosophy. But we also had private lives and secret lives, which, in the current atmosphere about female productions, only served to give critics more ammunition to convince people to ignore her work and message. I amplified by saying her private life was known to her immediate family and close friends. Others might see pieces of this private world, or might guess about it, but it was all speculation. In a fashion, a person's home life was not a totally closed book.

However, there was the secret life, unknown to even family and friends. Everyone, regardless of who they might be, had secrets they did not want to extend into their public persona or private life. We guard this secret world and the embarrassing moments or past mistakes that would diminish, if not destroy, our public personae or private lives. We tell no one, absolutely no one, about this secret life. We take these secrets to our graves. The "Gleaner" must stay hidden and never expose her secret world to scrutiny. And with a stern emphasis, I asked if she understood.

I had given her much to think about, she replied. She never thought in terms of public, private, and secret lives. Her problem was that she had never been ashamed about who she was. She had drawn her essays from personal experience, the private life as I called it, and she needed to ensure personal experiences did not stray to the point they reflected on her directly. She would never endanger the secret world as I had termed it. I could see she was contemplating the problem, thinking it through and then, with a wide smile and eyes sparkling with enthusiasm, she said there was a solution to the identity problem. She then went on to outline her answer in a fashion that impressed me with its creativity.

Her response was subtle and effective. In describing the life and issues confronted by the protagonist, Margaretta, she could couch her identity by assuming a male persona, the "Gleaner," while using a female alias, Constantia, to show authorship. She would position herself in the narrative as the dominant male voice dispensing advice to fictitious male and female correspondents. This technique would confuse her gender to the point that the author's sex became irrelevant to the themes and messages of the stories. She then looked at me and asked what did I think?

I responded that her solution was perfect, elegant in fact. It would keep everyone guessing, to the point the readers assumed she was a man. I then noted I knew of no author who had devised or used a similar technique, adding I would find it interesting to see how it was received by the public. I then told her I looked forward to being her first subscription and asked her to tell me more over dinner about her other plans. But before doing so, we decided to stroll the estate and enjoy the delightful weather on this last day of her visit. We kept the conversation casual.

At dinner, she spoke of another play in the planning stage, *The Traveler Returned*. The story focused on Mr. Montague, the traveler, who deserted his family because his young wife was flirting or worse with other men. As she spoke, I thought to myself, *The subject was very provocative and racy, and Abigail would love it. It would feed her love of rumor and gossip, wondering who the play was really about.* When he reappeared in a disguise sometime later, he found his wife had endured and, unlike other doomed heroines, had neither died nor been consumed with guilt. Rather, she had become a scholar. She hoped the theme would further disparage the widely believed assumptions about the intellectual inferiority of women. Besides the *Gleaner* and her two plays, she would continue publishing her poems in the *Massachusetts Magazine*.

I told her the theme would help discredit the notion that women needed men to fulfill their lives. I especially liked the storyline about a man leaving his wife over real or imagined transgressions with other men. The play would turn heads and start tongues wagging. It was suggestive and spicy without being lurid, while the play's theme was new to the American stage. I could only imagine how the religious martinets would panic in their pulpits, preaching hellfire and damnation to all who attended the play. In their haste to condemn, their protestations would fill seats and ensure her success. Her play was the perfect example of a person's private and secret lives intersecting without casting aspersions on its author. It would leave the audience guessing and chattering about it after they left. I told her it was great, and James said he could not wait to see it performed. He could only imagine the looks on people's faces at such a titillating story. Her broad smile said it all, and I first saw a mischievous twinkle in her eyes.

I then noted that I could follow her poems moving forward but asked if she could send me some of her earlier ones, as I would very much like to read them. She nodded and has not disappointed, sending poems dealing with moral, religious, philosophical questions, and impressionable events, such as monologues about contemporary plays. One poem, in particular, I found fascinating because it argued against capital punishment. Overall, her poetry was enlightening, reflecting the personality of the woman I had come to know these three brief days. But I again am digressing from my main narrative.

I demurred asking about her opinion of the current state of our nation and, in particular, the increasing factionalism among the political class, especially the debate between the Anti-Federalists and Federalists over governance. From our earlier conversation, I knew she supported the Federalists with their belief in a strong central government, while I was an Anti-Federalist who advocated for a balance between states' rights and central governance. If I had learned anything about discussing politics, it was the fastest way to lose friends or create unnecessary personal discomfort. I had friends in the Federalist camp, which was why I kept my authorship of the *Observations* secret. I did, however, ask if she had read the *Observations* and the *Bill of Rights*. She said yes without offering an opinion on either document. She noted, however, that until women were given equal status, the *Constitution's Bill of Rights* were only words on paper. I left the conversation on that note, thinking to myself that it was best to concentrate on our similarities, not the everchanging differences of the political class.

During supper on our last evening together, we conversed about the struggles of being female authors in a male-centered society. We both agreed if society came to accept female productions, the message of the women's intellectual equality would be one step closer to reality. We then found ourselves returning to the subject of female education and the need to convince conservative-minded men that educated young girls and women posed no threat but were assets to them, bringing different strengths to relationships and society. Not an easy task considering the embedded sexism of American society, but we needed to try.

After we retired for the evening, I remember telling James I would miss this unique lady and thanked him for his patience these last few days. He looked at me, kissed my forehead, and said that he had not seen me this engaged in serious conversations since Catharine's visit. "You and Judith have a great deal in common, and I can see why she idolizes you, and you her," he said. He noticed a deference in her countenance when I spoke, saying that she was admiring me while we educated each other. He said he was proud of me and, by the by, I was certainly not too old to learn new ideas. With that, he planted another kiss on my cheek.

At breakfast, Judith and I were quietly eating when James declared that we both looked as if we had just returned from a funeral, adding that our cook might think we were not enjoying breakfast, and we knew how sensitive she was about her cooking. Judith apologized, saying she would have liked to have stayed longer. I told her the visit had passed too quickly, but I promised we would see each other again at her play's opening night, if not sooner.

Before she left, I gave her an autographed copy of my *Poems, Dramatic and Miscellaneous,* for which she thanked me and promised to send me a copy of *The Gleaner*. I reminded her of my promise to subscribe to the work, but I wanted a signed copy. As I watched she and James in the coach disappearing over the horizon, I felt the same sense of loss when Catharine and William left. Here was an exceptional woman whose career I had influenced but who had exceeded me in talent and intellectual gifts. For the time she was with me, I felt more the student. This delicate lady with penetrating, sparkling eyes and delicate fingers taught me the promise of the Revolution was alive and well in women who were demanding more freedom and equality. We, of course, continued to correspond, and I did see her multiple times: at the openings of her three plays in Boston, her visit with me after the death of James in 1808, and my visit to her in Boston a year later when her husband suffered a stroke. In between, we continue communicating by letter.

When James returned after dropping her off, he said the trip was uneventful, except she did all the talking, and that meeting me was a dream come true. She found me a like-minded spirit who believed in the same things and had the same aspirations for women. She just could not stop speaking of me in glowing terms. At one point, she had James promise, he would intercede on her behalf to have my plays staged. She said in a very authoritative voice that my name being iconic in Boston, no less the state and country, she was convinced the Federal Street Theatre would want to produce the renown Mrs. Warren's plays. She then added she would raise the subject directly in a future letter. He then gave me a carefully wrapped package containing Mary Astell's *By a Lover of her Sex, A Serious Proposal to the Ladies for the Advancement of their True and Greatest Interest presents*, and *A Serious Proposal Wherein a Method is offered for the Improvement of their Minds*. He could not find deGournay or de Genlis, but Thomas and Andrews promised to buy copies for me. I simply smiled and thanked him, kissing him on the cheek.

I continued to follow Judith's career, reading her essays and poems in the *Massachusetts Magazine,* and, as promised, James and I attended opening night and the next evening's performance of *The Medium, or Virtue Triumphant* when it debuted at the Federal Street Theatre in 1795, the first play by an American woman author performed in Boston. As we had suspected, the play's opening night suffered because of a hastily rehearsed performance, but the second night was much better. The cast seemed to have gotten over their opening night jitters. But a damaging review by Robert Treat Paine Jr., son of my revolutionary compatriot and supporter, implied the author was her husband. Besides being an outright lie, the review was slanderous and intended to damage her reputation. After reading this piece of verbal trash, I dashed off a letter to her. I noted the play did not receive critical acclaim because of a biased review by a jealous man who was a failed playwright and a social conservative that did not subscribe to female productions. As expected, her response was brief, saying such attacks only served to make her redouble efforts as a playwright.

The following year, James and I attended opening night and the second performance of *The Traveler Returned*. Although the audience enjoyed the performances and spoke glowingly about the storyline, it also was not well-received because, once again, Mr. Paine wrote a critical review. He seemed intent on thwarting her career as a dramatist. I wrote to Judith, telling her not to despair; this was obviously the work of a man who feared successful women. Once again, she told me so long as the theatre staged them, the managers supervised production, and actors appeared in them, she would continue writing; Mr. Paine be damned.

I remember receiving my signed copy of, *The Gleaner, A Miscellaneous Production*, which was a masterful crafted series of essays and wonderfully devious. How creative, disguising herself as a male with female pseudonym, dispensing advice and opinions on social, financial, and political matters to fictitious male and female characters corresponding with the "Gleaner." The best part came at the end in her last essay when she announced that she, the male Constantia, was in fact a female, and that the "Gleaner's" correspondents were of her own invention. A truly virtuoso performance. The great Machiavelli himself would have been proud beyond words: the triple pleasure of deceiving the deceived by a deceiver. Her talent was in the tradition of Macaulay, Montagu, Wollstonecraft, Astell, More, and others of our sex arguing for female equality, and told her so in my next letter.

Then in 1802, I received a letter announcing she had founded a school for girls in Dorchester. I wrote that this was a great personal achievement and showed her commitment to women's education and equality. Simply said, she had done what she had promised. She mentioned in the letter that I was the subject of one of her lectures, citing me as a real-life example of a married woman who was recognized by our Founding Fathers as an expert in constitutional law, as well as a poet, playwright, historian, and revolutionary activist. I told my students that I proved women were as intellectually capable as men. She even had her students read my plays and poems, to which I felt very flattered and humbled. In my next correspondence, I applauded her accomplishment as a major step toward women's equality.

In 1804, James and I attended the opening of *The African*, but it too did not receive critical recognition. Once again, Mr. Paine was the antagonist with his typical criticism of a female production. I found it difficult to imagine any woman wanting to be with this insufferable fool. He was certainly not his father's son. The Robert Treat Paine I had known was an intelligent, well-spoken, and open-minded gentleman who would have been repelled by his son's behavior. The following year, Judith sent me a wonderful letter, informing me that she had received her signed copy of my history. Within weeks, I received another correspondence telling me the work would propel me into the annals of history as the first woman to pen a history of our struggle for independence. Her last correspondence, not more than a month ago, informed me she would visit soon, John's health permitting. An interesting aside is that each time we meet, I continue to be fascinated by her eyes. They opened a window into her mind and soul.

Plymouth, Friday, 4 March 1814

Chapter 18

A LIFE WORTH LIVING

I close this journal with reflections on my achievements, failures, and regrets. As I look back on my life's journey, Dante's opening lines come to mind as he was standing at the gates of hell in the *Divine Comedy*: "Midway upon the journey of our life I found myself within a forest dark, For the straightforward pathway had been lost." There were moments in my life when I could not see the path forward but continued my journey in the hope of reaching personal fulfillment. I faced these moments of doubt by confronting the obstacles hindering my quest, husbanding the inner strength to not surrender to despair.

This journal will remain a secret, an unpublished one. Rather, this narrative is for future generations of the Warren family to know their ancestor's participation in and contribution to the founding of our great country, and about the family and celebrated personages who influenced my personal and intellectual journey. I have spoken with Henry, Mary, and James Jr., expressing the wish that they, and later heads of households, male or female, read the journal to their children when they reach majority. In this way, my history, the family's history, and the history of America's founding is passed down to future generations.

I could not include everyone who passed through my life but adding these vignettes would have made the journal too long. I have tried to describe my family as best as possible, but the exclusion of some does not diminish their importance in my life. My beloved James and my five sons, of whom only Henry and James Jr. remain, are my greatest achievements. I had the good fortune of falling passionately in love with a man who was as much a partner and confidant as he was a husband. He was throughout our marriage an enthusiastic supporter of my intellectual goals and activities, lifting my spirits during those times when tragedy struck or I doubted my abilities. To this day, I think of this loving and caring man every day.

I am immensely proud of what my sons accomplished and, to this day, mourn the three lost. As they matured, I grew with them and even though we might disagree, I always felt their love, respect, and admiration. My only regret was not having a daughter with whom I could share my love of knowledge and experiences of life; a little girl whom I could spoil and who, as an adult, would have demanded more from our society about the role of our sex.

My first accomplishment, other than surviving my birth and the illnesses that cut short so many young lives, was my non-traditional education. I had the rare opportunity, available to very few young girls of my generation, to study the great authors and ideas with my brother and uncle. I had full and free access to Uncle's extensive library and, more importantly, was able to have spirited discussions with a liberal-minded man who challenged me at every turn. Uncle Jonathan treated me as an equal, no different than any other male student. He was demanding, teaching me not just about what to read but how to think objectively and perceive an author's meaning. I learned to look for the hidden meanings by reading between the lines of the narrative to understand the author's context and motivation. He was my Virgil, guiding me through the labyrinth of learning and to whom I owe my intellectual achievements.

Less a regret and more a wish, I would have liked to have attended Latin School and Harvard College, if only to experience the formal learning process in environments where I could challenge my intellectual knowledge and skills with groups of male peers and instructors. Of course, if my friend Hannah Winthrop's letters were any indication, I would not have fitted in with the ruckus lifestyle she described. But it would have been interesting if only for a fleeting time. Someday, I hope young ladies will have access to the formal education process and the opportunity to enter those professions currently denied them because of our sex.

My study of the law was the next achievement. From Uncle Jonathan, my brother, and father, I learned to love the law and how it formed the foundation of ordered societies and cultures. I learned the law evolved from the legal systems of ancient Greece and Rome to English Common Law to the *Declaration of Independence* and *Constitution*. Recognized as an expert in constitutional and English Common Law by the powerful men founding our nation was a singular triumph because it proved a woman could reach the same intellectual heights as any man. I corresponded or spoke with the Founders of our great nation about constitutional and legal issues and how they applied to our situation, whether it was prior to or after the Revolution.

My only regret, more a frustration, was not being able to practice the law which I loved. I would have enjoyed litigating an important case in front of a tribunal, using my knowledge and passion to win a victory for a client or larger cause affecting society. Even today, it still rankles that as a female, I was denied my wish because of antiquated social conventions. I hope in the future America allows women to practice law because I believe in my heart we would make effective advocates, bringing a feminine perspective to jurisprudence.

My accomplishments as a poet, dramatist, and historian are other successes of which I am proud. But it was not simply that as a woman I wrote in these genres; it was the reason for their publication. My five plays supported our revolutionary cause. I was honored to take part in and contribute to the fight for liberty and creation of our great nation by using my pen. However, I do have regrets about my plays. I would like to have seen my dramas staged. I certainly had an advocate, more an unofficial agent in Judith, who wrote that she believed the Federal Street Theatre would be extremely interested in producing the work of the famous Mrs. Warren.

But this regret was only an excuse to conceal my fear about bad reviews. Having seen the poor reviews of Judith's plays, I was concerned my dramas would suffer the same fate because I was a woman, regardless of name recognition or reputation. Unlike my dear friend, who took criticism without umbrage, I would have exploded, being someone who did not suffer fools, especially sexist fools. In the end, I lacked the courage to take the chance. To her lasting credit, Judith has never let me feel awkward about my decision, continuing to tell me they deserved staging so audiences could bear witness to my talent and contribution to American independence.

My next regret was not having the first five plays included in the *Poems, Dramatic and Miscellaneous*. My reasoning at the time was it would have made the work a two- or three-volume collection with the associated problem of making subscriptions more difficult. Furthermore, I had just completed my last two plays, *The Sack of Rome* and *Ladies of Castille*, was doing research on the history, and preparing the *Observations*, and my recurring health problems drained my strength, making it difficult to pursue the idea. But I could have published them separately and have no excuse for not doing so. Just another regret, but not one over which I lose sleep.

My greatest achievement and contribution to our country's founding was the *Observations on the New Constitution*. This pamphlet, written at the request of the Constitutional Convention's Anti-Federalist faction, was different from my plays and poems, which were satirical propaganda devices supporting the fight for liberty. The *Observations*, my first journey into contemporary real politics, blended my knowledge of history, philosophy, and constitutional and English Common Law to challenge the arguments in the *Federalist*. I was gratified that some of my recommendations became amendments in the *Bill of Rights*.

My biggest regret was not issuing the pamphlet in my name. At the time, the decision for anonymity was based on the potential political consequences for my husband and sons, who I believed would lose patronage positions in the new federal government if my authorship became known. I was wrong, my political acumen having abandoned me. Now, in hindsight, I should have known better. I forgot no secret stays a secret for long when political power struggles were involved. I am now convinced my authorship was known by those in the Federalist camp, like Messrs. Jay, Madison, and Hamilton, who had read my earlier works and knew my literary style and political leanings. In the end, the patronage jobs never appeared from either Presidents Washington or Adams. And now, even though they may have known it was me who authored *The Observations*, they would have not advertised it publicly because this knowledge would have forced them to admit to Americans that a woman influenced the amendments in the *Bill of Rights*.

The next contribution of which I am proud was the publication of the three-volume *History of the Rise, Progress, and Termination of the American Revolution*, the first written by an American woman. The book encompasses the period from the *Stamp Act* crisis to the ratification of our Constitution. As critics pointed out, the work held controversial views about the Revolution, but I stand by my opinions regardless of their criticisms. Although I began the history in the 1780s, it was finally published in 1805 because of my involvement in the constitutional debates, publication of my last two plays, the *Poems, Dramatic and Miscellaneous*, and the deaths of three of my sons, dear friends, and my increasing health problems. But in the end, it was published.

My regret was my loss of perspective as an objective observer because Mr. Adams had not offered a government position to my husband James or my sons Henry and James Jr. Based on personal animus over the patronage issue, I besmirched his good name. I paid the price for this error in judgment with the estrangement from my dear friend

Abigail. I can only thank Mr. Gerry for brokering our reconciliation. Although John and Abigail have forgiven my dreadful behavior, for me, it was a stain on my history I cannot forgive. I would be negligent as a historian if I did not speak briefly on the recent and other contemporary events I believe important to America.

When Mr. Jefferson took the office as America's Chief Magistrate in 1800, the country was rift with factionalism between the old-line Federalist and new Jeffersonian Democratic-Republican factions. Even though Messrs. Jefferson and Adams had drafted the Declaration of Independence together, they became political rivals starting with the election of 1796, which saw Mr. Adams, a Federalist, become president. Mr. Jefferson, placing second, become vice president, and later defeated Mr. Adams in a poisonous election in 1800 to become president. Since then, these two old friends have not spoken. This was one result of the evil specter of party factionalism.

As president, Mr. Jefferson did a great deal. He actively supported our young nation's shipping and trade interests, defeated the Barbary pirates, and worked against aggressive British trade policies. In 1803, he promoted western expansion by buying the Louisiana Territory, which increased our land area, and dispatched Captain Meriwether Lewis and Lieutenant William Clark to explore the newly acquired lands. Unfortunately, he began the repugnant processes of removing native tribes from their lands to make room for the new settlers and allowing slavery to flourish in the new territory. Another result of the peace negotiations with Napoleon Bonaparte allowed him to reduce the size of our army which, as later events proved, was not a clever idea.

During his second term, he confronted the treason trial of his former Vice President, Aaron Burr, and weakening foreign trade when he implemented the *Embargo Act* in response to British threats to American shipping interests. This action laid the foundation for our current war with Britain. But to his credit, he signed the *Act Prohibiting Importation of Slaves,* but this did little to stop the import of Africans to the southern states.

Although I could respect his political judgement and successes in many cases, I cannot forgive his support for the odious three-fifths compromise to get the Constitution ratified by the southern states, his support of the abhorrent institution of slavery, and his personal ownership of hundreds of enslaved Africans. In this regard, he proved my maxim that the human character opens at once a beautiful and deformed picture of the soul. It was his aristocratic southern plantation class whose excess of wealth and train of domestic slaves had banished any sense of liberty for those so shackled and deserving of the rights and privileges spoken of in the *Declaration of Independence* and *Constitution*. Our country will rue the day this evil institution continues to thrive in a country built on the foundations of liberty and equality.

Our nation's current Chief Magistrate is James Madison and our old and dear family friend, Eldridge Gerry, his Vice President. But we are now engaged in a war after the failure of negotiations with the French and British. Of course, this War of 1812 is just another one of those never-ending European hegemonic conflicts that the continent seems impossible to escape. We read in the press the reason for this war is America's national honor. To this, I say balderdash. It is really about the economic and trade disputes between the America, Britain, and France, but the direct cause for the war involved the British navy, who saw fit, in their hubris, to stop and seize American ships on the open ocean and impress their crews who they claimed were British subjects but included American citizens. No country has the right to seize another country's ships on the high seas and hold its citizens hostage without a charge of piracy leveled against the offending party or parties.

Although the British have had success in their land battles, our infant navy has acquitted itself well, and our army did defeat Chief Tecumseh, a British ally, and his native confederacy at the Battle of the Thames in our northwest territory, recovering the eastern part of this territory from the British. How long this conflict will continue I do not know, but I believe we will prevail because our cause is just. I believe history and present events can say much about what might happen in the future, so I offer my opinion as a historian about where I see America moving forward.

In a country founded on liberty and equality, it is unfathomable that half the population is denied basic political rights and equal educational opportunities because of their sex. Democratic principles are the result of equality of condition. At some point in the future, America must address the dismal condition of the female sex, which is no better than indentured servitude. The same is true for the institution of slavery, outdated laws of coverture, and the treatment of the native tribes who have inhabited America for centuries and whose property rights are ignored to accommodate the new settlers.

Their treatment begs the question, do not women, slaves, and native tribes have the same rights as any other American? Are they not citizens of our country? If the words of the *Declaration of Independence* and *Constitution* hold any value, then for me, it is self-evident these groups are all created equal to everyone else and endowed by our Creator with the same unalienable rights as everyone else to wit, life, liberty, and the pursuit of happiness. If America cannot provide these basic liberties to large, oppressed minorities, then the words in these documents are not worth the paper upon which they are written. If these injustices remain uncorrected, I fear it will lead to revolution or civil war, which might well end our republican experiment. Of equal import to our nation's survival is the evil of factionalism.

President Washington warned against the threat of factionalism or political parties, which over the course of time become a powerful mechanism and, through the cunning of ambitious and unprincipled men, subvert the power of the people and assume for themselves the reins of government. I agree with his statement, for there are few men with sufficient virtue to withstand the highest bidder. But when factions or political parties are fighting for power, they are prone to ignore the needs and rights of the people. This was the main reason

I recommended term limits to minimize the corrupting influence of money, which will have an adverse influence on government policy, laws, and sound governance. I remain convinced there exists a tendency among humans to tyrannize their fellow man because the bulk of humanity fall prey to greed and ambition.

I would also combine sectionalism with factionalism, which can also have a corrupting effect on good government. We in the north are predisposed to manufactures, while those in the south are wedded to the land. We in the northern states are individualists who are manufacturers, merchants, businessmen, seamen, and farmers, while our southern brethren rely on chattel slavery to produce cotton and tobacco, living like European aristocrats in blissful denial that they are treating other human beings as subhuman. These differences will influence the social and political landscape of America, and I can assure the reader the corrupting influence of power and money will be at the center.

Finally, *the Preamble to the Constitution* states that we the people of the United States, in order to form a more perfect union, I find disingenuous. There is no perfection because we humans are imperfect creatures. We might strive in our endeavors to reach perfection, but we will inevitably fail. The best we can hope for is to create the most favorable outcomes possible, recognizing history is replete with examples of societies whose search for perfection led to imperfect and destructive results. Realizing the words in our *Declaration of Independence* and *Constitution* will be a never-ending search to achieve as near to perfection as humanly possible. The people must always be aware that change is inevitable, but we the people must always guard against would-be tyrants, promising perfection while destroying liberty. I will now turn my concluding thoughts to the dearest friends, Abigail, Catharine, and Judith, who influenced my life and shared my aspirations.

Having spoken of Abigail in an earlier chapter, there was one more factor explaining her growth from the reticent, young woman to the woman I know today. As she matured, she found herself married to a powerful man charting the course of the republic. She rose to the occasion by using her personal skills and intellect to not only support her husband but strengthen his position of power. She saw herself as an equal partner in John's rise, even if he did not recognize it. I had always believed, and still do, that John was a powerful man, but when it came to Abigail, he was less the empowered man than he or anyone realized.

She was a complex woman, like all of us, with various sides to her personality. The controlling, flirtatious, manipulative, and puckish Abigail, who looked to control situations or people, concealed her insecurity as a woman existing on the margins of a society that considered women as nothing more than wives, mothers, and domestic managers with no voice in public affairs. I know of no woman who did not feel this way, and I include myself in this assessment. To hide this vulnerability, we offered reasons, more excuses, to conceal this weakness. I used a pseudonym as a protective shield to avoid confronting criticism for stepping outside my designated social role as a woman. For my friend, her power rested in the ability to read people. Rumors were the fodder for her to exercise control. Gossip was not idle talk; it was about exercising power over those she perceived as competitors to her husband or family.

We were opposites. I saw my life as a balance between distinct roles, two different worlds. I was proud of being the traditional wife and mother who was also a recognized legal scholar, poet, dramatist, pamphleteer, historian, and revolutionary activist. My power existed in the pen, but I was no less insecure and vulnerable as Abigail or any other women existing on the margins of a sexist society. I would be less than candid if I did not admit that I fed off her personality. She brought out the side of my personality that would not have existed without her presence. I lived vicariously through her experiences and, in doing so, found a person who I could call friend. We all have our strengths and weaknesses, and my personal observations do not take away from the truth that she is my dearest friend, who has always supported me in my endeavors. Yes, we were opposites but that was the strength of our bond.

My friendship with Catharine was a different, unique experience. From our first letters, we both sensed an instant bond based on shared aspirations and intellectual goals for our respective countries and sex. Like me, the pen was her weapon. When she and her husband visited us, our bond became stronger. She was my mentor, the woman who I looked to emulate. She was celebrated throughout the realm as the leading historian and activist with no consideration for her sex. For me, meeting her and sharing conversations about diverse topics was a dream come true, but she too had her vulnerabilities. These did not diminish her person or celebrity in my mind, but they proved we women lived on the fringes of narrow-minded societies who patronized our intellectual abilities until we crossed an imaginary line defined by the social conventions established by men.

Whereas Abigail closely guarded her public, private, and secret lives, Catharine was more open. She was a woman with a very public persona. Where I hid behind a pseudonym, she published in her name, which meant she was open to criticism for supporting unpopular causes. This took great courage because England was as sexist as America. But she was the celebrated Mrs. Macaulay, which kept her critics silent, fearing the backlash from her supporters. Her public and private lives was continually under scrutiny. She appeared often in newspapers, who reported on her health, dining habits, and who visited her. Print sellers and street vendors sold her portraits, and she was even honored with a porcelain doll. She was even mentioned, in jest of course, as a future candidate for Parliament, the next royal historiographer, or the person who best personified the muse of history. But she had a wonderful sense of humor for one in the public eye. When I asked about the rumor that she had allowed herself to be worshipped like a queen by male admirers, she noted this was malicious gossip and then wrote cheerily that her being a queen was absurd, and that

Queens Cleopatra, Zenobia, and Elizabeth would be turning somersaults in their graves, laughing until their sides ached.

She had no private life and even her secret life was subject to speculation, especially after her marriage to William, a man half her age. The hateful attacks would have affected most men, no less a woman, but not Catharine. She weathered the storm of the vicious gossip and effects of being spurned by former friends. As I learned, she cared nothing for rumors and gossip mongers. She was who she was and that was that. She continued to voice her support for dissidents and causes she believed important to all Englishmen and women. Regardless of the professional and personal attacks, she was still an international celebrity, a woman of great intellectual and emotional depth.

Her candor was refreshing and insights into good governance enlightening. She argued eloquently for the rotation of members of Parliament, which I later used in my *Observations* to argue for representative term limits. She also was intuitive, blaming the corruption in government on a press which did not report on important political issues for fear of retribution. She knew an unfettered, responsible press was vital in controlling the excesses of government, but as she noted, the English press had become a party to the corruption by focusing on celebrities, gossip, scandals, and fashion. This became another point I emphasized in the *Observations*. In fact, her insights into our government organization led her to comment that we needed a constitutional convention to correct the failings in the *Articles of Confederation*, something that happened within two years of her visit to America.

I know her visit with other revolutionary leaders, including General Washington, only proved what I had told her; she would have been welcomed as an American heroine should she choose to stay in our country. Later, during the latter part of the constitutional debates, she guessed I authored the *Observations* and, to her credit, took my secret to the grave. In two short weeks, she became a treasured friend who I truly wished had stayed in America. When she passed in June 1791, my heart experienced an empty and melancholy feeling for weeks. I remember her each day in the same way I do my husband James, children, parents, my brothers and sisters, and Uncle Jonathan and Aunt Mercy, most of whom I have outlived. She was that one special person who crosses once in a lifetime, and I am proud to say I am honored she crossed mine.

The third woman who influenced me was the youngest but as equally intelligent and intuitive as Catharine, but with a different, adventurous spirit. As noted previously, our meeting happened through a series of coincidences, which I can only describe as ethereal. Judith's petite frame and delicate features concealed a strong-willed, blunt, and religious woman who dedicated her intellect to woman's independence from the shackles of the male-centered society. She was very much an example of the new generation of women who were demanding better opportunities for our sex. Where Catharine and I wrote about women's political and legal equality and education, Judith did something about it. When she spoke of founding a female academy, she did it. She did not just theorize; she acted. There were no hidden meanings in her conversations or writings.

Judith, like Catharine and myself, had experienced a similar education, but her reading concentrated on female authors and leaders from history who exemplified the idea that educated, independent, and strong women could be as successful as men in any profession. In her view, a good education would allow women to make independent decisions about their futures and free themselves from the constraints of outdated social norms concerning marriage and motherhood. I believed Judith did not subscribe to the idea of Republican Motherhood or thought the idea of spinsterhood somehow demeaning. So long as a woman was happy with her life choices, why should she be concerned about whether she married? I could not help but agree with her arguments, as they were so well-crafted. She believed marriage and children was a normal social convention for women and men, but matrimony was a partnership of equals with shared responsibilities, not one based on male dominance or subservience to tradition.

Not being an overly religious partisan myself, I found her Universalism appealing. Their dogma was a breath of fresh air when I thought of having attended the structured Puritan observances, listening to fire-and-brimstone sermons preaching hell and damnation. I definitely agreed with Universalism's support of women's education, defense of dissidents, and the separation of church and state. What also impressed me was that she was not a proselytizer looking to convince me of the worthiness of her denomination versus another. She simply described the dogma and left it at that. But this and other traits also opened a window into her personality.

I found in Judith a woman much like Catharine, who showed courage and decisiveness, and a woman determined to succeed regardless of the obstacles put in her path. She reacted to the criticism of her plays by continuing to show self-confidence in herself and enthusiasm for her art. She was a free spirit born in the vision of our revolution, believing anything to which she applied her mind was possible. But with all these attributes, she was a kind, gracious, and thoughtful woman who, to my everlasting frustration, continues to push me to stage my plays. She is a a genuine friend for whom I have a deep affection and admiration.

As I look back on my life and the momentous events in which I particpated, they do not come near to those persons who brought joy into my life. I had the good fortune to marry a man who treated me as an equal and a partner. I had children who, regardless of their different personalities, always made me proud. As to my close friends, like Abigail, Catharine, Judith, and other family members and friends, I could not have asked more. They were genuine, considerate, and giving of their time, respect, and affection. For my family's future generations, for which this journal is penned, I offer the following message.

Remember the words of the great Roman poet, Virgil: "Time passes irrevocably." So, cherish each day as if it is your last. Live each day knowing you live in a country of boundless potential, opportunity, and energy. Do not be a spectator, drifting through life because in the end, the measure of a successful life is your participation in and contribution to yourself, your family, your friends, and your country. Be tolerant and respectful of others, especially with those with whom you disagree and bear no one ill will. And at the end of day, thank the Lord you have lived a good life, if only for that day. So ends my journal, my journey through a life worth living. A final thought, one thing I do know for sure: Uncle Jonathan would be pleased; there are no marginalia.

Fini
Plymouth, Thursday, 7 April 1814

APPENDIX
MERCY WARREN'S READING LIST

Mercy Warren's reading history is a revised version of the original published in the author's dissertation and includes books and authors discovered through additional research. The books were cited in her personal correspondence and published works, as well as her other readings from the Latin School and pre-university tutorial curricula. The revised list does not include all the newspapers, pamphlets, broadsides, and periodicals which Mercy Warren would have read in much the same way we read newspapers, magazines, and online news today. The reader should note an eighteenth-century young girl's education was limited to learning how to read and subjects associated with her future responsibilities as a wife, mother, and household manager. Mercy Warren was an exemption to the rule because she demanded more for herself and achieved a level of excellence recognized by our Founding Fathers. The reading history offers an illustration of the extent of her reading experience, literary preferences, and intellectual development.

READING CATEGORIES

HISTORY

John Adams,
> *Dissertation of the Feudal and Canon Law; Thoughts on Government* ... (1776)
> *A Defense of the Constitution of the United States* (1787).
> *Discourses on Davila* (1790)

William Aglionby, *The Present State of the United Provinces* (1669)

John Arbuthnot, *The History of John Bull* (1727)

George Anson, *Voyage Round the World* (1748)

Johann Eustachius Görtz, *The Secret History of the Armed Neutrality* ... (1792)

Jean Barthelemy, *Travels of Anarcharsis* (1790)

William Blesham, *Memoirs of the Reign of George III* ... *1793*, 4 Vol. (1795)

James Bowdoin, *A Short Narrative... of the Massacre in Boston* (1770)

Hugh Brackenridge,
> *The Battle of Bunker Hill* (1776)
> *The Death of General Montgomery...* (1777)
> *Insurrection in the Western Parts of Pennsylvania* (1795)

William Bradford, *History of Plymouth Colony* (1630)

Patrick Brydone, *Tour through Sicily and Malta* (1775)

Leonardo Bruni, *History of the War Against the Goths, tr.* by Arthur Golding

Julius Caesar, *The Commentaries of Caesar,* tr. by Arthur Golding (1565)

Antoine Cerisier, *Tableau de l'Histoire Generale des Provinces-Unis* (1777)

A Compendium of the Most Approved Modern Travels. Containing a distinct account of the religion, government, commerce, manners, and natural history of several nations (1757)

Gabriel Francoise Coyer, *The History of John Sobieski, King of Poland* (1767)

Philip Francis, *A state of the British authority in Bengal ...* (1780)

William Findley, *History of the Insurrection in ... Pennsylvania, in the Year 1794* (1796)

Edward Gibbon, *Decline and Fall of the Roman Empire* (1776-1789)

Frederick II of Prussia & Leopold II Holy Roman Emperor, *Declaration of Pillnitz* (1791)

Gaius Julius Solinus, *The Polyhistor of Gaius Julius Solinus*, tr. by Arthur Golding

Francis Godwin, *Annales of England* (1706)

Thomas Godwin, *Romanæ Historiæ Anthologia. An English Exposition ...* (1614)

Alexander Gordon, *The Lives of Pope Alexander VI, and His Son Cesare Borgia* (1779)

William Gordon, *The History of the Rise, Progress ... of the United States of America* (1788)

Catharine Sawbridge Macaulay Graham,
   The History of England from the Accession of James I ... 8 vol. (1763 – 1783)
   Loose Remarks on Certain Positions to be found in Mr. Hobbes's ... (1767)
   Observations on a Pamphlet Entitled Thoughts ... on the Present Discontents (1770)
   An Address to the People of England, Scotland, and Ireland ... (1775)
   Treatise on the Immutability of Moral Truth (1783)
   Observations on the Reflections of the Rt. Hon. Edmund Burke ... (1790)
   Letter on Education (1790)

David Hartley, John Adams, Benjamin Franklin, John Jay, *The Definitive Treaty of Peace ...*

Benjamin West, *Treaty of Paris* (1783)

John Jay, *The Treaty of Amity, Commerce, and Navigation, Between His Britannic Majesty and the United States of America* (1794)

Herodotus, *The History of Herodotus*, tr. by Isaac Littlebury (1737)

Marcus Junianus Justinus, *The Abridgement of the histories of Trogus Pompeius*, tr. by Arthur Goldyng (1564)

William King, *An Historical Account of the Heathen Gods and Heroes ... the Ancient Poets* (1711)

Titus Livy, *Roman History*, tr. by Edmund Bohun (1686)

Gabriel Bonnot de Mably
   Observations sur les Romain (1751)
   Remarks Concerning the Government of the United States of America (1784)
   Observations on the Greeks (1770)
   Observations sur l'Histoire de France (1765).

John Marshall, *The Life of George Washington* (1804)

John-Thomas Minadoi, *The History of the Warres betweene the Turkes and the Persians...* tr. by Abraham Hartwell

Edward Montague, *Reflections on the Rise and Fall of the Ancient Republics* (1759)

Marchamont Nedham,
  The Case of the Commonwealth of England Stated (1650)
  The Excellence of a Free-State (1656)
  A Short History of the English Rebellion (1661)

Marcus Porcius Cato, *Grammatically Directing for Understanding ...*, tr. by John Brinsley (1612)

Francis Osborne,
  Traditional Memoirs of the Reigns of Q. Elizabeth and King James I (1658)
  A Seasonable Expostulation with the Netherlands (1652)
  Political Reflections upon the Government of the Turks (1656)

Thomas Osborne, *A Universal History, from the Earliest Account of Time ...* (1747-1768)

Odoardo Lopez, *A Report of the Kingdome of Congo, a Region of Africa And of the Countries that border ... Drawen out of the writings and discourses of Odoardo Lopez ... by Philippo Pigafetta,* tr. by Abraham Hartwell (1597)

Pelopidas, *Life of Pelopidas in the Lives of Illustrious Men,* tr. by Hon. Mr. Finch, Mr. Creech, and others (1713)

Pliny the Elder, *Pliny the Elder's The Historie of the World,* tr. by Philemon Holland (1601)

Plutarch, *Plutarch's Morals, Laconick Apothegms, or remarkable sayings of the Spartans,* tr. by Thomas Creech (1684)

Plutarch, *Lives of Solon, Pelopidas, and Cleomenes in Plutarch's Lives,* 5 vols., tr. by Thomas Creech (1683-1686)

Lucius Plutarch, *Lives of Illustrious Greeks and Romans,* tr. by John Dryden (1683)

Polybius, *The History of Polybius ... with A character of Polybius,* tr. by John Dryden (1698)

Pomponius Mela, *The Geography of Pomponius Mela,* tr. by Arthur Golding (1585)

Publius Cornelius Tacitus,
The Modern Courtier: or the morals of Tacitus upon flattery (1687)
Works of Tacitus with Political Commentary ... tr. by Thomas Gordon (1753)

Samuel Pufendorf,
Introduction to the History of the Principal Kingdoms and States of Europe (1719)
History of Sweden (1702)
Of the Law of Nature and Nations (1729)

Walter Raleigh, *History of the World* (1621)

Allan Ramsay, *Historical Essay on the English Constitution* (1771)

David Ramsay, *The History of the American Revolution* (1789)

Edmund Randolph, *Essay on the Revolutionary History of Virginia 1774-1782*

Guillaume Raynal, *History of the Two Indies* (1751)

William Robertson,
History of the Reign of the Emperor Charles V (1764)
History of America (1776)

Charles Rollin,
The Roman History (1768)
The History of the Arts and Sciences of the Ancients (1768)
The Ancient History of the Egyptians, Carthaginians, Assyrians, Babylonians ... (1768)

Seneca the Younger, *The De Beneficiis of Seneca the Younger,* tr. by Arthur Golding (1578)

William Sewel, *The History of the Rise, Increase, and Progress ... called Quakers ...* (1728)

George Shelvocke, *A Voyage Round the World by Way of the Great South Sea* (1723)

Suetonius, *The Historie of Twelve Caesars*, tr. by Philemon Holland (1606)

Tobias Smollett,
A complete history of England: from the descent of Julius Caesar ... (1758)
Travels through France and Italy (1766)

Lazaro Soranzo, *The Ottoman of Lazaro Soranzo. Wherein is delivered ... a full and perfect report of the might and power of Mahomet the third, ... peoples, Countries, Cities, and Voyages ... present Warre in Hungarie*, tr. by AbrahamHartwell (1603)

John Swinton, et. al., *A Universal history, from the earliest account of time ...* (1763)

Stanbury Thompson, *The Journal of John Gabriel Stedman, soldier and author ... to Surinam in 1772* (1797)

Thucydides, *History of the Peloponnesian War*, tr. by Thomas Hobbes (1628)

George Washington,
Articles of Capitulation, Yorktown (1781)
Farewell Orders to the Army of the United States (1783)

Alexander Wedderburn, *American Revolutionary Era notes and Writings* (1773-1778)

Samuel Williams, *Natural and Civil History of Vermont* (1794)

Mary Wollstonecraft,
An Historical and Moral View ... of the French Revolution (1795)
A Vindication of the Rights of Woman ... (1794)

Xenophon, *Xenophon's Cyropaedia*, tr. by Philemon Holland (1632)

PHILOSOPHY, POLITICAL THEORY, LAW

Parliamentary Enactments,
> *Doomsday Book*
> *Assizes of Claredon*
> *Magna Carta*
> *English Bill of Rights of 1698*
> *Writ of Assistance of 1761*
> *The Proclamation of 1763*
> *The Currency Act of 1764*
> *Sugar Act of 1764*
> *Quartering Act of 1765*
> *Stamp Act of 1765*
> *Townshend Act of 1767*

Aristides, *Orations I and II*, ed. by Robert Dodsley (1765)

Aristotle,
> *A Treatise on Government*, tr. by William Ellis (1776)
> *Aristotle's Masterpiece*, publisher William Salmon (1680)

Mary Astell,
> *Six familiar essays upon marriage, crosses in love, sickness, death, loyalty ...* (1696)
> *An Essay in Defense of the female sex* (1697)
> *A Serious Proposal to the Ladies .... By a Lover of Her Sex* (1697)
> *A Serious Proposal Wherein a Method ...* (1700)
> *Some Reflections Upon Marriage ...* (1700)
> *A Fair Way with Dissenters and their Patrons* (1704)
> *An Impartial Enquiry into the Causes of Rebellion and Civil War ...* (1704)
> *The Character of the Wisest Men* (1704)

Saint Augustine, *Meditations*, tr. by George Stanhope (1701)

Francesco Algarotti, *Sir Isaac Newton's Philosophy Explained for the use of Ladies, in six dialogues on Light and Colours*, tr. by Elizabeth Carter (1739)

Francis Bacon,
Essays (1597)
Advancement of Learning (1605)
New Method (1620)
The Elements of the Common Laws of England, Maxims of the Law ... (1630)
The Learned Reading of Sir Francis Bacon upon the Statute of Use (1642)

Matthew Bacon,
The Complete Arbitrator or the Law of Awards and Arbitraments (1731)
A New Abridgement of the Law, 8 vol. (1736)

Augustin de Barruel, *Memoires sur les Jacobinisme* (1797-1798)

William Belsham,
Examination of an Appeal from the Old to the New Whigs (1792)
Remarks on the Nature and Necessity of Political Reform (1793)
Memoirs of the Kings of Great Britain of the House of Brunswick-Luneburg (1793)
Memoirs of the Reign of George III to the Session of Parliament 1793 (1795)
A History of Great Britain from the Revolution to the Accession ... (1798)

Cesare Beccaria, *An Essay on Crimes and Punishments* (1775)

William Blackstone, *Commentaries on the Laws of England, 4 Books* (1765-1769)

Henry Bolingbroke,
Dissertation on Parties (1735-38)
A Collection of Political Tracts (1748)
The miscellaneous Works of ... St. John, Lord Viscount Bolingbroke (1773)

Reading Categories

Nicolas-Antoine Boulanger, *Anecdotes Physiques de l'Histoire de la Terre*, 2 Vol. tr. by John Wilkes (1764)

Robert Boyle, *The works of the Honorable Robert Boyle ...*, ed. by Thomas Birch (1744)

Edmund Burke,
    Selected Works (1770)
    Lessons to a Young Prince ... (1790)
    Reflections on the Revolution in France (1790)

Samuel Butler, *Hudibras* (1663-1678)

Sallust, *The Works of Sallust ...*, tr. by Thomas Gordon (1744)

Anthony Ashley Cooper, *Characteristics of Man, Opinion, Times* (1773)

Roger Cotes, *Preface to the Second Edition of Newton's Principia* (1713)

Tench Coxe,
    An Examination of the Constitution of the United States (1788)
    A View of The United States of America ... Between the Years 1787 And 1794

Declaration and Resolves of the First Continental Congress (1774)

Constitution of the United States (1789)

Declaration of Independence (1776)

Declaration of Indulgence (1687)

Declaration of Rights (1689)

Denis Diderot & Jean le Rond d'Alembert, *Encyclopaedia* (1751-1772)

Rene Descartes, *Meditations*, tr. by Duc de Luynes (1642)

John Dickinson, *Letter from a Pennsylvania Farmer* (1767-1768)

William Drayton, *The Letters of Freeman ...* ed. by Robert M. Weir (1774)

Daniel Dulany, *Considerations on the Propriety of Imposing Taxes ... British Colonies ...* (1765)

Desiderius Erasmus,
    A Devout Treatise upon the Paternoster tr. by Margaret Roper (1524)
    Colloquies (1671)
    The Praise of Folly, tr. by John Wilson (1668)

Robert Filmer, *Patriarcha or the Natural Power of Kings* (1680)

Bernard Le Bovier de Fontenelle, *The Plurality of Worlds*, tr. by Aphra Behn (1688)

John Fortescue-Alland,
    A Learned Commendation of the Politique Lawes of England (1567)
    The Difference between an Absolute and Limited Monarchy ... (1714)

Benjamin Franklin,
    Experiments and Observations on Electricity (1751)
    Poor Richard's Almanac (1732-1758)
    Silence Dogwood (1722)
    Letters, 1766-1773 (1789)

William Godwin, *Enquiry concerning Political Justice* (1793)

Mary deGournay,
    Equality Between Men and Women (1641)
    Complaints of Ladies (1641)
    Apology for the Writing Women (1641)

Hugo Grotius,
    On the Law of War and Peace, tr. by Thomas Manley (1665)
    Introduction to Dutch Jurisprudence (1631)

Matthew Hale,
    Contemplations, moral and divine in two volumes by Sir Matthew Hale ... (1677)
    A History and Analysis of the Common Law of England (1713)

The History of the Pleas of the Crown (1736)

Alexander Hamilton, James Madison, John Jay (aka Publius), *Federalist Papers* (1787-1788)

James Harrington, *The Oceana of James Harrington* ... ed. by John Toland (1700)

Claude Helvetius,
> *On the Spirit* (1758)
> *A Treatise on Man and His Education* (1772)
> *Refutation of The Man of Helvetius* in the "Encyclopedia," ed. by Denis Diderot (1775)

Thomas Hollis, *The Moral and Political Works of Thomas Hobbes* (1750)

David Hume,
> *A Treatise of Human Nature* (1740)
> *Essays* (1741)
> *Enquiry Concerning Human Understanding* (1748)
> *Enquiry Concerning the Principles of Morals* (1751)
> *The Natural History of Religion* (1758)
> *History of England to the Revolution of 1688* (1762)
> *Dialogues Concerning Natural Religion* (1778)

Thomas Jefferson,
> *A Summary View of the Rights of British America* (1774)
> *Declaration of the Causes and Necessity of Taking Up Arms* (1775)
> *Memorandums Taken on a Journey from Paris into the Southern Parts ... 1787*
> *Notes on the State of Virginia* (1782)

John Locke,
> *Letter Concerning Toleration* (1689)
> *Second Letter Concerning Toleration* (1690)
> *Third Letter for Toleration* (1692)
> *Two Treatises of Government* (1689)
> *Some Thoughts Concerning Education* (1693)
> *Essay Concerning Human Understanding* (1690)

The reasonableness of Christianity as delivered in the Scriptures (1695)
Vindication of the Reasonableness of Christianity (1695)

Nicolo Machiavelli, *The Works of the Famous Nicolas Machiavel: The History of Florence, The Prince, The Discourses, The Art of War* by John Starkey (1675)

James Mackintosh, *Defense of the French Revolution* (1791)

Bernard Mandeville,
The Pamphleteers: A Satyr. London (1703)
Aesop Dressed; or a Collection of Fables Writ in Familiar Verse (1704)
Typhon: or The Wars Between the Gods and Giants; A Burlesque Poem ... (1704)
The Grumbling Hive: or, Knaves Turned Honest (1705)
A Treatise of the Hypochondriac and Hysteric Passions ... (1711)
The Mischiefs that Ought Justly to be Apprehended from a Whig-Government (1714)
The Fable of the Bees: or, Private Vices, Public Benefits (1714)
The Fable of the Bees Part II (1729)
Free Thoughts on Religion, the Church and National Happiness (1720)

John Milton,
A Complete Collection of the Historical, Political ..., ed. by John Toland (1698)

John Hughes, *A Complete History of England, 3 vol.* (1706)

Michel de Montaigne, *Essays*, tr. by John Florio (1603)

Charles de Montesquieu,
On the Spirit of Law (1748)
The Complete Works of M. de Montesquieu (1777)

Thomas More, *Utopia* (ca. 1550)

James Otis,
>   *Vindication of the Rights of the Province of Massachusetts Bay* (1762)
>   *The Rights of the British Colonies Asserted and Proved* (1765)
>   *A Vindication of the British Colonies* (1765)
>   *Brief Defense of the Halifax Libel on the British-American Colonies* (1765)
>   *Considerations on Behalf of the Colonies in a Letter to a Noble Lord* (1765)

Thomas Paine,
>   *Common Sense* (1776)
>   *American Crisis* (1776)
>   *Rights of Man* (1791)
>   *Age of Reason* (1794)

William Paley, *Principles of Moral and Political Philosophy* (1785)

Henry Pemberton, *A View of Sir Isaac Newton's Philosophy* (1728)

William Penn, *Frame of Government of Pennsylvania* (1681)

William Pitt,
>   *Speeches in the House of Commons, Jan. 4, 1778*
>   *On the Right to Tax America* (1766)

Plato, *The Republic*, tr. by Harry Spens (1763)

William Pym, *Asserts Parliamentary Supremacy* (1765)

Josiah Quincy, *Observations on the Act of Parliament Boston Port Bill* (1774)

Matthew Robinson-Morris, *Considerations on the Measures ... in North America* (1774)

Jean Jacques Rousseau,
>   *A Discourse upon the Origin and Foundation of the Inequality among Mankind* (1761)
>   *Du Contrat social* (1742)
>   *Emile* (1762)
>   *Esprit, Maximes e Principes* (1764)

La Nouvelle Heloise (1764)
A Treatise on the Social Compact (1764)

Charles-Irénée Castel, abbé de Saint-Pierre, *Discours sur la Polysynodie* (1718)

Jonathan Sewall, *Philanthrop* (1767)

Adam Smith.
The Theory of Moral Sentiment (1759)
Inquiry into the Nature and Causes of the Wealth of Nations (1776)

William Smith, *The Politicks and Views of a Certain Party, Displayed* (1792)

Philip Stanhope, Earl of Chesterfield,
Letters to His Son on the Art of Becoming a Man of the World ... (1774)
Man of the World (1775)
Principles of Politeness and of Knowing the World (1791)

Algernon Sydney,
Discourses Concerning Government (1698)
The Works of Algernon Sydney, ed. by Joseph Robertson (1772)

John Trenchard & Thomas Gordon,
Cato's Letters (1720-23)
Independent Whig (1720-1721)

Emerich Vattel, *The Law of Nations, or Principles of the Law of Nature* ... (1760)

Voltaire,
Letters Concerning the English Nation (1733)
Candide (1759)

Joseph Warren, *Oration Delivered March 6, 1775, on the Boston Massacre*

Reading Categories

NOVELS, POETRY, PLAYS

Joseph Addison,
> *The Miscellaneous Works, In Verse and Prose ...* (1726)
> *Cato, A Tragedy in Five Acts* (1713)
> *The Spectator* with Richard Steele (1711-1714)
> *The Guardian* (1713)
> *The Freeholder* (1715–16)

Aesop,
> *Select Fables of Aesop and Other Fabulists*, ed. by Robert Dodsley (1744)
> *A Collection of Poems in 5 Volumes by Several Hands* (1763)
> *The Fables of Aesop, with Instructive Applications*, ed. by Samuel Croxall (1722)

Dante Alighieri, *The Divine Comedy*, tr. by Charles Rogers (1782)

Joel Barlow,
> *Visions of Columbus* (1787)
> *Conspiracy of Kings* (1792)
> *The Hasty-Pudding* (1793)
> *Political Writings* (1796)
> *View of the Public Debt, Receipts and Expenditure of the United States* (1800)

Aphra Behn,
> *Love-Letters Between a Nobleman and His Sister* (1684)
> *Poems upon Several Occasions* (1684)
> *Miscellany, Being a Collection of Poems by Several Hands* (1685)
> *A Miscellany of New Poems by Several Hands* (1688)

James Boswell,
> *The Life of Samuel Johnson* (1791)
> *An Account of Corsica, The Journal of a Tour to That Island ...* (1768)
> *The Journal of a Tour to the Hebrides* (1785)
> *No Abolition of Slavery* (1791)

Pierre de Beaumarchais,
    Eugénie (1767)
    L'Essai sur le genre dramatique sérieux (1767)
    Les Deux amis ou le Négociant de Lyon (1770)
    The Barber of Seville (1775)
    La Lettre modérée sur la chute et la critique du "Barbier de Sérville" (1775)
    Narrative Respecting Count Pulaski (1777)
    The Marriage of Figaro (1784)

Anne Bradstreet,
    The Tenth Muse Lately Sprung Up in America from the Manuscripts ... (1650)
    Several Poems (1678)

John Bunyan, *The Pilgrim's Progress from This World, to That Which Is to Come* (1678)

Miguel de Cervantes Saavedra, *Don Quixote*, tr. by Peter Anthony Motteux (1700)

Richard Cumberland, *The Carmelite* (1784)

Geoffrey Chaucer, *The Canterbury Tales* (1687)

William Congreve.
    Poetical Miscellanies (1704)
    Works (1710)

Pierre Corneille, *The Chief Works, with remarks by Voltaire* (1758)

Thomas Corneille, *Works* (1758)

William Cowper,
    Complaints of an Old Bachelor (1756)
    On conversation (1756)
    On keeping Secrets (1756)
    A Letter from Mr. Village (1756)
    Olney Hymns (1779)
    John Gilpin (1782)
    The Task (1785)

Prosper Crebillon, *Oeuvres* (1772)

Daniel Defoe,
    The True-Born Englishman (1701)
    The Shortest Way with Dissenters (1702)
    The Further Adventures of Robinson Crusoe (1719)
    Serious Reflections … of Robinson Crusoe (1720)
    Captain Singleton (1720)
    Memoirs of a Cavalier (1720)
    A Journal of the Plague Year (1722)
    Colonel Jack (1722)

John Dryden,
    The Works of John Dryden (1691)
    Fables Ancient and Modern … Homer, Ovid, Boccacio, & Chaucer … (1700)

Francois Fénélon,
    The Adventures of Telemachus (1699)
    Dialogues of the Dead … tr. by George Lyttelton (1760)

John Gay,
    The Shepherd's Week. In Six Pastorals (1714)
    Poems on Several Occasions (1720)
    The Captives (1724)
    Fifty-one Fables in Verse (1727)
    The Beggar's Opera (1728)
    Achilles (1733)

Thomas Godfrey, *The Prince of Parthia* (1767)

Oliver Goldsmith,
    Account of the Augustan Age in England (1759)
    The Citizen of the World (1760)
    The Life of Richard Nash (1762)
    The Hermit (1765)
    The Deserted Village (1770)
    She Stoops to Conquer (1773)
    The History of England, from the Earliest Times to the Death of George II (1771)

> Dr. Goldsmith's Roman History Abridged by Himself for the Use of Schools (1772)
> An History of the Earth and Animated Nature (1774)

Eliza Haywood,
> *The Female Spectator* (1744 – 1746)
> *Memoirs of a Certain Island, Adjacent to Utop*ia (1724)
> *The Secret History of the Present Intrigues of the Court of Caramania* (1727)
> *Memoirs of an Unfortunate Young Nobleman* (1743)

Homer,
> *The Iliad*, tr. by Alexander Pope, ed. by Bernard Lintat (1753)
> *The Odyssey*, tr. by Alexander Pope, ed. by Bernard Lintat (1753)

William Hogarth,
> *The Analysis of Beauty* (1753)
> *Industry and Idleness* (1747)
> *The Four Stages of Cruelty* (1751)

Charles Hoole, *Corderius's School Colloquies, English and Latin* (1657)

Horace, *Works of Horace*, tr. by Anne Dacier (1735)

William Jones, *Poems, Consisting Chiefly of Translations from the Asiatick Tongues* (1772)

Juvenal, *Satires of Juvenal and Persius*, tr. by John Dryden (1693)

Juvenal, *The Thirteenth Satire of Juvenal, with notes, in the translation by Mr. Dryden and ...*, tr. by Thomas Creech (1693)

Jean Baptiste Moliere, *The Works of Moliere, French and English in Ten Volumes* (1739)

Hannah More (aka Will Chip),
> *Sir Eldred of the Bower* (1776)
> *The Search after Happiness* (1762)
> *The Fatal Falsehood* (1779)
> *Slavery* (1788)
> *Strictures on the Modern System of Female Education* (1799)

Lady Mary Wortley Montagu,
> *Collection of Poems in Six Volumes*, ed. by Robert Dodsley (1763)
> *The Nonsense of Common-Sense* (1738)
> *Woman not Inferior to Man* (1739)
> *The Turkish Embassy Letters* (1763)
> *Observations on the Genius and Writings of Shakespeare* (1769)

Arthur Murphy, *The Grecian Daughter* (1772)

Judith Sargent Murray,
> *The Gleaner* (1798)
> *Desultory Thoughts... Self-Complacency, Especially in Female Bosoms* (1784)
> *On the Equality of the Sexes* (1790)
> *On the Domestic Education of Children* (1790)
> *The Repository* (1792–94)
> *The Reaper* (1794)
> *The Medium, or Virtue Triumphant* (1795)
> *The Traveler Returned* (1796)
> *The African* (1805)

Ovid, *Metamorphoses*, tr. by Arthur Golding (1567)

Ovid, *Several Elegies from Ovid with the Second and Third Eclogues of Virgil* ... tr. by Thomas Creech (1684)

Alexander Pope, *The Works of Alexander Pope*, ed. by Bernard Lintat (1753)

Jean Racine, *Oeuvres de Racine*, ed. by J.F. Bernard (1722)

Allan Ramsay,
> *Poems* (1720)
> *The Tea-table Miscellany* (1724)
> *The Ever Green* (1724)
> *The Gentle Shepherd* (1725)

Andrew Michael Ramsay, *A New Cyropaedia ... Travels of Cyrus*, tr. by Nathaniel Hooke (1729)

Samuel Richardson,
> *Pamela; or, Virtue Rewarded* (1740)
> *Clarissa; or The History of a Young Lady ...* (1748)

William Shakespeare, *Works*, ed. by Nicholas Rowe (1709)

Richard Sheridan,
> *School for Scandal* (1777)
> *The Rivals* (1775)
> *The Critic* (1779)

Sophocles, *Oedipus: A Tragedy, dramatic adaptation* by John Dryden (1679)

Jonathan Swift,
> *Miscellanies in Poems and Verse*, ed. Bernard Lintat (1712)
> *Gulliver's Travels* (1727)
> *The works of Dr. Jonathan Swift: with the author's life and character* (1768)

Publius Terentius (Terence), *Comedies*, tr. by George Coleman (1768)

Theocritus, *Idylliums of Theocritus, with Rapin's Discourse of Pastorals*, tr. by Thomas Creech (1684)

James Thomson,
> *The Four Seasons, and Other Poems* (1735)
> *The Tragedy of Sophonisba* (1729)
> *The Castle of Indolence* (1748)

John Trumbull, *The Progress of Dullness* (1772-1773)

Royall Tyler, *The Contrast* (1787)

Virgil, *The Works of Virgil ... Pastorals, Georgics, and Aeneis*, tr. by John Dryden (1697)

Edward Young, *The Complaint: or Night Thoughts on Life, Death, and Immortality* (1773)

RELIGION

King James Bible, Book of Common Prayer, Psalter, Catechism, Sermons

Jonathan Edwards,
> *Some thoughts concerning the present revival of religion in New-England ...* (1742)
> *A Treatise Concerning Religious Affections* (1746)
> *An Inquiry into the Modern Prevailing Notions of the Freedom of the Will...* (1754)

John Fothergill, *An Account of the Life and Travels ... of John Fothergill ...* (1754)

Cotton Mather,
> *Magnalia Christi Americana* (1702)
> *The Christian Philosopher* (1721)

Jonathan Mayhew.
> *A Discourse Concerning Unlimited Submission and Non-Resistance ...* (1750)
> *Observations on the Charter and Conduct of the Society for the Propagation ...* (1763)

Richard Watson, *A Collection of Theological Tracts* (1785)

Phillis Wheatley, *Poems on Various Subjects, Religious and Moral* (1773)

James Winthrop IV,
> *Attempt to Translate the Prophetic Part of the Apocalypse of St. John* (1794)
> *Attempt to Arrange Scripture Prophecies Yet Remaining Unfulfilled* (1803)
> *Appendix to the New Testament* (1808)

EDUCATION

Rhetoric (works of Cicero, John Locke during pre-university tutorial)

Arithmetic; English Dictionary; Geography; Primer (often included a catechism); *Speller*

Anna Barbauld,
Lessons for Children from Two to Three Years Old (1778)
Lessons for Children of Three Years Old (1778)
Lessons for Children from Three to Four Years Old (1779)
Hymns in Prose for Children (1781)
Lessons for Children, Part Three (1787)
Lessons for Children, Part Four (1788)

George Bickham, *The Universal Penman* (1743).

Stephanie deGenlis,
Théâtre d'Éducation (1779–1780)
Les Annales de la Vertu (1781)
Adèle et Théodore (1782)

Hester Chapone, *Letters on the Improvement of the Mind* (1773)

Charles Demarville, *The Young Lady's Geography...* (1757)

François Fénelon, *Treatise on the Education of Daughters* (1681)

James Fordyce,
Sermons to a Young Woman (1765)
The Character and Conduct of the Female Sex (1776)

James Gregory, *A Father's Legacy to His Daughters* (1761)

Jedidiah Morse,
The American Gazetteer (1762)
The American Geography (1789)
The American Universal Geography (1793)
The American Gazetteer (1797)

King James I of England, *A Counterblaste to Tobacco* (1604).

Charles Rollins, *The Method of Teaching and Studying the Belles Lettres; or an introduction to anguages, Poetry, Rhetoric, History, Moral Philosophy, Physics, etc.* (1769)

Juliana-Susannah Seymour (aka John Hill), *On the management and education of children...* (1754)

REFERENCE TEXTS

The Complete Farmer: or a General Dictionary of Husbandry (1756)

John Abercrombie, *The British Fruit-gardener; and Art of Pruning* (1779)

Zabdiel Boylston, *A historical account of the small-pox inoculated in New-England, ...* (1724)

Richard Bradley, *New Improvements of Planting and Gardening* (1718)

William Buchan, *Domestic Medicine: or a Treatise on the Prevention and Cure ...* (1769)

William Ellis, *The Modern Husbandman* (1750)

Edward Kimber, *The Ladies Complete Letter-writer* (1763)

Benjamin Franklin, *Poor Richard's Almanac* (1732-1758)

Hannah Glasse *The Art of Cookery Made Plain and Easy* (1747)

John Morgan, *A Recommendation of Inoculation to Baron Dimsdale's Method* (1776)

Thomas Osborne, *Mr. Hoyle's Treatises of Whist, Quadrille, Piquet, Chess ...* (1748)

Benjamin Rush, *Inquiry into the Effects of Spirituous Liquors on the Human Body and Mind* (1790)

William Smellie, *A Treatise on the Theory and Practice of Midwifery* (1752-1764)

Eliza Smith, *Complete Housewife* (1727). Reprinted by Hugh Gaine in 1760s

Adam Thomson, *A Discourse ... Preparation of the Body for the Smallpox* (1750)

John Winthrop IV,
    Relation of a Voyage from Boston to Newfoundland for the Transit of Venus (1761)
    Lecture on Earthquakes (1755)
    Answer to Mr. Prince's Letter on Earthquakes (1756)
    Account of Some Fiery Meteors (1755)
    Two Lectures on the Parallax (1769)

BIBLIOGRAPHY

The bibliography provides the reader with additional sources describing the eighteenth-century colonial society in which Mercy Otis Warren lived. When I was doing the research for my doctoral thesis in the 1990s, the internet was not as robust as it is today which required more time in libraries to find sources supporting my hypothesis. So, in conducting research for the historical novel, I was grateful for and surprised by the plethora of information available on the internet allowing me to explore a wide variety of topics like eighteenth-century children's games, food, diseases, courtship and marriage rituals, pregnancy and childbirth, old colonial sayings, Christmas traditions, and women's fashion, to cite a few.

For example, while investigating the internet, I discovered details which surprised me like the game of Rounders whose description sounded like contemporary baseball. Other citations include collections of correspondence, published writings, and studies by historians which are useful for the reader in framing the socio-cultural and political world of eighteenth-century colonial America. These websites and books allowed me to build on the facts of Mercy Warren's life and blend speculation and fiction which filled in the gaps of this unique woman's life. I hope the reader takes advantage of the opportunity to delve into the suggested readings because this important period in our history saw the creation of the American republican experiment and who we have become as a country.

ABIGAIL ADAMS

Quotes. https://www.azquotes.com/author/71-Abigail_Adams

Abigail Adams. https://en.wikipedia.org/wiki/Abigail_Adams

Adams Family Correspondence, 6 vol. edited by Lyman H. Butterfield (Cambridge, Harvard University Press, 1963). https://www.hup.harvard.edu/catalog.php?isbn=9780674004009

Diary and Autobiography of John Adams, 4 vol., edited by Lyman H. Butterfield (Cambridge, Harvard University Press, 1961) https://www.bestofdocument.com/pdf/diary-and-autobiography-of-john-adams/

Abigail Adams and "Remember the Ladies." https://americainclass.org/abigail-adams-and-remember-the-ladies/

New Letters of Abigail Adams, 1788-1801, edited by Stewart Mitchell (Ann Arbor, University Michigan Press, 2005). https://quod.lib.umich.edu/g/genpub/ABP4380.0001.001?rgn=main;view=fulltext

Abigail (Smith) Adams, First Lady of the United States Genealogy. https://www.geni.com/people/Abigail-Smith-Adams-First-Lady-of-the-United-States/6000000010340691844

Smith, Page. *John Adams* (NY, Doubleday & Company 1962). https://archive.org/details/johnadams01smit

Akers, Charles. *Abigail Adams, An American Woman* (Boston, Harper Collins, 1980).

Bober, Natalie. *Abigail Adams, Witness to a Revolution* (NY, Simon and Schuster, 1995).

Gelles, Edith. *Portia, The World of Abigail Adams* (Bloomington, Indiana University Press, 1992).

Levin, Phyllis. *Abigail Adams, A Biography* (NY, St. Martin's Griffin, 1987).

Withey, Lynne. *Dearest Friend, A Life of Abigail Adams* (NY, Atria Books,2002). https://archive.org/details/dearestfriendlif0000with

CATHARINE SAWBRIDGE MACAULAY (GRAHAM)

Quotes.
https://quotefancy.com/catherine-mcauley- quotes#:~:-text=Catherine%20McAuley%20Quotes%201.%20%E2%80%9C%20We%20must%20strive,Resolve%20to%20do%20good%20today%20and%20better%20tomorrow

Catharine Sawbridge Macaulay. https://en.wikipedia.org/wiki/Catharine_Macaulay

Catharine Sawbridge Macaulay. https://plato.stanford.edu/entries/catharine-macaulay/

Catharine Macaulay. https://plato.stanford.edu/entries/catharinemacaulay/?msclkid=7ef1480bc27011ecbd7bdaba45e1347d

Green, Karen, *The Correspondence of Catharine Macaulay*, (Oxford, Oxford University Press, 2019). https://bookszone.net/books/the-correspondence ofcatharine-macaulay.html?msclkid=600beabac27111ec97186d3f29a6536f

Catharine Macaulay. Observations on the Reflections of the Right Hon. Edmund Burke, on the
Revolution in France: in a letter to the Right Hon. the Earl of Stanhope by Macaulay, with introduction by Mercy Otis Warren, (Boston,Thomas & Andrews, 1791) https://archive.org/details/obser-vationsonre00macauoft/page/2/mode/2up?msclkid=f668424ac35011ec84f880af4d96e15f

JUDITH SARGENT MURRAY

Quotes. https://www.azquotes.com/author/31176-Judith_Sargent_Murray

Judith Sargent Murray. https://en.wikipedia.org/wiki/Judith_Sargent_Murray

Judith Sargent Murray Genealogy. https://www.geni.com/people/Judith-SargentMurray/6000000017467274010

Judith Sargent Murray to Mercy Otis Warren (1728–1814), Autographed Letter, March 1796. http://bostonliteraryhistory.com/chapter-6/judith-sargent-murray-mercy-otis-warren-1728%e2%80%931814-autographed-letter-march-1796.html

The Gleaner, edited by Nina Baym (Schenectady, Union College Press,1992).

Selected Writings of Judith Sargent Murray, edited by Sharon Harris (NY, Oxford University Press, 1995).

Judith Sargent Murray Papers (Jackson, Mississippi Dept. of Archives and History, 1998).

Judith Sargent Stevens, Some Deductions from the System Promulgated in the Page of Divine Revelation, Ranged in the Order and Form of a Catechism (Norwich, Judith Sargent

Murray Society,1782).

Hurd, Bonnie Smith. *From Gloucester to Philadelphia in 1790: Observations, anecdotes, and thoughts from the 18th century letters of Judith Sargent Murray* (Cambridge, Judith Sargent Murray Society, 1998).

Shiela Skemp, *Judith Sargent Murray, A Brief Biography with Documents* (NY, Bedford St. Martins, 1998).

JAMES OTIS

Quotes. https://www.azquotes.com/author/11177-James_Otis

James Otis, https://en.wikipedia.org/wiki/James_Otis_Jr.

11 Fascinating Facts About James Otis, the Revolutionary Who Went Insane. https://www.newenglandhistoricalsociety.com/11-forgotten-facts-james-otis-insane-revolutionary/

The Rights of the British Colonies Asserted and Proved (1764). https://archive.org/details/cihm_20373/page/n7/mode/2up?ref=ol&view=theater

Considerations on Behalf of the Colonists. In a letter to a noble lord (1765). https://archive.org/details/considerationson00otis_0/page/n9/mode/2up

A Vindication of the British Colonies, against the aspersions of the Halifax gentleman, in his Letter to a Rhode-Island friend (1765). https://archive.org/details/vindicationofbri00otis

A vindication of the conduct of the House of Representatives of the province of the Massachusetts-Bay: more particularly, in the last session of the General Assembly (1762). https://catalogue.nla.gov.au/Record/2440690

MERCY OTIS WARREN

Quotes. https://www.azquotes.com/author/15312-Mercy_Otis_Warren

Mercy Otis Warren. https://en.wikipedia.org/wiki/Mercy_Otis_Warren

Warren-Adams Papers, 1767-1822. Massachusetts Historical Society. https://www.masshist.org/collection-guides/view/fa0306

Mercy Otis Warren Papers,1709-1841. Massachusetts Historical Society.
https://www.masshist.org/collection-guides/view/fa0235

Correspondence between John Adams and Mercy Warren relating to her "History of the American revolution," July-August 1807 (Boston, Massachusetts Historical Society, 1878).
https://onlinebooks.library.upenn.edu/webbin/book/lookupname?key=Warren%2C%20Mercy%20Otis%2C%201728%2D1814

History of the Rise, Progress and Termination of the American Revolution, Biographical, Political and Moral Observations, 3 vol. in "Parallel Lives" by Richard Seltzer. (Boston, 1805).
https://onlinebooks.library.upenn.edu/webbin/book/lookupname?key=Warren%2C%20Mercy%20Otis%2C%201728%2D1814

The Adulateur, A Tragedy, Acted in Upper Servia in "Parallel Lives" by Richard Seltzer. (Boston, Concert Hall, 1773).
https://onlinebooks.library.upenn.edu/webbin/book/lookupname?key=Warren%2C%20Mercy%20Otis%2C%201728%2D1814

The Defeat in "Parallel Lives" by Richard Seltzer (1773)
https://onlinebooks.library.upenn.edu/webbin/book/lookupname?key=Warren%2C%20Mercy%20Otis%2C%201728%2D1814

The Blockheads: or the Affrighted Officers, A Farce in "Parallel Lives" by Richard Seltzer (Boston, John Gill, 1776).
https://onlinebooks.library.upenn.edu/webbin/book/lookupname?key=Warren%2C%20Mercy%20Otis%2C%201728%2D1814

The Group: A Farce in "Parallel Lives" by Richard Seltzer. (Boston, Edes and Gill, 1775)
https://onlinebooks.library.upenn.edu/webbin/book/lookupname?key=Warren%2C%20Mercy%20Otis%2C%201728%2D1814

Bibliography

The Motley Assembly, A Farce, published for the entertainment of the Curious in "Parallel Lives" by Richard Seltzer (Boston, NathanielCoverly,1779).
https://onlinebooks.library.upenn.edu/webbin/book/lookupname?key=Warren%2C%20Mercy%20Otis%2C%201728%2D1814

Poems, dramatic and miscellaneous. By Mrs. M. Warren (Boston, Thomas & Andrews, 1790).
https://onlinebooks.library.upenn.edu/webbin/book/lookupname?key=Warren%2C%20Mercy%20Otis%2C%201728%2D1814

Observations on the new Constitution, and on the Federal and State Conventions. by a Columbian Patriot [Mercy Otis Warren] once erroneously attributed to Elbridge Gerry, Sic Transit gloria Americana, Boston 1788.
https://onlinebooks.library.upenn.edu/webbin/book/lookupname?key=Warren%2C%20Mercy%20Otis%2C%201728%2D1814

An Additional number of letters from the Federal farmer to the Republican, leading to a fair examination of the system of government, proposed by the late Convention, to several essential and necessary alterations in it; ... Together with Oberservations on the new Constitution, and on the Federal and State Conventions by a Columbian patriot (NY 1788).
https://onlinebooks.library.upenn.edu/webbin/book/lookupname?key=Warren%2C%20Mercy%20Otis%2C%201728%2D1814

Sans Souci. Alias Free and easy: or an evening's peep into a polite circle. An entire [sic] new entertainment. In three acts (Boston, Warden and Russell, 1785).
https://onlinebooks.library.upenn.edu/webbin/book/lookupname?key=Warren%2C%20Mercy%20Otis%2C%201728%2D1814

Mercy (Otis) Warren (1728–1814) Genealogy.
https://www.wikitree.com/wiki/Otis-42

Davies, Kate. *Catharine Macaulay and Mercy Otis Warren: The Revolutionary Atlantic and the Politics of Gender*, (NY, Oxford University Press, 2005). https://www.deepdyve.com/lp/university-of-north-carolina-press/catharinemacaulay-and-mercy-otis-warren-the-revolutionary-atlantic-sivkDg9WkP

Brown, Alice. *Women of Colonial and Revolutionary Times: Mercy Warren* (NY, Leopold Classic Library, 2016).

Cibbarelli, William. *Libraries of the Mind: A Study of the Reading Histories of Mercy Warren, Abigail Adams, and Judith Sargent Murray 1728-1820* (Ann Arbor, UMI, 2000).

Ellet, Elizabeth, *The Women of the American Revolution* (Philadelphia, Baker & Scribner, 1900) https://archive.org/details/womenofamerican00elle/page/n1/mode/2up

Fisher, Nicole. *Meet The Revolutionary Woman Mercy Otis Warren* https://thefederalist.com/2016/03/09/meet-the-revolutionary-woman-mercy-otis-warren/

Nicolay, Theresa Freda. *Gender Roles, Literary Authority, and Three American Women Writers: Anne Dudley Bradsteet, Mercy Otis Warren, Margaret Fuller Ossoli* (NY, Peter Lang Inc., 1995).

Richards, Jeffrey H. *Mercy Otis Warren* (NY, Twayne Publishers, 1995). https://openlibrary.org/books/OL1122353M/Mercy_Otis_Warren

Stuart, Nancy Rubin. *The Muse of the Revolution: The Secret Pen of Mercy Otis Warren and the Founding of a Nation* (Boston, Beacon Press, 2008).

Zagarri, Rosemarie. *A Woman's Dilemma, Mercy Warren and the American Revolution*

(Oxford, John Wiley & Son, 2015). https://www.fly-unicorn.com/lp_ta/index.cfm?_=1645714717911&T=102199

18ᵀᴴ CENTURY SOCIAL – POLITICAL–CULTURAL HISTORY

Eighteenth Century London: Politics and Society, Whigs and Tories. https://www.anglistik.uni-kiel.de/de/tl_files/EnglSem/Fachbereiche/Kultur%20und%20Medienwissenschaften/Projekte/18th_century_london/whigs.html#etymology

Boston Tea Party. https://en.wikipedia.org/wiki/Boston_Tea_Party

Children's Games. https://classroom.synonym.com/childrens-games-in-the-18th-century-13583117.html

Christmas in England. https://www.julieratcliffe.co.uk/an-eighteenth-century-christmas/

Christmas in France. https://en.wikipedia.org/wiki/Christmas_in_France

Colonial & Early American Fare. https://www.foodtimeline.org/food-colonial.html#colonialfare

Constitution of the United States. https://constitution.congress.gov/constitution/?msclkid=5ddf5ff8c42411ec95820ec589304c54

Declaration of Independence. https://declaration.fas.harvard.edu/resources/text?msclkid=c5c1c376c42411ec9fd89324dd48a880

Disease in Colonial America. https://en.wikipedia.org/wiki/Disease_in_colonial_America

Education in Colonial America, https://fee.org/articles/education-in-colonial-america/

Federalist Papers.
> https://www.thefederalistpapers.org/wp-content/uploads/2012/12/The-Complete-Federalist-Papers.pdf?msclkid=4b9f4a89c26c11ecbddc12f6ebbd92d8

French and Indian War.
> https://en.wikipedia.org/wiki/French_and_Indian_War?msclkid=dbbb35bbc26b11eca8e733bd537d0247

Gaspee Affair.
> https://en.wikipedia.org/wiki/Gaspee_Affair#:~:text=The%20Gaspee%20Affair%20was%20a%20significant%20event%20in,in%20and%20around%20Newport%2C%20Rhode%20Island%2C%20in%201772.?msclkid=21eb2eb6c27511ec87e6a926f97cdc88

Harvard in the 17th and 18th Centuries
> https://guides.library.harvard.edu/c.php?g=405381&p=6465805

How to Read 18th Century British-American Writing.
> https://dohistory.org/on_your_own/toolkit/writing.html?msclkid=f163e748c40511ecbb90cc27158efaad

Indentured Servitude. https://en.wikipedia.org/wiki/Indentured_servitude#North_America

King James I of England, *A Counterblaste to Tobacco* (1604).
> http://laits.utexas.edu/poltheory/james/blaste/blaste.html

Legal Status of Women in Ancient Rome.
> http://www.womenintheancientworld.com/legal%20status%20of%20women%20in%20ancient%20rome.htm?msclkid=20282164c26f11ecb9c838e43002118e

Life in New England. http://strategy2design.com/PVMA/revolution/main.html

Old Colonial Sayings We Use Today.
> https://williamsburgprivatetours.com/old-colonial-era-idioms-sayings-we-use-today/

Pregnancy & Childbirth. https://18thcenturydiary.org.uk/childbirth-2/

The Academy: Curriculum and Organization. https://archives.upenn.edu/exhibits/penn-history/18th-century/academy

The Role of Women in the Colonies. https://courses.lumenlearning.com/boundless-ushistory/chapter/the-role-of-women-in-the-colonies/?msclkid=0581ba98c40311eca60b95ee7c20ef75

United States Census Data (1790 -1810). https://libguides.lib.rochester.edu/GOV/Census/1790

Women's Clothing & Accessories. http://www.larsdatter.com/18c/women.html

Writ of Assistance. https://en.wikipedia.org/wiki/Writ_of_assistance#:~:text=A%20writ%20of%20assistance%20is%20a%20written%20order,enforce%20an%20order%20for%20the%20possession%20of%20lands%22.?msclkid=625243c4c27411ecae5a62bf3803ecff

XYZ Affair. https://en.wikipedia.org/wiki/XYZ_Affair?msclkid=51ba1c83c27e11ec9ea7816e3b96beb1

Boylston, Arthur. *The Origins of Inoculation.* Journal of the Royal Society of Medicine, 2012 July https://www.ncbi.nlm.nih.gov/pmc/articles/PMC3407399/

Canada, Mark. *Colonial America was divided over smallpox inoculation, but Benjamin Franklin championed science* (Jul 6, 2021). https://www.msn.com/en-us/news/us/colonial-america-was-divided-over-smallpox-inoculation-but-benjamin-franklin-championed-science/ar-AALQgFD

Cott, Nancy. *The Bonds of Womanhood: Women's Sphere in New England, 1780-1835* (New Haven, 1977). https://archive.org/details/bondsofwomanhood00cott

Davidson, Cathy, *Reading in America, Literature & Social History* (Baltimore, Johns Hopkins University Press, 1989).

Davies, W. J. Frank. *Teaching Reading in Early England* (NY, Pitman, 1974).

Hawke, David. *Everyday Life in Early America* (NY, Harper & Row, 1988).

Hayes, Kevin J. *A Colonial Woman's Bookshelf* (Knoxville, Wipf and Stock, 1996).

Littlefield, George. *Early Schools and School Books of New England* (NY, Russell & Russell, (1965).

Morrison, Samuel. *Three Centuries of Harvard, 1636-1936* (Cambridge, Belknap Press,1936).

Ulrich, Laurel Thatcher. *A Midwife's Tale, The Life77 of Martha Ballard, Based on Her Diary, 1785-1812* (NY, Simon & Schuster, 2002). https://is.cuni.cz/studium/predmety/index.php?do=download&did=73231&kod=JMM654